Religious, Feminist, Activist

Religious, Feminist, Activist

Cosmologies of Interconnection

Laurel Zwissler

University of Nebraska Press
Lincoln and London

Acknowledgments for the use of previously published
material appear on page 207, which constitutes an
extension of the copyright page.

Library of Congress Cataloging-in-Publication Data
Names: Zwissler, Laurel, author.
Title: Religious, feminist, activist: cosmologies of
interconnection / Laurel Zwissler.
Description: Lincoln: University of Nebraska Press, [2018]
| Series: Anthropology of contemporary North America |
Includes bibliographical references and index.
Identifiers: LCCN 2017038775
ISBN 9780803285705 (cloth: alk. paper)
ISBN 9781496205025 (pbk.: alk. paper)
ISBN 9781496205933 (epub)
ISBN 9781496205940 (mobi)
ISBN 9781496205957 (pdf)
Subjects: LCSH: Women—Religious life—North
America. | Feminism—Religious aspects. | Women
political activists—North America. | Religion and
politics—North America.
Classification: LCC BL625.7 .Z95 2018 |
DDC 201/.7082—dc23
LC record available at https://lccn.loc.gov/2017038775

Set in Charter ITC by Mikala R Kolander.

For my participants, without whom there would be no book,
and for the members of the Centre for Women and Transpeople,
University of Toronto, 1998–99,
whose conversation and camaraderie first inspired it

Contents

Illustrations

Acknowledgments

This project is the culmination of many collaborations, gifts, and debts. First off, I would like to thank each of the amazing women who participated in this project and all the members of the Yarrow Collective, the Clearwater United Church, and the Toronto Catholic Worker. By taking time out of your lives to speak with me, you made this work possible. You have new names in the text that follows, but I hope that you nonetheless recognize yourselves within it. My goal in sending this book out into the world is that your words and work can reach far beyond the communities into which you welcomed me and help others envision ways to make change in their own. I offer you profound respect and gratitude.

The strengths of this book have come into being through many iterations, each made better than the last by the contributions of generous people. Their insights have made this a better work and me a better scholar. At the University of Toronto, Pamela Klassen significantly influenced the shape of this project. I have benefited in countless ways from her careful readings, questions, and challenges. This work also improved through the care and attention of Judy Taylor, Amira Mittermaier, Lynda Lange, and Amy Mullin. Courtney Bender, at Columbia University, contributed as an external reader of the initial project. She continued to offer frank advice as I navigated the challenges of finding a good home for this book. Anthropology of Contemporary North America series editors James Bielo and Carrie Lane created what has turned out to be that good home with University of Nebraska Press. Mary Keller and an anonymous reviewer provided invaluable recommendations for improving the manuscript.

Professional organizations have also provided mentors, conversation partners, and friends. Ron Grimes is always deeply supportive and a pleasure to think with. His mobilization of the Southern Ontario Religious Studies Fieldworkers Group, along with fellow members, including Ellen Badone and Carol Duncan, created an important space to ask big questions about ethnographic methods and the purpose of anthropological work at a crucial time in my research. The American Academy of Religion, particularly the units of Anthropology of Religion, Ritual Studies, New Religious Movements, and Contemporary Pagan Studies, provided me venues in which to share my ideas. I thank especially Sarah Pike and Doug Cowan for feedback and guidance. The Society for the Anthropology of Religion, a subgroup of the American Anthropological Association, has also been a valuable source of both critique and support and has allowed new acquaintances to become old friends. Special gratitude goes to Simon Coleman for his mentorship and buoying insistence, when my spirits flagged, that this work was important. Lastly, the International Association for the History of Religions has allowed me to deepen conversations with friends in Europe, especially Anna Fedele and Kim Knibbe.

My partners in crime at the Centre for the Study of Religion at the University of Toronto are as fine a pack to run with as I ever could have asked. Here I will rat out specifically Arlene MacDonald, Kerry Fast, honorary csrer Chris Klassen, and David Perley. I would also like to thank colleagues at Central Michigan University for their ongoing support of my work. Particularly, in the Religion Area, Guy Newland has encouraged my commitment to research, Pam Jones has been an excellent resource on African American women's religious history, and Sara Moslener suggested sources on anti-Catholicism. Thanks also to Alec Burch and Myra Fearn. In Philosophy, Robert Noggle talked "cosmology" with me, and Andy Blom is a diplomatic Women and Gender Studies coconspirator. In Anthropology, Laura Cochrane is a much-needed, one-woman anthropology of religion conversation group. Lastly, representing that elusive blend of immediate colleague and true friend, Kelly J. Murphy helps make it possible for me to go into work in the morning and also to go home at night, community service projects in which she is supported by John, human, and Gilgamesh, canine.

Over the course of this project, some friendships have deepened into

Muppet Family. Sylvia Zwissler understands the honor of being in this category and has earned it through a superhero's heart. She also provides urban sanctuary and the company of Oliver and Batman, feline. Sarah King and her accomplices Henry, human, and Rocky and Pickles, feline, share their home, and often their sanity, with me on a regular basis. Ken Derry is probably the best person I know, that I suspect anyone knows, but he is so lovely that he will just be confused by this declaration. Michael Ostling has seen me through slumps and rages but somehow always insists that I am great, which is actually pretty great of him. Sarah Boyce, aka Gwisdalla, is a piece of my heart, and hers—Greg, Zinnia, and Camilla, all human—are mine.

Liz Clayton was right around the corner for a good portion of this work, with Geneva, feline, and I will always be grateful for the opportunity she provided me to know Jeff Chapman, model human, and Foot-Foot and Woodward, feline, all of whom are missed. I am thrilled now to embrace Ed Gil and Leonora Hermalinda, human, along with Guillaume, feline, under Liz's patronage. The Basran Taekwondo club, especially Master Gary Basran and Master Maria Prieto, provided structure, moral support, and opportunities to kick hard and yell loud, things that turn out to be my favorite, even when it means I get kicked back. Stan Byrne and David Robson, along with the late Dolly, canine, shared food, space, and good coffee with me. Stan and David now share food and space, but presumably not the coffee, with Holden and August, human, and Bambi, canine. Conversation with Carol Borden, in the company of the late Minstrel, Clea, and Spider, feline, always led to new insights. Pretty Boy Floyd, the Goblin King, feline, sustained me through the ups and downs of research and writing and life. He is passed; my love is not.

Finally, David Ferris, Men's Auxiliary to the University of Toronto Centre for Women and Transpeople: in the chaos of Quebec City, he reached for my hand. We never let go.

Religious, Feminist, Activist

Introduction

I never see a disconnection between religion and activism.
It seems to me if you were really, truly religious . . .
you couldn't help being a social activist.

FRANKA, United Church Protestant

I don't see how anybody can be spiritual
without having it come in action.

LAVENDER, contemporary Pagan

If you're going to push yourself as an activist, or as a
Christian activist, the natural outcome is that you
become radicalized, because you're looking at issues
of social justice and, once you fully analyze the issues,
you're going to end up a radical.

ANGEL, Catholic

This book is about people who combine in their lives and communities
deep commitments often taken as fundamentally incompatible by
others: feminism, progressive political engagement, and religion. In
fact, despite the emergence of spiritual feminism in North America in
the last half century, I have found that trying to talk about this project,
even with academic colleagues, elicits surprise. Popular discourses
intimate that social justice commitments, especially to gender and
sexual equality, do not mix with institutional religion, yet my participants thrive on this supposedly impossible, or at least dangerous, potion.
More complicated explorations about religion and social justice in the

public sphere reveal creative spaces and potential rapprochements between apparently discrete communities. This project explores political and religious identity among feminist political activists in Toronto, Canada, activists who also identify as United Church Protestant, Catholic, or contemporary Pagan, and contributes to new conversations about what it means to be both religious and politically engaged in North America today.

Gender analysis is crucial to this investigation. Disputes about the validity or impossibility of combining religion and politics in North America are implicitly androcentric, both in terms of who typically gets to participate and in terms of who participants assume the hypothetical models for citizenry to be. Despite their lack of authority in public deliberation, or perhaps because of it, women often symbolize religious tradition in debates around the role of religion in civic discourse.[1] Through appearance—Muslims' hijab, Catholic schoolgirls' uniforms, Hasidic women's covered hair, Buddhist nuns' shaved heads—or through gendered standards of behavior such as chastity, modesty, maternity, and caretaking, women become the examples of religious virtue or repression. The lack of women's voices in discourse about the dangers and advantages of religion in civic space is especially striking when one considers the many ways women symbolize both the private sphere and traditional religious values. To better understand the implications and possibilities of combining religion and democratic politics, we must expand our view beyond these limitations and integrate into our discussions other modes of being religious in civic space.

In this introduction I begin by exploring current debates, within North American popular culture more generally and within academe, about the role of religion in public space. Because feminism is an important touchstone for both my participants' activist projects and my own analysis, I outline the interface of feminist theory and the academic study of religion, using a discussion of Progressive Era (1880–1920) women reformers to provide historical context for my participants' efforts to combine religion and politics in social justice work. Returning to the present, I outline my research methodology and introduce the participant groups that generously contributed to this project.

Refusing the Secular-Religious Split

Much academic study of religion allows for more nuanced understandings about the role of religion in the public sphere, and in the greater part of this book I am delighted to join these disciplinary conversations. However, the complexities of such scholarly analyses do not often filter into mainstream discourse. Because my ethnographic work is grounded in the experiences of women who negotiate their religious and political identities largely in this other milieu, it is imperative to trace popular discussions of religion before removing to the privilege of academic discourses.

In exploring the dichotomous nature of popular discourse, I want to make it clear that it reflects *false* categories. The world does not neatly split into secularists and conservatives. This study is specifically about women who engage their religions and politics in combinations that offer alternatives to such partitions. In doing so, they must nonetheless respond to binary assumptions about what it means to be both religious and politically active in contemporary North America. Avoiding this discussion would seriously neglect important social contexts for my ethnographic work.

Somewhat ironically, I begin my analysis of popular discourse about the role of religion in the public sphere with a dualism, but it is one that I believe sheds light on the construction of others. In her discussion of women-focused traditions, anthropologist Susan Starr Sered distinguishes between "this-worldly" and "other-worldly" religions. This-worldly religions are concerned with problems of this life, "concrete concerns."[2] Other-worldly traditions emphasize transcendence, setting aside quotidian concerns as insignificant compared to what comes after this earthly experience. Contemporary North American culture generally shares an assumption that religion is, by definition, other-worldly.

This assumption of other-worldly orientation has been true, for the most part, for the religions that have found mainstream acceptance in North America, particularly the popular forms of Protestantism, so significant in shaping common values of personal autonomy and accessible public discourse. A focus on transcendence combines neatly with the Protestant sense that religion should remain a private affair, outside of the public sphere of material strivings.[3] Religions deviating from this abstract ideal, such as Mormonism, Spiritualism, and even Catholicism, have historically been met with suspicion at best.[4] While the players in the debate have changed over time, earlier historical conflicts underlie contemporary hostility directed toward religious discourse in the political sphere and feed popular assumptions about the benefits of teleological secularization.[5]

The plethora of atheist manifestos published by celebrities such as evolutionary biologist Richard Dawkins, journalist Christopher Hitchens, and neuroscientist Sam Harris serve as fine examples.[6] Like history professor Mark Lilla, each decry religious faith as backward and dangerous.[7] Most significant for my analysis is that all of these authors have expressed particular disdain for moderate believers, arguing that liberal religion provides cover for dangerous extremism. Their books have topped best-seller lists, and each of these authors has frequented the North American talk show circuit. Although people buying their books do not necessarily agree with all their views, these authors represent a significant trend in mainstream Western discourse about religion and politics. Adding to such voices are pundits such as comedian Bill Maher, who has likened religious belief in otherwise reasonable people to "schizophrenia."[8]

In contrast, those on the Religious Right vocally oppose the complete rejection of religion as a legitimate element of political discourse. They interpret such privatization as a sign of the weakness, moral decay, and preposterous irrationality of Western liberalisms.[9] A well-worn example clearly explicating such views is the notorious conversation between Pat Robertson, the founder of the Christian Coalition, and the late Jerry Falwell, the founder of the Moral Majority. On Robertson's *700 Club* Falwell placed blame for the September 11 attacks on his political opponents, saying, "I really believe that the pagans, and the abortionists, and the feminists, and the gays and the lesbians who are actively trying to make that an alternative lifestyle, the ACLU, People For the American Way—all of them who have tried to secularize America—I point the finger in their face and say 'you helped this happen.'"[10] Straddling a dichotomous identity of both beleaguered oppression and triumphalism, public figures such as Robertson, Falwell, James Dobson (founder of

Focus on the Family), and Tim LaHaye (late author of the *Left Behind* Rapture-fantasy series and founder of the American Coalition for Traditional Values) have insisted that true democracy properly rests on their idiosyncratic theology.[11]

The viewpoints of secularists and conservative Christians, explicitly built in dialectical opposition to one another, divide the world up into the saved and unsaved, or the enlightened and those suffering false consciousness.[12] Proponents of both perspectives understand themselves as inherently rational and the other side as blind or even purposefully malicious and exploitive. These positions are based in concerns over what they understand to be rejections of the "right" way to live and what they perceive as the intentional prevention of access to it by anyone else.

Their aggressive opposition manifests in a nearly endless catalog of cultural conflicts, including accessible abortion, same-sex marriage, sex education and abstinence programs, appropriate gender roles, transgender identity, birth control, environmental stewardship, family discipline and domestic abuse, HIV/AIDS treatment and prevention, control of the media, global capitalism, and militarization. At the heart of these struggles is the conflict between standards for behavior focused on otherworldly ends and standards of behavior focused on the pragmatics of diverse democracy in the here and now. In creating the so-called culture wars,[13] both sides contribute to a rhetoric that winnows multiple options down to a single choice: a public space meticulously policed to protect it from the repressive infringements of religion, or a public space meticulously policed to conform to the strictures of a neoconservative Christianity. As Janet Jakobsen and Ann Pellegrini write: "While there is no doubt that some religious formations are dominating, it is both a poverty of imagination and a continued entanglement in the various assumptions that go along with the secularization narrative that leave us in the bind where we must choose between (supposedly) conservative religion or (supposedly) progressive secularism. Not only does this opposition force us to ignore or deny the ways in which religion can be central to progressive politics and the ways in which secularism can limit such politics, it limits our imagination of secularism to only one narrative."[14]

Collectively, these positions also assume particular race and class positions as central.[15] The forced choice such worldviews require is no more realistic today than it has been historically, which is to say, it is not. Religion and politics have a long history of interaction in North America far more complex than the Manichaean versions these positions reflect.

It's (Also) about Sex

The conflict over the role of religion in public space is also about the problem of sex. Part of the secular-religious dichotomy outlined here focuses on an imaginary of transgressions perpetrated by and/or inflicted upon particular gendered and sexualized bodies, especially those of women and LGBTQ (lesbian, gay, bisexual, transgendered/transsexual/ trans, and queer) people, as the example of the North Carolina "bathroom wars" attests. Popular North American discourse frequently scapegoats religion for justifying misogyny and violence against women.[16] At the same time, traditionalist religious groups denounce secularization as sexually predatory and degrading.[17]

These conflicting assertions raise a number of pragmatic questions that cut across variously drawn political lines but have taken on special urgency in social justice movements because they posit specific configurations of religion and power. They raise questions about the connection between religion in general, or of specific religions, to the oppression of women. Does religion contribute to misogyny? Do religions hold special sway over other aspects of culture? The chances for success in programs for social change hinge on the perceived causality of this relationship. If religion is a root cause of misogyny, as some feminists and proponents of secularization argue, then logic dictates that an important step toward ending gendered oppression is ridding society of religion. If, on the other hand, as other feminists have understood it, religion is one cultural complex among many that work together to create, enforce, or subvert gendered oppressions, then the type of religion an individual, community, or nation practices becomes crucially important, both because it reflects power dynamics at work in other areas and because it has the potential to create social change. For social justice movements to be effective, they must correctly diagnose the relationship between religion and other aspects of culture.

Feminist theory has important responses to these entanglements. Feminism is today a transnational movement involving grassroots efforts around the world.[18] Despite its current contributions to global change, mainstream feminism emerged out of Western political and philosophical trajectories.[19] Here I primarily discuss Western feminism, with a focus on North American movements, and trace intersecting threads: the relationship of religion to feminism as a political movement; the role of feminism in religions, especially Western traditions; and contributions of feminist criticism to the academic study of religion.

Feminism and Religion: Chimerical Terms

Feminism and religion are unsettled categories. One could as easily say that there are as many feminisms as there are feminists as one could say that there are as many Christianities as Christians or as many religions as religious people. Personal interpretations of spirituality may abound,[20] yet institutional religions remain great power brokers in contemporary societies. Despite a diversity of forms, people around the world, and religious studies scholars in particular, seem to generally agree that there is something at the heart of the human phenomenon of "religion" that is worth examining, even if the purpose of that examination may ultimately be deconstruction.[21]

If religion is difficult to pin down, feminism is equally so; it rests on more than one slippery idea. Feminism encompasses multiple means of seeing, acting in, and thinking about the world. Feminism is an analytic perspective, attainable by people of any gender, that explores the relationship of women to power, on both interpersonal and structural levels, and takes as fundamental that gender should not impede recognition of a person's humanity, access to equality, or exercise of self-determination.[22] Power is enacted, diffused, exercised, and imposed in dizzyingly complicated ways throughout Western modernity.[23] Women's access to power is impeded by sexism, which can be identified in two related but different forms: androcentrism, which is the ignorant, nonmalicious, but nevertheless damaging assumption that male experience is normal, average, or primary; and misogyny, which is hatred, deliberate silencing, or suspicion of women based on the assumption that they are inherently inferior to men.[24]

There is also the problem of defining "women." Is there actually such a group of people prior to their creation through social customs?[25] Within feminism there is a schism between those who believe that there is something inherent that constitutes women and men, something on the level of biology or essence, and those that argue that gender, like other socially weighted categories, such as race, is culturally constructed.[26] These varying understandings of women are responsible for much diversity within feminist theory.

To further complicate the issue, there are several different ways feminist ideas can manifest in practice. Feminism is a political movement that ebbs and flows throughout North American history and coalesces in diverse ways during different time periods. In discussing the various versions of feminism in twentieth-century North America, both scholars and activists alike have used the metaphor of "waves" to assert continuity and to signify difference between: first, the push for women's rights in the Progressive Era into the early twentieth century (1880–1920), which centered around suffrage—the right to vote—and full recognition under the law; second, struggles for gender equality that started to draw serious public attention in the 1970s; and third, some current theory and political activism, which incorporates serious critiques of the previous two. Like all overarching narratives, the metaphor of first, second, and third waves is useful when used as shorthand for similarities and differences that are far more complex than those phrases convey but detrimental if mistaken for the total reality of what happened historically.[27]

Feminism is also a theoretical tool, mutually inspirational to feminism as a political movement. Feminist theory takes gender as a crucial lens through which to analyze social relations and cultural production.[28] Feminist academic methods are interdisciplinary, drawing on diverse sources, including the social sciences, literary criticism, and philosophy, and can be applied widely.[29] One of the tenets of feminist criticism is that questions about gender are not optional but imperative to any rigorous analytic perspective.[30] Hence, gender is a crucial consideration in method and theory in the academic study of religion.

Historical Relationships between
Feminism and Religion

The first wave of feminism during the Progressive Era in North America emphasized women's suffrage, but this was only a part of a broader project of "feminine" social reform that explicitly invoked religious values. Drawing on Victorian ideas of natural gender roles, women's reform work focused on extending the private sphere of women's influence into civic life. Projecting the home into public space, reformers advocated a private model for the solution of social problems.[31]

Historian Peggy Pascoe discusses four different projects in the American West that were created and administered by eastern women's associations and based in the ideology of the Christian home: one group sponsored a home loans program and a medical mission on an Omaha, Nebraska, reservation, which included sending Susan LaFlesche, an Omaha woman, to medical school.[32] Other groups sponsored rescue homes, one for unmarried mothers in Denver, one for second wives of Mormon marriages in Salt Lake City, and one for Chinese women who wished to leave the sex trade in San Francisco.[33] As the work of Caroline Strange and Mariana Valverde demonstrates, the city of Toronto had its own share of reform movements rooted in feminine domesticity, which "blurred the lines of public and private," in the words of historian Jane Jenson.[34] With their ideal of the "Christian home," white, Victorian women reformers tackled such diverse social issues as urban and rural poverty, single motherhood, sexual violence, polygyny, prostitution, and labor exploitation.

Grounding public activism in notions of the Christian home carried special power for women of color. In her study of New York's Black YWCA during this era, Judith Weisenfeld describes the process through which African American women created "mobile private space" through the discourse of home. Writes Weisenfeld, "By transporting the mantle of respectability, as engendered in the space of the YWCA, these women sought to overcome the vision of African American women as carriers of moral disease."[35] Particularly for women of color, the politics of carrying the home into the public sphere expanded the activities they could perform and the places in which they could perform them, pushing against limitations of public racism and sexism.[36] Evelyn Higginbotham argues that ideologies of Christian home supported a "politics of respectability" that were crucial for the participation of women of color in North American civic spaces.[37]

It was not only women within Protestant Christianity who were able to mobilize gendered discourses to their advantage. Interacting with the same dominant society, women in the newer religions of Spiritualism, New Thought, and Mormonism also negotiated with the "cult of true womanhood" prevalent in Victorian notions of gender and morality. They, too, found within their traditions ways to turn notions of women's proper place into justifications for their reform efforts.[38]

While these feminine reformers understood their religions to be useful in improving their worlds, each example also provides evidence that religion can be detrimental to women. The Victorian gender ideology women embraced as justification for their activism restricted both women and men to very specific social roles and, in many cases, perpetuated the structural inequalities they were fighting. Peggy Pascoe relates, for example, that rescue home workers understood the women who came to them for help to have been abused, but this understanding did not lead to a reassessment of male privilege or traditional gender roles, nor did it contribute to an anti-rape discourse.[39] Locating women's moral authority in their biology—and the presumed passivity, gentility, and domesticity that accompanied such embodiment—limited women's public actions and self-expression.[40] The racial dimensions of such ideology buttressed social injustices, as did classist and imperialist assumptions.[41] Religion was not unequivocally good for Progressive Era women reformers or for solving the problems that concerned them; however, religions did provide space and support for many first-wave social reform efforts.

When feminism again burgeoned in the late 1960s and early 1970s, the movement focused on women's empowerment through facilitating access to positions of authority, deconstructing hierarchical structures of social inequality, and creating safety from rape and other forms of sexual violence.[42] Feminists analyzed structural oppression as fundamentally based in gender: patriarchy, the power of men within society exemplified by the power of the father over the family, was the foundation of inequality.[43] Cultural feminism, popular in the second wave, rooted women's oppression in sexual difference: men's discomfort and jealousy over women's reproductive role led to a prehistoric revolution in which peaceful, matriarchal societies were conquered and enslaved by violent, patriarchal invaders, forming the basis of present-day gender relations.[44]

According to the logic of cultural feminism, if women's oppression stems from men's violence and if women have been collectively indoctrinated for millennia to believe that they are weaker, less intelligent, and naturally inferior to men, then to correct inequality, women should take leave of men, or at least spend time in women-only spaces, to explore who they might be outside of this patriarchally constructed stereotype of femininity.[45] Thus, only in starting over, rethinking what it means to be a woman, is it possible to discover the essence of womanhood, or Woman, the universal female experience. For those cultural feminists who understand religion as a possible resource in such recovery, exploring and creating visions of female divinity is crucial.[46]

The relationship between religion and second-wave feminism is much more ambivalent than that between suffrage activists and other Progressive Era reformers.[47] Women's liberation leaders in the late 1960s were involved with Christian organizations.[48] However, after the height of the Civil Rights movement, leftist activists began to move away from Christianity and embrace Marxist understandings of religion as an oppressive tool of the bourgeoisie for spreading false consciousness.[49] Following popular trajectories of secular humanism, many activists saw religion as colluding with other institutions—government, family, media—to maintain social hierarchy and the subjugation of women. Some feminists came to understand all forms of religion as oppressive. Oral historian Alice Echols, for example, quotes prominent feminist Ti-Grace Atkinson: "Whenever 'religion'—whatever its alleged genesis—has resurfaced in a Movement, it has historically been a sure sign of decadence and reaction. Any religion is too much religion."[50] It is during this second wave that we can see the beginning of divisions between those feminists who embrace a spiritual dimension to their political work and those who reject such a notion. Many of the current debates among progressive activists about the legitimacy of religion in political work stem from this split.

Not widely discussed outside of Goddess spirituality and new religious movements scholarship is the exploration of alternative religious practices by second-wave feminists. While some distanced themselves from religion as patriarchal and illusory, others began experimenting with goddess rituals, meditation, and trance states.[51] Institutionalizing these practices, women founded Goddess spirituality groups, which continue to constitute a major component of contemporary Paganism (for example, in the form of Wicca, among predominantly white women's communities) and to mutually influence Caribbean Creole and other Afrocentric traditions (such as Ifa, Yoruba, Santeria, and Vodou) and Latina spiritual orientations drawing on Indigenous knowledge (such as Gloria Anzaldúa's articulation of Chicana "*Mestiza* consciousness").[52] Although the second wave is largely presumed to be a radically secular movement and religion continues to be absent from most discussions of contemporary feminisms,[53] religion was nonetheless an important presence in this phase.

In the 1980s voices from within the feminist movement began to critique cultural feminism, the inspiration for much of this religious exploration, for its biological reductionism and ethnocentrism.[54] By choosing a specific cultural experience of gender to represent all women everywhere, one that looks eerily similar to the Victorian gender dichotomy of the first wave, cultural feminism leaves out people who do not fit this image. Women of color argue that their experiences of gendered oppression are different from those of white women both because the sexism they encounter also interacts with racism and because they understand themselves to be in solidarity with men in their communities in working against racism.[55] By insisting that biological sex was the cause of all women's oppression everywhere, white women could avoid confronting ways that they were complicit in structural racism, colonialism, and other forms of imperialist exploitation.[56] Working-class women made similar arguments about socioeconomic positionality.[57] And lesbian, bisexual, and non-gender-conforming women argued that they did not see themselves represented in the visions of Woman that cultural feminism posited, often in heterosexist ways, based on traditional stereotypes of gender complementarity.[58]

As a result, women who felt themselves excluded from cultural feminism began to articulate different visions of a movement to end gender oppression. Some women of color, arguing that feminism did not adequately account for racism as a tool of women's oppression, identified as part of the same struggle for women's empowerment but as allies, rather than as "feminists." Activists and theorists took up Alice Walker's term *Womanism* to describe a movement for women's empowerment that takes the experience of African American women as central.[59] Similarly, Chicana and other Latina women may describe themselves as "Mujeristas."[60] Lesbian, bisexual, and trans women may identify more with queer theory or LGBTQ activism.[61] Critiques and alternatives that directly address issues of race and sexual diversity are often called "third-wave" feminism. For many, especially younger, activists today, *third wave* describes the types of feminism in which they are engaged and with which they identify.[62]

Feminist Theory Inside and
Outside Religious Communities

Feminism works to redress inequality at the societal level. This political project influences and is influenced by feminist theory, which analyzes women's marginalization with the goal of ending it. Feminism impacts understandings of gender within and about religious traditions. Using feminist theory, it is possible to examine particular religious traditions for their contributions to oppression and empowerment of women within society. If the goals of such inquiry are to reform religious traditions to be more egalitarian, then the undertaking falls within the rubric of feminist theology. If the goals are to reform academic traditions, then it fits within the academic study of religion.

Feminists critically evaluate what sacred texts and religious practices have to say about women, femininity, and sexual difference. Feminist criticism looks past the assumed gender-neutrality of cosmologies, laws, and rituals and asks what kind of audience is central to scripture and doctrine. What kind of religious subject is imagined at the heart of a particular faith tradition? Is this subject implicitly male? Heterosexual? What does the tradition have to say about women? What kinds of messages does the tradition send about gender, sexuality, social power, and authority? This critique connects to other methods, such as critical race theory and queer theory, in order to investigate what religious traditions convey about the most marginalized people. While their tools are similar, their different goals generally mean that feminist theology and feminist criticism in the academic study of religion engage in divergent projects. Nonetheless, shared methodologies and commitment to feminist change place these disciplines in frequent conversation.[63]

Feminist Theologies

Women face different challenges in each religion.[64] Feminist movements in religions focus on identifying aspects of these religions that are woman-positive and those that are less so. This process is not a new one, nor is any text or ritual simply transparent, with obvious meaning. Saints and mystics, feminist and otherwise, have been engaged in struggles to understand and interpret their roles throughout religious history.[65] Feminists reinterpret or discard components of a religious tradition that are detrimental to women's personal well-being and social empowerment; they prioritize and embrace those that contribute to a feminist future.

The gendering of deities, for example, is an especially important issue for women in Abrahamic traditions, such as Christianity, Judaism, and Islam, that worship a single god. While polytheism does not guarantee respect for human women,[66] it also does not foreclose the possibility of feminine traits being considered sacred in the same way that exclusively masculine monotheisms do. Feminists argue that when there is only one image of the Divine, one God, then the gender of that God has implications for how human gender is understood.[67] As theologian Mary Daly famously put it, "If God is male, then the male is God."[68] This connection helps explain suspicious attitudes toward women throughout the histories of Western religions.

Agreeing on cause does not necessarily mean agreeing on solution. Feminists within Judaism, Christianity, Islam, and Goddess traditions have responded differently to the cycle of misogyny caused by masculine monotheism. Within Judaism and Christianity, feminists explore ways to reenvision the gender of the deity. Exploring Goddess imagery—or doing "thealogy," as Carol Christ has called it, following Naomi Goldenberg— involves efforts to understand the Divine as feminine, or to reimagine

God as Goddess.[69] Feminists may focus on feminine attributes in praying to God/dess, such as using feminine pronouns, addressing Deity as "Mother," instead of the traditional "Father," or using resources within their traditions that offer nongendered alternatives. The Hebrew Bible provides visions of Deity as friend, sacred place, even mother bear.[70] Feminists may search for images of the divine, besides Deity, that have traditionally taken on feminine traits or been understood as female. Examples include Lady Wisdom and Shekinah (internal sacred energy) in Judaism and Sophia and the Holy Spirit in Christianity.[71] They may also creatively explore exemplary human women in scripture and tradition, such as Eve, Miriam, and Deborah in the Hebrew Bible and Mary, mother of Jesus, and Mary Magdalene in the Christian Gospels as well as other historical figures in the tradition.[72]

Islam provides stories of strong human women with whom feminists within the tradition may engage;[73] however, it does not offer the same flexibility in metaphors for Deity. Nonetheless, the iconoclasm that underlies prohibitions against creating new images of God can also be used to feminist advantage. Within Islam it is heretical to mistake any specific image for Deity. Therefore, while masculine gender is used to refer to Him in the classical Arabic of the Qur'an, mistaking that linguistic label for the physical equivalent of human masculinity can be interpreted as *shirk*, or idolatry, mistaking maleness, especially human maleness, for the Divine.[74] Muslim feminists can use this understanding to argue that while images of Allah as female are unacceptable and heretical, anthropomorphic images of Him as a human man are equally so. Judgments about the relative worth of women and men based on assumptions of sacred maleness therefore also need to be rethought.

Jewish, Muslim, and Christian feminists work to critically analyze and reform their religions to better meet the needs of women; however, some feminists from these faiths respond to sexist traditions by leaving altogether. For those who continue to seek a spiritual practice, Goddess traditions offer an alternative.[75] Fitting under the broader rubric of "feminist spirituality," these include contemporary Pagan groups, such as Wicca, groups that draw on African, Latina, and/or Indigenous heritages, and looser collectives of women who come together to explore historical and existing goddess traditions as a corrective to exclusively male god imagery.[76] Not restricted to particular scriptures or theologies, Goddess spirituality frees feminists to draw on diverse feminine images of divinity. They may investigate specific goddesses from other religions or work together to help explore members' personal visions of the Goddess.[77]

Even among advocates of feminist religion, however, there is dissent about what sorts of theologies might be included. Members of Goddess religions and contemporary Paganisms sometimes dismiss feminist Christianity, Judaism, and Islam as oxymorons, suggesting that reform of such traditionally patriarchal religions is impossible. They advocate leaving them in favor of explicitly feminist Goddess religions.[78] On the other hand, feminist theologians from Christian and Jewish traditions may dismiss contemporary Paganisms and Goddess spirituality as too new and decentralized to deliver any of the benefits of religious community.[79] An example of this type of conflict can be found in debates within Womanist circles over whether such a theological project must be inherently Christian or Pagan or whether Womanist spirituality, rooted as it is in the experiences of women in the African diaspora, can accommodate both cosmologies.[80] Echoing disagreements within the larger movement, feminists outside Goddess spirituality may also be concerned about aspects of cultural appropriation in the embrace of goddesses from other religions and cultures.[81] The same arguments may be turned toward Western conversion to transplanted Eastern traditions, such as Buddhism and Hinduism, and Indigenous traditions, such as Native American spirituality.[82]

Despite divisions of religion and denomination, North American feminists of faith have much in common with each other.[83] They often explicitly acknowledge their shared interest in religious experience as personally empowering, beneficial for participation in community, and supportive of political action. Such mutual recognition was apparent, for example, at the conference "Religion and the Feminist Movement," held at Harvard Divinity School in November 2002, which drew together leaders from feminist movements in Judaism, Christianity, Islam, and Goddess spirituality.[84]

Feminist Theory in the Study of Religion

While feminist theologies provide opportunities for practitioners to reenvision their religions in new, more just ways, feminist criticism in the study of religion offers provocative interventions into social theory, spurring scholars to reevaluate dominant models. Despite its self-understanding as objective and impartial, the Western academy has its own traditions of androcentrism and misogyny, its own cosmologies and value judgments.[85] What happens when scholars of religion put women at the center of their analysis, rather than treating them as perplexing exceptions to theories that take men's experiences as foundational? What is typical religious experience and practice? What criteria have scholars been using to determine such things? What role do gender assumptions play in the creation of the category of religion itself as well as main terms such as *theology, ritual, mysticism,* and *sacrifice*?[86]

Focusing on women's experiences and practices calls into question the traditional privileging, based on Western models, of religions focused on other-worldly concerns.[87] Popular definitions of religion that prescribe transcendent deities communicating mainly through sacred texts, hierarchies of authority with identifiable leaders, and cosmologies that emphasize the afterlife exclude from the beginning many social practices that would fit under broader definitions of *religion,* especially non-Western and Indigenous religions, new religious movements, as well as women's practices.[88] In taking the experience of women and other marginalized people seriously, feminist critics argue that there are many alternative ways of being religious to those traditionally recognized by scholars.

In her discussion of spirit possession, for example, anthropologist Susan Starr Sered draws on feminist ethnographies of both woman-dominated religions and women in male-dominated religions.[89] Sered considers why spirit possession, a common ritual practice that allows communities to encounter their deities face-to-face, has been treated by scholars as exceptional and in need of special explanation.[90] She asks what would happen if instead of assuming that spirit possession by women is an aberrant and eccentric ritual practice, we reorient our perspective: "Could it be that possession trance is a normal and healthy part of human experience, but men have trouble with it because they have trouble with relationships?"[91] Asking new questions helps unmask the androcentrism behind supposedly objective theories.

Likewise, historian Ann Braude reconsiders models of a "feminization" of American religion, in which a masculine Christianity, supported by a majority of male practitioners, has been giving way to a supposedly sentimental, diluted theology endorsed by predominantly female church attendees. In examining historical trends in churchgoing, she discovered that the image of a masculine church with a majority-male congregation is based on what is actually an exceptional period in American colonial history.[92] To rephrase, women have traditionally made up the bulk of church attendance in America: "Women's history *is* American religious history."[93] Only by viewing these trends through a sexist lens, in which women are less desirable than men, do we get a tragedy in which the robust masculinity of the American church is compromised by feminization.

Feminist scholarship in religious studies not only enriches the field but also contributes to interdisciplinary debates. An area of fruitful controversy at the intersection of feminist theory, the social sciences, and philosophical ethics focuses on agency and resistance among women in traditionalist religions. Women converting from mainstream liberal society into religious communities, such as Orthodox Judaism, conservative Pentecostal Christianities, and the conservative mosque movement in Islam, trouble models of progress built on the assumption that the world is on a predictable path away from restrictive religious traditions and toward liberal secularism. When women voluntarily limit their personal autonomy in favor of religious community, this disrupts notions of the primacy of personal freedom at the heart of Western modernity.[94] Yet women within conservative traditions negotiate for their own needs and interests within such limits, challenging the boundaries of their communities at the same time that they endeavor to conform to their strictures.[95]

To dismiss women in more conservative movements as lacking agency, or to only recognize agency when it takes the form of resistance to social norms and values, is to engage in what Lila Abu-Lughod has termed "the romance of resistance," based on Western values of autonomy over and against community and tradition.[96] She argues that personal agency is something that all subjects, including women—and more specifically, women in conservative traditions—enact in all their practices. Responsible feminist research examines not only those behaviors that contradict social expectations but also those that reinforce them.

Anthropologist Saba Mahmood observes, for example, that women in the conservative mosque movement in Egypt must struggle against mainstream suspicion of their religion in order be part of it. In embodying their traditionalist understandings of women's proper behavior, attitudes, and roles to the fullest, these women are enacting personal agency just as much as women who buck them.[97] Similarly, R. Marie Griffith's fieldwork among women in the Christian Women Aglow movement in North America demonstrates that members work very hard to perform the visions of Christian women, wives, and mothers that their religion promotes. Not only do they strive to enact these gendered standards, but within this women's movement they are part of creating them, albeit in interaction with men and patriarchal tradition.[98] As the work of these ethnographically engaged theorists highlights, scholars can't have it both ways: that women are agents when dissenting but victims when they embrace nonfeminist values.[99]

Feminist Criticism, Religion, and Social Change

Certainly religions can have detrimental effects on women as well as other marginalized members of society. Religious traditions are necessary components of discussions about a range of problems, including intimate partner violence and child abuse.[100] However, they are especially luridly denounced in discussions of culturally specific practices, such as honor-anxiety crimes, female genital cutting, and dowry murders, not to mention heated controversies around female veiling, abortion and other forms of birth control, and same-sex relationships.[101] This continues a long history of accusations about religiously sanctioned mistreatment of women being used as justification for Western colonial projects, such as the British in India and North America, the French in Egypt, and the Dutch in Indonesia, and as rationalization for repressing religions at home, such as Catholicism and Mormonism.[102] It is important to acknowledge both that religions can repress women and that women's repression is a convenient excuse for cultural chauvinism and religious intolerance.

Women in secularized contexts are killed by ex-partners out of jealousy. Wives and daughters are physically punished by men for being perceived as dressing in "inappropriate" ways, speaking or behaving immodestly, or for sleeping with the wrong people under the wrong circumstances. It turns out that people still care a great deal about policing women's behavior, especially their sexuality, even outside explicitly religious contexts.[103] Religion does not have an exclusive hold on gender oppression.

Moreover, marginalized people find religious resources for liberation from oppression precisely because religions are an important part of many people's lives, in fact most people's lives, around the world. Christian theologian Virginia Ramey Mollenkott advocates feminist scriptural interpretation as a strategy for transforming the most misogynist traditions. Because many Christian women take the Bible as the literal word of God, they have no recourse when feminists argue that scripture is inherently misogynist. On the other hand, it is liberating for women in conservative traditions when feminist theologians can offer alternative interpretations to misogynist passages and new criteria for being good women within their traditions.[104]

In contrast to misogynist movements that justify themselves in the name of Islam, Muslim feminists such as Amina Wadud, Riffat Hassan, and Azizah al-Hibri argue that justice is a core value in Islam and the major message that Allah is trying to convey through the prophet Muhammad in the Qur'an.[105] All scriptural interpretations must be made in light of this fundamental sacred principle.[106] In choosing between interpretations of particular passages, it is the duty of individual Muslims and the Islamic community to prioritize interpretations that favor equality and human rights for women as well as other marginalized people. Arguing that sexism is not an original part of Islamic religion but rather an outside influence allows feminist Muslims to position gender equality at the heart of their tradition.[107] Therefore, educating women to be experts in Qur'anic interpretation and jurisprudence is one of the most practical strategies for improving their status.[108]

Feminists of faith argue that religion itself is not the core cause of misogyny but rather that male-dominated religious traditions reflect broader structural inequalities that oppress and denigrate women. It is naive to think that if everyone woke up tomorrow an atheist, no one would continue to be sexist, racist, or homophobic. These negative values suffuse society and transcend particular cultural systems. Blaming religion for these problems means not having to acknowledge how deeply ingrained hierarchy and oppression are within contemporary societies and obscures the violence inherent in the nation-state.[109]

The relationship between feminism and religion is multifaceted. Religions have played and continue to play important roles in feminist political movements. Feminist criticism, in turn, influences religious traditions, the traditions of the Western academy, and the ways that scholars study and theorize about religions.

Academic Context

Although there is significant literature on contemporary conservative women, there is sparse literature with a rigorous, scholarly approach that addresses how religion and politics may intersect for feminist women in North America. Exceptions to this trend include some good historical work on the first wave of the feminist movement, mostly, but not exclusively, exploring the role of Christianity for the movement.[110] However, once scholars move from the explicit religious interests of first-wave feminists, religion seems to disappear from the story of feminist history.[111] The second wave is largely presumed to be a radically secular movement, and religion is equally absent from most discussions of contemporary feminisms.[112]

Women who do not fit these frames are often left out of the discussions, and the exclusion of religion parallels earlier absences in women's studies.[113] Barbara Smith points out that, for example, in scholarship of the second wave, feminist scholars often say that its real transformative power was "over" by the early to mid-1970s, precisely the time that women of color, Jewish women, and working-class women began to become involved and bring their critiques to the community.[114] Similarly, Sherna Berger Gluck and her coauthors argue that the traditional conception of second-wave feminism only focuses on white women on the East Coast of the United States who specifically articulated their activism as having gendered dimensions. Using examples from groups of working-class women of color in California, Gluck and her coauthors point out that there was a lot going on in places scholars chose not to look.[115] Becky Thompson argues for a historical reassessment of feminism that includes the influence of the Civil Rights and Black Power movements as well as major contributions by women of color.[116]

The majority of scholarship on the relationship between religion and politics for women in contemporary North America focuses on the relationship between Christianity and political conservatives.[117] While there are exceptions to this trend,[118] very little work directly investigates contemporary relationships between religion—whether Catholic, Protestant, or contemporary Pagan—and progressive political action. There is some confessional literature from current activists on the Left.[119] Religion and feminist politics surface in Christian thea/theological works; however, in these the focus is on the theory, with concrete applications serving as examples.[120] The confessional and thealogical literature of contemporary Paganism and women's spirituality, similar to Christian feminist theology, also does not focus on politics and activism, but instead these arenas appear as anecdote or example, the means to or expression of a spiritual experience.[121]

Some descriptive social science work on women's spiritual groups— Christian, contemporary Pagan, and comparative—mention politics and activism, but it is in passing.[122] One survey study of woman-focused, North American, Christian women includes a section on political involvement but merely links women-focused Christianity with political involvement, rather than investigating that link.[123] One survey study of women in Dianic Wicca focuses on political activism, concluding that Wiccan religious orientation does not preclude political involvement.[124] Three ethnographic studies—one of women in the Feminist Spirituality movement, one of North American contemporary Pagans, and one of queer women's spirituality in Los Angeles—include attention to political action.[125] There is very little work, however, outside the context of confessional literature that focuses specifically on the ways religious and political commitments interact for contemporary feminist women in North America.

Method and Description

This project is a multisited, ethnographic study of religion among feminist activists in Toronto, Canada. It focuses on women who identify as political activists and as feminist Catholic, feminist United Church Protestant, or feminist contemporary Pagan. My main sources are ethnographic interviews with informants in the Toronto area. Of the sixty-one women interviewed, all identify as feminist political activists, and within that group, twenty identify as feminist Catholic, twenty-two identify as feminist United Church Protestant, and nineteen identify as feminist contemporary Pagan.[126] In addition to interviews, I engaged in participant-observation within feminist Catholic, United Church, and contemporary Pagan groups.[127] The three groups in which I conducted fieldwork are the Toronto Catholic Worker community, Clearwater United Church, and the Yarrow Pagan Collective, a contemporary Pagan group strongly influenced by Reclaiming Witchcraft. Reclaiming Witchcraft is a contemporary Pagan Witchcraft tradition founded in the San Francisco Bay area around 1980 by Starhawk, among others, such as M. Macha NightMare.[128] I participated in events such as group planning meetings, public demonstrations, and religious rituals.

Both the participants and the researcher inevitably influence ethnographic work, which is an inherently social enterprise. As a young woman pursuing an academic degree in religious studies and gender studies and as someone with connections in Toronto activist communities, I was received by my participants and their groups in particular ways. Because of who I am, or was perceived by others to be, I heard specific stories and was privy to particular participant-observation experiences. This dynamic becomes especially important to keep in mind when evaluating my research, as it is the result of particular conversations between particular people. My participants greeted my fieldwork project with enthusiasm, and I came to my participants sympathetic to their political and religious projects. In many ways I was treated more as an insider than, for example, an older, politically conservative man working on a newspaper story might have been. Another researcher, even using similar methods in the same communities, may have come away with different impressions, experiences, and narratives.

Because each of these groups works hard to subvert traditional authority hierarchies within their traditions, conducting participant-observation within them was not as fraught as it might have been within other ethnographic research environments. Each group with which I conducted fieldwork is generally welcoming to the public and, even for closed rituals, does not require initiation. This is most significant for my participant-observation of the Catholic Worker liturgies. Because these rites are not High Mass, I was welcome to participate in the rite of Communion and share bread and juice with the rest of the community.

On only one occasion was I questioned about my own religious affiliation in a manner that expressed anxiety on the part of a participant and that made me uncomfortable.[129] I understand this lack of concern on the part of my participants to be an anomaly in the field of religious ethnography. In general my participants did not expect me to identify myself as part of their religions, though I did receive questions about my religious background, usually in interview contexts when a participant was relating her own experiences and checking for understanding on my part. Simply saying, "I was raised Presbyterian," satisfied all such inquiries across disparate contexts including a United Church member describing her positive religious experiences and a contemporary Pagan member talking about leaving a homophobic church as a teenager.

Building on participant-observation of public protest demonstrations beginning in 2000, I carried out fieldwork in these communities during 2003 and 2004, and I conducted interviews with women members. While I did not formally interview men within the communities, with the exception of Bill, Clearwater's pastor, my participant-observation naturally included men, and many informal discussions with men contributed to this study. Further, I conducted interviews with women who came to me through my call for participants; not all of my participants belonged to one of these specific groups, although all identified with one of the religious communities. I also took part in religious rituals and public demonstrations with my participants and their groups.

Inclusion Criteria

While much abstract debate around religion in the public sphere is by men and is often implicitly androcentric, women are major actors in religion in North America, as they have been historically.[130] I centered my research on women who actively participate in political discourse in the public sphere and who do so at the same time that they hold religious affiliations among the three groups in my study. I sought participants who identify as "feminist," as "political activists," and as members of specific religious traditions. Rather than try to define *feminism* in a particular way and then seek out women who met my arbitrary definition, I chose to make self-identification my criteria. If a woman considers herself feminist, she is feminist in my study.

The second selection criterion I used for participation was political activism. I was looking for a specific kind of activism in that I did not include, for example, anti-choice protesters or people who protest gay marriage. In large part self-identification as feminist screens for conservative political affiliations, but "activism" is still very broad. My participants vary greatly in terms of the kinds of activist work they do. I have spoken with women who participate in guerrilla street theater, who work with developmentally disabled people in group home settings, who make organic body care products, who participate in formal political structures, who shun formal politics, who graffiti, who write letters to their representatives in government, who do all sorts of diverse and contradictory things. What can political activism mean if the women I talked to are engaged in such different activities?

I was pushed to be more specific in defining *political activism* by someone who had seen my flyer. She called me, very eager to be interviewed. She said that she was a very busy woman and could only give me an hour of her time. She would only agree to participate in the study if I could guarantee her I would use her real name. It was also very important to her that I promise to get my work published. She had some suggestions about how I might do this.

It turned out that she was a freelance, corporate training consultant, and she wanted to participate to get publicity from being in the project. She happily told me over the phone that she was a "goddess spirituality activist." In her trainings for companies, such as large telecom corporations and global food distribution companies, she brought the "goddess into the workplace" and emphasized power sharing and anti-oppression. It became clear to me that the kinds of activist undertakings I was interested in studying and the kind of activities in which she engaged with her corporate training were two very different things. Yet she identified as an activist. My interactions with her highlighted for me that I needed to be more specific in what I was looking for in a political activist.

For the purposes of my study, I define a political activist as someone who has participated in at least one street demonstration and is engaged, in one form or another, in efforts they define as "social justice" work. *Social justice* is a term that is used by groups that perform the kinds of activism in which I am interested and not used by groups engaged in more conservative causes. For example, Focus on the Family does not use the term, nor do institutional consultants, but Christian Peacemaker Teams do. Social justice activism beyond public protest takes many forms: volunteering with local organizations; attending political meetings and rallies; letter writing; public education campaigns. Each individual participant may not engage in every one of these activities, but all of the women I included in my study dedicate time and resources, beyond money, to projects of social change.

As the third inclusion criterion, I chose specific religious institutions, instead of activists who identified exclusively as "spiritual," in order to address the challenge that religious institutions pose to secularist assumptions within political activist communities, as opposed to a generic spirituality, which accommodates negative assessments of religion. I sought out three religious traditions that were explicitly present at public demonstrations in the city and with whom I was familiar through personal contacts.[131] These groups clearly promoted the incorporation of their religious practice into public action. Each group was vocal about refocusing their personal religious practices and their congregations' energies on "this-worldly" concerns.

Two of these groups are Christian: Toronto Catholic Worker and Clearwater United Church. The third, Yarrow Collective, is contemporary Pagan. Each of them is explicit about incorporating politics with religion, though each also belongs to a larger tradition that does not exclusively involve itself with active social reform projects. These groups, while not new religious movements in that they all claim a relationship to more established traditions, can nonetheless be thought of as "new movements in religion." Feminist reinterpretation and ritualizing of

Christianity function explicitly as reform movements within the tradition, reinterpreting Scripture and reworking ritual to emphasize the social justice messages that they understand to be at the heart of their traditions.

Feminist contemporary Pagans, on the other hand, often present their religion as an alternative to Christianity, a relinquishing rather than reformation, an opting out rather than staying to reform the oppressive structure from inside.[132] However, feminist contemporary Paganisms, particularly feminist Wicca and feminist Witchcraft, can also be seen as reform movements, like feminist Christian theology, in that theology, rituals, and symbolism have been modified, particularly from their British High Magic roots, inherited from Gerald Gardiner, among others.[133] Nonetheless, feminist Witches argue that, at the very least, female symbolism and leadership roles for women have always been a part of Wicca, even if they relied on traditional European understandings of gender and essentialized ideas of women's nature.[134] In addition, Yarrow members distinguish themselves from other contemporary Pagan groups in town, whom they understand to be apolitical.

I chose to investigate both Catholic and Protestant groups not only because they form the dichotomy of religious hegemony in Canada but also because main arguments in the debate about religion and public discourse trace back to the basic identity difference between these groups, an issue I explore in chapter 3. Moreover, both the Toronto Catholic Worker and Clearwater United Church explicitly strive to subvert the hierarchy and privilege they receive as official Christian institutions in Canada. I chose contemporary Paganism because it is a popular alternative to Christianity within activist circles. Many of the participants from the Yarrow Collective explained that they had at one time been Christian of one sort or another.

In many ways *Christianity* is the default for *religion* in North American discussions of religion in public space. Moreover, a reductionist caricature of Catholicism lurks behind some of the most vehement dismissals of religion as speciously harmful and restrictive. Ironically, Catholicism is also the most widely embraced of the permutations of Christianity, so it is both the most widespread centralized hierarchy and the most globally populist of the Christian traditions.

Participant Demographics

I did not plan my study to limit participants beyond the criteria described here; nonetheless, certain kinds of women responded to my call for participants and welcomed my presence. A large number of my participants were white Anglo Canadians;[135] however, I do not want to dismiss the importance of my participants who are women of color. Glossing my study as predominantly white obscures these women and obfuscates their contributions, something I am loath to do. Yet I also believe it is significant that the majority of women who were attracted to the labels of "feminist" and "political activist" in my call for participants are not women of color.

As much effort as feminist movements in North America have expended to attract women of color and as sharp as the critiques of internal racism have been, I suspect that most self-identified feminists, at least in Canada, remain white. This does not mean that women of color are not engaged in combating gender oppressions but rather that many choose to do it outside the rubric of feminism.[136] Women engaged in work against gender-linked oppressions may not self-identify as feminist for several reasons: it may make them uncomfortable in relation to nonfeminist women and men; it may prioritize gender oppression above other forms of oppression in their lives and work; or they may feel alienated from the term *feminism* for other reasons. Because *feminism* conjures for many people the image of a white, middle-class, liberal women unconcerned with oppressions other than gender, there are likely many social justice activists with religious affiliation who do not identify this way, many of whom do identify as "Womanist," "mujerista," and/or "anti-oppression" activists.[137] A few white informants told me as much when at the end of interviews I would ask them if they knew of other women with whom I should talk. They would suggest someone and then think twice, saying, "Oh, but she doesn't like the term *feminist*."

Most of my participants are highly educated, and many have advanced degrees, some in areas very similar to this project, such as gender studies, the study of religion, and systematic theology. Some had done fieldwork themselves for various projects. A great number read feminist theory and attend feminist-oriented conferences and workshops. Several are published authors. Their occupations include a professor of law, former and aspiring pastors, and a former Canadian senator. One of the distinctive strengths of this anthropological project is that I have been able to study people who are normally understood as socially privileged, that is, white feminists. However, there was wide class diversity among my participants, with several living below the poverty line. Further, I would estimate that about a third of my informants identify as lesbian, bisexual, trans, or queer.

Feminist ethnographers R. Marie Griffith and Saba Mahmood engage in work to humanize, to "unother," the "other"—that is, nonfeminist women. Griffith's *God's Daughters: Evangelical Women and the Power of Submission* looks at predominantly white women in America who are part of the conservative Women Aglow movement in Christianity. Mahmood, in her *Politics of Piety: The Islamic Revival and the Feminist Subject*, looks at Egyptian women who are part of the conservative mosque movement in Islam. Both Griffith and Mahmood study women who resist liberal Enlightenment discourses.

Despite my different focus, I understand this study in relation to those of Griffith and Mahmood. I turn to women who for the most part embrace liberal ideals of autonomy, freedom, and equality and consider themselves rightfully central to such discourses. My participants position themselves as subjects, rather than marginal objects, to progressive social aims. In analyzing particular forms of feminist discourse and practice via my participants' narratives and activities, this project offers a useful connection between the thought experiments of some recent feminist theory and ways that feminism is actually practiced in North America, providing insight into translations of feminist theory into popular practice.

My participants' identification with Enlightenment subjectivity does not mean, however, that they are not also critical of mainstream liberalism. Their concerns are that, as Charles Long writes of the critique brought by the African American religious experience, the West is "not *being* the West" in "not living up to its cultural ideals."[138] My participants are painfully aware that values of equity and justice remain unfulfilled in the contemporary world and disgustedly cite selfish politicians, rapacious corporations, and misguided social conservatives as obstacles in the way of necessary change. In this sense they have something in common with women in Marla Frederick's study of the Black Church in North Carolina.[139] Frederick's participants share deep suspicions of "Progress" born out of the historical failure of projects meant to improve their communities. Nonetheless, like Frederick's participants, the women I spoke with continue to work for change.

The biggest potential challenges to my identity as a researcher and as a person dedicated to issues of equity and just social change came in moments when my participants articulated ideas and goals very different from my own under rubrics of movements with which I identify, such as feminism and social justice activism. Many women, some of my participants included, conceive of their feminism in ways that contradict my own. For example, I find essentializing ideas of "Woman's Power" alienating and consider them counterproductive in the project of eliminating gender-based oppressions. Some of the activities in which my participants engage as part of their political activism are not ones I would view as particularly politically savvy or useful for wide scale social change. On many such issues, in fact, my participants disagree with each other too.

I consider this diversity of viewpoints among my participants to be a positive attribute of the study. The goal of my project is to describe and analyze ways that women live their feminisms, rather than determining prescriptions for how feminism *should* be lived.[140] I bring tools of critical analysis to this project, but it is not solely, or mainly, criticism. While my own opinions and attitudes inescapably shape my fieldwork experiences and writing, my aim is to describe my participants and their worldviews in ways that they will recognize. At the same time, however, as Griffith has articulated in describing her own ethnographic project, "The lived worlds of human experience, after all, are not identical to people's descriptions of these worlds."[141] I have tried to take what my participants have shared with me seriously. That includes critical engagement with their words and actions. I have attempted to think about things that they might not have, to make connections and comparisons particular to the perspective that this project has afforded me. My regard for the work in which these women and their communities engage is inherent in this analysis.

Toronto Catholic Worker

The organization of Catholic Workers was founded in Chicago in 1933, the heart of the Great Depression, by Dorothy Day and her friend Peter Maurin.[142] They created a community model of hospitality, care of the poor, and simple living based on Catholic principles, with active roles for women.[143] Day's important role as founder provides a template for women's participation and leadership. The organization has been politically active from the beginning, blending a commitment to Catholic pacifism with direct action tactics.[144] In her later years Day went to jail four times for protesting nuclear weapons.[145] Through both public action and its newspaper, the *Catholic Worker*, the organization has had great influence on North American understandings of civil disobedience and nonviolent action in advocating for peace and care for the poor.[146] Catholic Worker communities are locally based, with loose affiliations with the rest of the approximately 185 communities worldwide.[147]

The Toronto Catholic Worker community was founded in 1991 and is located in a series of rental houses on the west side of the city in an economically challenged neighborhood with many immigrant families. The Gardiner Expressway divides the neighborhood from the lakefront at the southern edge of the city. Although it has gentrified a bit over the past decade, the neighborhood continues to have a reputation for drugs and other extralegal businesses. The Catholic Worker houses share the block with an elementary school and a city-run, in-patient rehab clinic, just down the street from what is regarded by many of the women I interviewed as one of the most conservative Catholic churches in the city. The community has about fifteen steady adult members and five children, but this number does not include people who are staying with the community, such as international students, refugees, and U.S. war resisters. These people stay on a more temporary basis and contribute to the community to the extent they are able.

The Toronto Catholic Worker is run as a cooperative. Workers live in each of the six houses. The main house, known as the Zacchaeus House, functions as the heart of the community. Zacchaeus House is organized and maintained by a woman and a man working together. For the duration of my fieldwork, the leaders were Regina and Neil. Both were in their midtwenties and friends of a friend. I knew Neil—friendly, witty, and ponytailed—from activism at the University of Toronto Centre for Women and Transpeople years earlier. I found Regina approachable, sometimes frighteningly smart, and always easy to like. She had just taken over the position at Zacchaeus House when I began my fieldwork and facilitated my access to the community. Regina and Neil were both very down to earth and seemed to work well together, dividing work, supporting each other, and sharing a sense of humor about their many commitments.

I was not the first researcher to do fieldwork in their community. Journalists had come through in years past. Partly because of this, Regina and Neil insisted that anonymity was not necessary for my fieldwork with them. "People know who we are," said Neil. "We don't really worry about that stuff." The result in this work is that members of the community receive pseudonyms, just as members of the Clearwater congregation and the Yarrow Collective do, but the name of the organization is not altered.

Part of the responsibility of running Zacchaeus House is that someone must be available at all times to help people in need of food, shelter, or emotional support. Zacchaeus House functions as a drop-in center, temporary shelter, and community kitchen. Dinners are communally served in Zacchaeus House, and anyone may drop in off the street. On Wednesday nights, after dinner, there is a community liturgy led on a rotating basis by different members of the community or friends of the community and held in the cozy living room. Several members of the community live in Zacchaeus House with Regina, Neil, and more transient guests. During my fieldwork most of the other housemates were international students. When I would call the house, the answering machine list of potential recipients of messages was impressively long.

The other five houses contain couples, families with children, and individual members living with friends. The house immediately next the Zacchaeus House is run by Agatha, a woman in her sixties known in the Catholic Worker community for her shy kindness and her talented knitting and by her working-partner, Arlene, who grew up playing the trombone in the Salvation Army. Their house is specifically dedicated to assisting international refugees, people trying to escape persecution in their home countries. The community is in a lot of ways very hand-to-mouth. There is not a lot of money floating around the co-op. They don't own their houses but rent them, even though they put a lot of effort into their upkeep and improvement.

The Catholic Worker community also has friends and allies who do not live in the co-op. Many of these people come by for community dinners or events. When they come, friends of the community may bring food for the kitchen or other small donations. Others may volunteer a bit of time. For example, the community had a special spring cleanup day in which they encouraged friends to come by and help spruce up the houses and yards.

Many of the women with whom I spoke were in their mid- to late twenties, as was Regina, but there were more venerable members as well, such as Agatha, who has made the Catholic Worker community an important part of her life for many years. In between are women like Maggie, a sociologist in her early thirties, who is raising her young children in the community together with her husband. In addition to being child friendly, the community is also explicitly welcoming to people of all sexual and gender orientations.

The Catholic Worker community is on the fringes of the larger Catholic Church. It is often viewed with suspicion by the establishment. Many of the Catholic women I interviewed had stories of distrust and frank insults from priests who dislike Workers. Some members, who still identify as Catholic, no longer attend the official rites of Mass or reconciliation (formerly called "confession") at Catholic churches but still participate in community liturgies.[148] In contrast, some members purposely seek out conservative parishes around the city to attend, hoping to challenge other Catholics through their meticulous adherence to church requirements in combination with their social justice politics and progressive lifestyle choices.

Not all of the Catholic women I interviewed were strongly affiliated with the Toronto Catholic Worker community, though many have personal or group ties to members. Almost all of them would ask if I was doing work with the Toronto Catholic Worker for my project and were pleased to hear that I was. Many of them had also participated in demonstrations or events with the Catholic Worker community at one time or another. For Catholic social justice activists within Toronto, the Catholic Worker community is an important hub of energy and activism, understood to be made up of Catholics who truly live their faith in action and embody Christian community through the way they live.

Clearwater United Church

In 1925 Methodist, Presbyterian, and Congregational churches joined to form the United Church of Canada.[149] The United Church is known as a liberal and socially engaged denomination,[150] though its membership also includes more conservative Christians who disagree with many of the church's policies, especially ordaining lesbian and gay pastors and performing same-sex marriages. A quick glance at the United Church homepage shows a tab for its "Social Action" page, which provides examples of current projects, such as earthquake relief, Amnesty International letter writing, and studies in racial and economic justice.[151]

Clearwater United Church is a small congregation of about fifty members that holds its Sunday services in an activity room of another, larger United Church's building. It is part of a collection of United Churches in an affluent neighborhood near the University of Toronto campus. The congregation itself is older but does include a few families, such as Annie, a professor of law at a local university, and her two teenage sons. Because it is small, the congregation is especially close-knit, but it is also welcoming to newcomers. There are several senior members who only make it out occasionally and are especially warmly greeted when they attend. One such member is Yoko, a Japanese Canadian woman who celebrated her eightieth birthday during my fieldwork.

From 1987 to 2000 the congregation was led by Franka, a striking older woman who founded one of the first fair trade projects in Canada. Franka retired as pastor in 2000 but still volunteers with the church and attends services with her partner, Sophie, a professional psychoanalyst originally from Germany. After a search, the congregation chose Bill, a sprightly and thoughtful middle-aged man with an interest in ecotheology, as a part-time pastor.

Clearwater consciously promotes and is known throughout Toronto for social justice activism. Weekly Bible studies held in members' homes focus on interpreting Scripture from this perspective. Weekly worship is organized with Bill and the worship committee. Each week a different member speaks during the main part of the service. During my time with Clearwater, the themes of focus included particular members speaking about their own spiritual journeys and personal experiences of activism.

A standard service includes a call to worship, hymns, a reflection, an offering, and an announcement period. After the service ends, members gather in the adjacent gymnasium for coffee and snacks. For those who wish to join, there is then a time for responding to the service, during which members regroup in the sanctuary in a circle of chairs and offer their thoughts, criticisms, and suggestions on the day's service.

Clearwater also has several different committees that deal with community work and church business. Among them are: the Social Justice, Peace and Environment working group; a committee that supports immigrating families that the congregation sponsors; and various liaisons to the other neighborhood United Churches and cooperative projects, such as the sponsorship of a street nurse who ministers to the local homeless people out of a church down the street, the Out of the Cold program, and the Homelessness Action group. In addition, the congregation plans its participation in political actions and demonstrations, such as anti-war rallies and marches in support of anti-poverty campaigns.

One of the foundational stories that Clearwater members tell about the congregation is that they once had a prominent building nearby, built in 1888, which they relinquished in 1985 and donated the money from its sale to charity. The old building now hosts a school for the performing arts and a local theater. For Clearwater members this act of renouncing their building is symbolic of their desire as a congregation to avoid the pitfalls of institutionalized religion. By coming together as a small group in borrowed space, they emphasize their commitment to fellowship and creative ritualizing, rather than to reified stone and traditional worship.

The congregation, while predominantly, though certainly not exclusively, white and older-middle-aged, is diverse in other ways. Since 1996 it has identified as an "affirming congregation"—that is, as a church that is open to members of all sexual orientations—and its membership reflects that commitment. The congregation performed its first same-sex marriage in June 2003. Moreover, there is at least one member who is openly HIV-positive.

Members also bring varying religious orientations to the church, including one member who identifies as Jewish and another who identifies as Buddhist. In addition, many members express personal interests in Hinduism, Native spirituality, and Asian spiritual traditions. The home-page at the church website includes the statement: "We understand the Spirit to be revealed not only in Jesus and in the Hebrew and Christian scriptures, but also in nature and in the spirituality of other traditions."

Deborah, an environmental scientist in her late forties and a member of the Clearwater worship committee, kindly facilitated my access to Clearwater. After we spoke, she took my request to conduct participant-observation to the membership and brought the approval back to me. It was her enthusiasm about Clearwater that attracted me to the possibility of working with this group. Most of my United Church interviews derive from this congregation. However, I also spoke with women from partner United Churches in the same neighborhood. These other churches share space, resources, volunteer programs, and occasional worship services with Clearwater.

Yarrow Collective

The Yarrow Collective was founded in 2002 as a way to bring together Toronto Pagans who wanted to more actively integrate their Pagan spirituality with their political activism. It serves as an umbrella organization; many members maintain affiliations with other covens in addition to being Yarrow members. In this sense Yarrow functions slightly differently than the Christian groups with which I worked. I heard about Yarrow through several friends and community groups and attended a collective meeting. I introduced myself and explained my project, asking the members of the group whether I might conduct research with them. They responded to my project description with enthusiasm and approved of my presence. Immediately following the meeting, several women volunteered to be interviewed.

Contemporary Paganism is a new religious movement made up of diverse groups and practices. One of the most well-known forms of

Paganism in North America today, Wicca, or Witchcraft, is a reinterpretation or conscious reconstruction of ancient Celtic and Anglo-Saxon religion, with a focus on the earth and earth cycles.[152] Wiccans usually worship a deity or deities who are connected to nature and the cycles of the year. Deity varieties usually include the Triple Goddess in her Maid-Mother-Crone aspects and range from Goddess-centered monism through a dual-theism of the Goddess and her consort-son, the Horned God, through radical polytheism with different goddesses and gods representing different facets of life, time, and experiences. Despite differences in deity choice, Wiccans collectively believe in pragmatic magic as a way of channeling personal energy and earth energy. In magic balance is emphasized, and the tradition is somewhat self-regulating in that Wiccans believe that whatever energy one sends out also returns to the sender.[153]

While not made up exclusively of Reclaiming Witchcraft members, the Yarrow Collective endorses the Reclaiming guiding "Principles of Unity," and several members belong to the same local coven, Celestial Circle, formed a few years earlier. Reclaiming Witchcraft is an explicitly feminist and social justice–oriented tradition.[154] Starhawk herself and Reclaiming members in general are acknowledged and respected by other activists for their participation in global justice protests,[155] such as those against the World Trade Organization meeting in Seattle in 1999 and against the Free Trade Area of the Americas (FTAA) meeting in Quebec City in 2001. Yarrow members look particularly to American Reclaiming groups, especially Starhawk's organization in San Francisco, to provide role modeling and inspiration to their burgeoning community.

The Yarrow Collective has a loose membership organized through meetings, a Listserv of about eighty subscribers,[156] and public events. This group's membership is made up predominantly of women. There was only one highly active male member during my fieldwork, though women occasionally brought male partners to public rituals. Betty, a woman in her midthirties who works in a women's studies program at a local university, explicitly spoke to this issue, saying that men were very welcome but tended not to stick around for one reason or another. However, in addition to welcoming people of all sexual orientations, Yarrow was also explicitly trans-positive—that is, welcoming of transgendered and transsexual people—and included at least one openly trans woman, Monica, a computer programmer.

Yarrow lacks a permanent meeting space and instead shifts gatherings from place to place. I attended meetings at the University of Toronto's Centre for Women and Transpeople and the lounge of the Women and Gender Studies Institute, the workshop space of a Goddess spirituality store, personal homes of members, restaurants, and public spaces such as Dufferin Grove Park, High Park, and the Toronto Islands. During my fieldwork there was discussion of a long-term plan to someday buy land for the collective to use as sacred space.

Membership among Yarrow, like the Catholic Worker, is a little younger than the majority of Clearwater. Yarrow had many mothers with young children. Along with married women and mothers raising their children on their own, there is a group of women alloparenting (community raising) a child, Lilly, Bea's daughter. Bea is working on a master's degree in environmental sciences and is actively involved with local electoral politics. She wants to raise her daughter in a supportive environment that disrupts the ideology of the nuclear family. Lilly, who turned one during my fieldwork with the group, is being raised by several members together, in a cooperative house, and she was present, gurgling happily or sleeping, for several of my interviews with Yarrow members.

Common Influences

There was much overlap between communities, and Toronto can sometimes be a rather small world. Participants of different religious affiliations often work on the same projects and know each other socially. They cross paths while volunteering for organizations such as Science for Peace, Food Not Bombs, the Toronto Public Space Campaign, and Out of the Cold or participating in coalitions such as those formed to protest the American war in Iraq or to support environmentalism. For those activists employed in nonprofit organizations, such as the former Ten Days for World Development, working together is sometimes part of the job, either as coworkers or as part of coalitions between different organizations.

Each of the three groups shares common religious and political influences and often have complementary ambitions. There were more similarities than differences between the Catholic and Protestant groups' worldviews and resources. The contemporary Pagan group also had much in common with these Christian groups. Many Yarrow members were raised Christian, and some attended churches into adulthood. In addition, because much religious writing in the English language assumes a Christian cosmology, available spiritual resources are often Christian.

Christian liberation theology is a major influence, even within Yarrow, if to a lesser extent. The reframing of political and economic injustices in terms of deviation from divine plans gives each group a religious mandate to rectify social injustice. The refraction of liberation theology through North American movements, such as black liberation theology and feminist liberation theology, is likewise a major contribution. Feminist theologians such as Rosemary Radford Ruether and Mary Daly influenced all three groups. Because they are explicitly feminist and because their approach to ritual affirms spontaneity and adaptation of new material, my participants actively seek out new work on women and religion, including systematic theology. In terms of influences for integrated models of religion and political activism, all three groups are deeply influenced by trajectories of religious engagement such as the Protestant and Roman Catholic presence in the Civil Rights movement and Catholic religious activism—Dorothy Day's movement against poverty and the Berrigan brothers' Vietnam protests, for example.

The same openness and emphasis on spiritual investigation leads not only my contemporary Pagan participants but also my Catholic and United Church participants to contemporary Pagan work. Women across traditions cited Goddess spirituality and contemporary Pagans as strong influences, both spiritually and politically. For example, Starhawk was cited by women from all three groups as someone to admire and emulate for so thoroughly integrating spirituality with activism. This interest in contemporary Pagan spiritualities overlaps with an interest in Native American spiritualities and a long tradition of North American nature religion more generally.[157]

In addition to models of religious and political activism, all three groups share the social milieu of Toronto more generally and its leftist political communities. These communities are heavily influenced by

Marxist understandings inherited from the New Left.[158] Despite conscious distancing from both U.S. foreign policy and popular culture,[159] Toronto activist communities are explicitly influenced by United States activism. One of the major conduits of such influence is the broader "anti-globalization," or "global justice," movement.[160] Moreover, many of the political organizations to which my participants belong maintain connections, both working relationships and personal ties, to U.S. organizations.

The religious groups do the same. Catholic Worker, as an organization, is connected to the base in the United States, but members also have personal connections to some of the other nearby Catholic Worker communities, such as the New York community, where they visit fairly regularly. Several Clearwater members were born, traveled for work, or have family in the United States. Yarrow is connected to the United States through Reclaiming Witchcraft, and members often attend "Witch-camps," religious training retreats, in the United States. They also host visiting teachers from the United States, such as Starhawk and other Reclaiming leaders, when they come through town.

As has become more visible since I completed my study, especially with the rise of the Idle No More movement, Toronto activist communities during my fieldwork are not only resisting the privileged place of Canada in a globalizing economy that exploits people in other nations but are also dealing with the ethical discomfort of living in a settler society at the expense of Canadian First Nations rights. Sometimes this issue was addressed explicitly within the groups, but often it was gestured toward more obliquely, in general conversations about Canadian racism and the illegitimacy of the government. As members of religious groups engaged in liberal networks that are often suspicious of religion as irrational and indulgent, my participants find themselves caught in several binds: defending the power of what has already been labeled "irrational" but trying to disrupt the shadows these assumptions have cast over Indigenous people; honoring what they have derived from learning about Native practices without stealing culture; trying to influence the policies of a government that is patently imperialist; and working to make change within an oppressive system.

Through the intersections of these different influences, there is a sense among my participants that they are part of a movement of spiritual people working to make the world a better place. That commonality reveals divisions between different trajectories of influence to be somewhat artificial. For many of the women with whom I spoke, there is not a stark distinction between reading the theology of Gustavo Gutiérrez, the environmental philosophy of Starhawk, or the autobiography of Nelson Mandela. All serve as resources in spiritual growth; all serve as tools for political activism. These divergent influences come together for them within an integrated and diverse movement for social justice.

Outline of the Book

Because ritualizing is a major activity of religiously motivated feminist activist communities, I begin chapter 1 with an examination of rituals my participants perform within their religious groups. Using these rituals as background, I investigate tensions within each religious group over the role, purpose, and form ritualizing should take. I explore common ritual elements shared by all three groups and reflect on how common rites signal membership in a larger movement of faith and social justice activism, despite disparate institutional affiliations. Lastly, I consider the kinds of selves, communities, and worlds reflected in their ritualizing.

Shifting from the discussion of rites performed within the confines of religious community, chapter 2 engages explicit ritualizing on the ground in anti-globalization protests. Such ritualizing is a visible way that activists bring their religions into the public sphere. Focusing on the anti-FTAA protest in Quebec City in 2001, I explore ways that religiously affiliated social justice activists incorporate ritual into political actions. Investigating this phenomenon gives insight into both mass anti-globalization demonstrations and into new ways that practitioners integrate religion and politics, particularly in the context of increasing cultural and economic globalization. Finally, I compare travel to global justice protests with another very public form of religion, that of the ritual of pilgrimage.

Not everyone in progressive activist communities understands the integration of religious and political identity as a positive development. In chapter 3 I explore the strategic use of the phrase "I am spiritual but not religious" by religiously affiliated feminist activists, women who explicitly *do* participate in religious communities. I argue that the distinction between *spirituality* and *religion* is rooted in cultural assumptions about the ideal relationship of the individual to institutional authority and community, the proper role of religion in the public sphere, and the desirability of secularization. Many of these assumptions stem from Protestant struggles to differentiate itself from Catholicism, but over time Protestant critiques of Catholicism as too institutional, rote, and controlling have diffused into critiques of religion in general. I argue that for feminists and others allied with those on the margins of both church and state, the category of spirituality may be especially attractive and politically expedient.

In chapter 4 I focus on my participants' articulation of an ethical system based on a cosmology of interrelationship. This ethical system of social justice reflects connections between the self and the global community and includes the well-being of the individual in determining the value of particular actions. I explore the types of projects this cosmology supports—such as fair trade, anti-globalization, and human rights work—engaging current feminist debates about agency and resistance. Lastly, I consider what implications a social justice cosmology has for cultural understandings of the "political."

The Power to Name

I end this introductory discussion with a brief note on my choice of words and stories. Throughout the text I engage with two main sources of language, my participant communities and academic scholarship. As a result, many terms appear here as multivalent. I balance emic usages of words, such as *spirituality*, *pilgrimage*, and *ritual*, with critical discussions of such terms across academic disciplines. This means that at the same time that I engage analytic deconstructions of concepts such as "religion," I also use terms in ways that reflect my participants' usage and the popular discourses with which not only they but also scholars in the academic study of religion are necessarily in conversation.

My use of *cosmology* is worth additional explication. While within astrophysics and world religions discourse *cosmology* is commonly used to describe understandings about the origin of the universe (e.g., Genesis, the Big Bang, Turtle Island), I am using the term in a manner consistent with the anthropology of religion.[161] My use is also influenced by philosophy; in metaphysics cosmology is an exploration not only of creation but also of the nature of the universe. As I use it here, cosmology encompasses not only how the sun got into the sky but also how all the things that happen under it are able to happen: the structure of the world. In other words, my deployment, while not explicitly excluding understandings about how things originated, is much more about how things work.

I choose the term *cosmology* to emphasize that feminist activists are making moral claims about the fundamental nature of the world, human existence, and relationships within and beyond material experience. In their perspective all individuals are already involved in relationships with, and ethically responsible for, the well-being of others, both intimate and distant, both human and other-than-human, whether or not they are consciously aware of these relationships and whether or not they have the courage to own up to them. Their cosmologies of interconnection motivate personal choices, the founding and tending of communities, and collective actions undertaken to create changes in society. In my participants' articulations morality is more than the separate sums of personal choices by autonomous individuals; it is both based in and enacts metaphysical connections between beings in the world.

As the discussion of word choice illustrates, the process of writing involves the power of selection, especially in the context of ethnography. Out of all I experienced during my fieldwork, this text can only reflect facets. My job as an anthropologist is to hold up particular pieces as part of a broader process of interpretation. Sometimes the stories I share are noble; sometimes they are messy; always they are human. I ask readers to work with my participants and me through occasional moments of conflict, even moments in which people are not necessarily their best selves. These stories are here because this book explores the deliberate creation of community, which requires honest engagement with tensions, misunderstandings, and disappointments. To misinterpret examples of internal conflict as reasons to dismiss my participants and the significance of their work is to miss the point entirely. These religiously motivated feminist activists ally by choice, not through ignoring their differences but by consciously working them out, in the service of creating more together than any one person could create alone.

1   Changing Rituals, Changing Worlds

Within their individual communities members of the Clearwater United Church congregation, the Catholic Worker community, and the Yarrow Collective spend significant time together planning and performing rituals. For them collective ritualizing creates community and affirms individuals within that community.[1] They value innovation, spontaneity, and experimentation in ritual actions. Their common understandings of ritual also create an environment in which playing with ritual expressions from other traditions is possible and desirable. In this chapter I use holiday and regular ritualizing to think through my participants' understandings of ritual and what it should accomplish and to address issues of ritual borrowing, authenticity, and tradition. In-depth discussion of shared ritualizing also serves as further introduction to these three communities and the values that each emphasizes as well as those they share across traditional boundaries.

Scholars continue to debate precise and cleanly bounded definitions of ritual and rituals, often very productively.[2] Nonetheless, here I am content to focus on a more popular understanding of rituals as "actions regarded as special" by my participants, a usage more in keeping with their perspectives.[3] As self-consciously voluntary members of religious communities who have very deliberately chosen their specific affiliations, the cooperative aspects of ritual are especially important to them. Together they devote energy, thought, planning, and reflection to creating rituals that will be emotionally satisfying, psychologically healing, and socially productive.

Ritual action is necessarily selective action. As Jonathan Z. Smith has argued: "Ritual is first and foremost a mode of paying attention. It is a process for marking interest."[4] Ritual enacts religious worldviews and through that enactment determines what is important within them, what is worth "paying attention" to. Smith also argues that the importance of ritual is found in the disjuncture between ideal events unfolding within sacred space and the chaotic events of everyday life.[5]

Approaching ritual as demarcating arenas of attention becomes especially significant within activist worldviews, in which society is seen as focusing on the wrong issues. Philosopher Philip Goodchild argues that within a secularized culture in which participation in the market replaces membership in religious communities, "the highest values are devalued: no longer can one be sure what is worth thinking about."[6] My participants deliberately use ritual to enact alternatives to what Goodchild has named modern capitalism's "theology of money," in which all value is ascribed through the dollar.[7]

If we look at the elements that Clearwater, Yarrow, and the Catholic Worker emphasize in their rites, we find that individuals feel empowered and valued, experience connection to nature and each other, and find strength in each other's company. This contrasts with an everyday world in which they feel disempowered and devalued, emotionally drained and disconnected from the earth and other people. My participants ritualize in order to set a broken world right.

Changing Ritual

Catherine Bell has criticized the field of ritual studies for historically assuming a split between thought and action in ritual. In this assumption ritual is supposed to express the innermost thoughts of the ritual participants, and the actions of the ritual participants are then supposed to be available to the academic observer for expression into thought, a Douglas Adams Babel fish translation. She writes of this theoretical approach, "Ritual is to the symbols it dramatizes as thought is to action; on a second level, ritual integrates thought and action; and, on a third level, a focus on ritual performance integrates *our* thought and *their* action."[8] As is clear in her description, this split reinforces condescension on the part of the observer, who presumes to know what the performers of ritual "really" mean by their rites. Ron Grimes has described this as the "assumption of a chasm between perceiver and perceived" that privileges the observer over those having the direct experience, reproducing a colonial ideology of superior knowledge through cultural distance.[9] Nikki Bado-Fralick intervenes in this emic-etic contest, writing, "Neither group automatically *misrecognizes*, but both scholars and practitioners may *differently*, yet also *legitimately*, recognize."[10]

Despite problematic assumptions that pit analytical thought against embodied action, the idea of ritual expressing internal thoughts and motivations is *made* real when religious communities decide it is accurate and design rituals around this idea. Many of my participants across the three traditions described ritual as doing precisely this. For example, Lavender, a contemporary Pagan, responded to my question "What is the significance of ritual for your politics?" by saying:

> Ritual is sort of speaking in metaphor, so I think it's very powerful from the therapeutic and empowerment point of view, which I guess is the same, anyway. It's kind of poetry in motion. I've just come back from the Sacred Circle dance camp, and there the ritual is dance, but it's just another form of expression, of focusing the energy and creating a safe and sacred space within which to do whatever kind of work needs to be done, which can be many kinds of work. I've done weaving and clay work and painting and singing and dancing and planning political actions, whatever, has all been done within sacred space.[11]

Regina, a Catholic, described ritual: "It's kind of an outward manifestation of what I feel like goes on in me sometimes, in terms of spirit confronting the construction of the messed-up parts of this world right now."[12] Lavender and Regina approach ritual as innovative and personally expressive.[13]

This understanding of ritual on the part of my participants shapes its practice within their communities. Each group has a committee dedicated to developing and experimenting with rituals to bring to the group. The Pagan collective divides tasks up into working groups called "petals"—for example, the "political action petal." Another one of these working groups is the "ritual planning petal." Anyone can join by showing up at one of the group's meetings or contacting them via its Listserv. The Catholic Worker rotates responsibility for planning its Wednesday night liturgies through individuals, pairs, or groups within the community who want to lead it. As the Workers who ran Zacchaeus House, the drop-in house that hosts the community dinners and liturgies, Regina and Neil planned slightly more liturgies than other people. They filled in when no one else expressed interest in putting together that week's service. Clearwater United Church plans upcoming services by means of a worship committee, made up of interested members and Bill, the pastor.

Each has mechanisms for emic criticism.[14] The Yarrow Collective has non-ritual-oriented organizational meetings, providing a forum in which people can discuss what bothered them or what they particularly liked about previous rituals. The Catholic Worker community often has informal discussions about ritual during community dinners and social time. Clearwater has a more formal and deliberate forum for feedback. After service there is time set aside for coffee and snacks in the gym outside the chapel, where the services are held. After coffee, however, anyone who wishes to participate migrates back to the chapel for a discussion of the service. This conversation includes praise, complaints, and personal reflections.

In each of these groups, most complaints are resolved by encouraging people to join the ritual planning group in order to design rituals more to their liking. This doesn't always work, however, especially when the disagreements over rituals are symptoms of deeper conflicts. For example, there was ongoing tension in the Pagan collective about communication with African spirits by a white member.[15] The tension was focused between Betty, a white woman who works at a local university and whose partner is a Caribbean Canadian woman, and Heidi, a white woman who identifies as a spiritual healer and who was called to and trained in a spirit possession tradition when she moved to South Africa with her first husband a decade earlier.

While there are specific traditions of deity possession, or "aspecting," within Paganism, practices of physically embodying divine forces focus mainly on versions of "drawing down the moon," embodying the Goddess and the God so that they can meet in the Great Rite, the culmination of a group's worship and magic working.[16] Alternatively practices influenced by the feminist spirituality movement focus on expressing an aspect of the Goddess that practitioners want to integrate into their lives.[17] Pagan possession rituals do not normally channel spirits or deities from other religious traditions.

Betty was concerned that Heidi was not being suitably respectful and was acting inappropriately by channeling African spirits, among others. More specifically, Betty felt that spirit possession, especially by spirits associated with people of color and their traditions, was rightfully the reserve of those people, not white women like Heidi and herself.[18] She regarded Heidi's practice as cultural appropriation. Heidi, on the other hand, considered her ability as one hard-earned through apprenticeship with a spiritual teacher. Well regarded by the group as a talented healer, she connected that spiritual gift with her ability to channel her inherited spirits. She seemed taken aback by Betty's objections.

The conflict came to a head at an event I did not attend, a ritual for the autumnal equinox in 2003. At the following meeting Betty apologized for having disrupted the ritual and told Heidi that she should have spoken with her privately about her discomfort. Heidi in turn insisted that Betty was not in the wrong and said, "Sometimes I just need to know when to shut up." While everyone, including Betty and Heidi, repeatedly discussed the issue of spirit possession and cultural appropriation and the group processed it in subsequent meetings, I was not able to extract specifics about what exactly had happened to bring their different cosmologies into conflict. While deflecting onto other subjects, those outside the pair dismissed the problem mostly in terms of a personality conflict between two strong community leaders.

Betty and Heidi continued to work together in the collective and in ritual, though it seemed evident there was continuing discomfort between them. For example, when the large, unwieldy reading group split into two of more manageable size, Heidi and Betty each organized separate groups, ensuring they would not see each other on a weekly basis. Because of scheduling, I ended up in Heidi's group with River, Sandra, Liz, and Christine. The closest the collective came to resolving this ritual concern was agreeing that they needed anti-oppression training to help them work through it.

Another example of ritual criticism that remains unresolved is from Clearwater. A particular section of the service, performed every other week or so, is called "Table Talk." During this time Bill or another member leading the service sits in a small chair at the low round table in the center of the chapel and reads from a book or tells a personal story. There is often an activity available at the table: coloring books and crayons, modeling clay, or Easter eggs to decorate. This part of the service is designed to address children, but there are very few children in the community. Some adults, usually women, may come to the table during this time to sit with the reader and do the activity.

However, at least one member of the congregation is bothered and annoyed by the Table Talk sections of the service. Wendy is an older member of the congregation, important both for the long time she has been involved and because she is the daughter of famous missionary parents who were involved in human rights struggles in revolutionary China.

During our interview in her apartment in a retirement community, she told me that she really hates the Table Talk part of the service. She thinks that it is silly and stupid. She is embarrassed for what newcomers might think, seeing the pastor sitting in a tiny chair reading a children's book to other adults, also scrunched in tiny chairs. Although she has made her dislike known during feedback time, to Bill personally, and to other members in more informal discussions of ritual, the congregation has decided to keep this element as part of its ritual repertoire. The practice continues to upset Wendy.[19] Other members' investments in continuing the Table Talk section of the service outweigh her objections. Because the procedures in place to critique ritual within the confines of Clearwater necessarily hinge on negotiation, this disagreement points to larger contestations about what functions ritual should fulfill within these groups.

My goal in sharing these conflicts is not to gossip or produce an exposé of internal tensions but instead to deal explicitly with the truth that communities, perhaps especially intentional communities, are challenging for those who participate in them. In the face of conflict, members must make conscious choices about how to continue to work together. Ritualizing is important to each group as a way to affirm commitments to each other and their shared work, but it is therefore also an area in which disagreements get laid bare. Rather than evidence of dysfunction, these conflicts over ritual are demonstrations of the effort each group puts into negotiating collective values and tolerating differences.

Chosen Rites

In order to take a more in-depth look at ritual and its functions in the Toronto Catholic Worker, the Yarrow Collective, and Clearwater United Church, I focus on Summer Solstice and Samhain (pronounced "SAH-wen") rituals in the Pagan collective and Easter celebrations in the United Church congregation and the Catholic Worker community as well as religious ritualizing at more regular group meetings. Most people who identify as contemporary Pagan will perform rituals, individually or with a group, and celebrate Samhain and Summer Solstice. Most people who identify as Christian will go to a church service and celebrate with family and friends on Easter. In this sense ritualizing on these holidays is part of what defines a practicing member of these religious communities.

Both Easter and Samhain are major holidays in their respective religious traditions and each highlights issues of death and rebirth. Easter celebrates Jesus's resurrection as the Christ after his crucifixion by the Roman state, the suffering through which he redeems humanity from sin. Although Christmas, with its celebration of Jesus's birth, sometimes outshines it, Easter is *the* foundational Christian holiday. The Catholic Worker community is well-known among progressive Catholics for its annual sunrise service. I started attending community liturgies just before Lent, and already people were asking Regina and Neil, the Zacchaeus House coordinators, about details for the service. Clearwater United Church, while not as elaborate, nonetheless planned a special service for Easter Sunday.

Samhain is one of the biggest holidays in the Pagan year, a time for interacting with departed loved ones and goddesses and gods. Coinciding with Halloween, this night is considered a time when "the veil between the worlds is thinnest." It is a night when people have especially good access to spirits and deities.

Another significant holiday within the contemporary Pagan year is the Summer Solstice. It celebrates life and warmth and the luxury of summer. For those traditions that include a masculine aspect of divinity, it is the height of the year for the romantic partnership between the Goddess and the God.

Yarrow Collective: Summer Solstice

We met on the Toronto Islands on Ward's Island beach around 4:00 p.m.[20] There were about twelve of us, mostly women with one woman's male partner. Heidi, a healer in her early thirties who sometimes spirit-trances, had her two children along as well. Sitting in a circle on the slope in the sun, we learned the songs for the ritual. Betty, an administrator at a local women's studies department in her early thirties, taught us a song to call the elements to the sacred circle. Heidi taught us a weaving song to go with the wish web we would make. River, also midthirties, who works in a nonprofit organization that advocates for mentally ill homeless people, said that she had done research to find a goddess for the ritual and had decided on a Lithuanian goddess of summer, sun, and spring. "The Lithuanian people were some of the last to become Christianized," she said. River also mentioned that Starhawk's Reclaiming Collective in San Francisco had a direct action against factory farming scheduled for the next day and that we could keep that in mind as we did our ritual.

We moved from the warm, dry sand and blankets to the wetter sand because it was flatter. There was some jovial grumbling. We formed a circle. Heidi's seven-year-old son stayed on the blankets and turned one of his mom's drums upside down and began calling into it. Heidi's five-year-old daughter ran around playing with string but then got upset because her brother wouldn't give "her" drum to her.

In the circle someone attempted to light cedar to smudge the circle, after asking if anyone was allergic. The wind kept the cedar from lighting, so Heidi suggested doing a ritual of physical clearing for each other. She began to go around the circle, but after she had cleared a few people, Heidi's daughter got sand in her eye and started crying, so other people finished going around. Betty cleared me.

We performed a ritual of forming the circle: "I'm Laurel, and from my hand to yours I spin the circle," linking hands as we went around. We stood in the circle and sang an elements song. River welcomed the Goddess. "We are now between the worlds, and what is between the worlds can change the world." We swung our arms up together and released hands.

Antonia, a woman in her early twenties interested in herbal healing and organic farming, led a grounding, a group meditation that emphasizes the place of the group in the universe. The purpose is to center concentration and get on the same wavelength as a group in order to more effectively do spiritual work together. First, we think about where we are, what the environment of the ritual is like. What is the ground we are sitting on like? What kinds of plants are around? Are there animals? Is there water nearby? What does the air feel like? Then we imagine connecting ourselves to the environment through rooting into the soil and expanding into the stars.

After the grounding we moved back to the sunny, dry sand for trance work. People sat around or lay down while Heidi drummed and Betty stood and led the trance. It was visualization from within into a spirit landscape. What kind of landscape? What time of day is it? Which direction are you facing? Look in each direction. Turn back to where you started. A path opens. Follow it. Are you alone? Who is there? Greet them. Notice what you have brought with you. How is the ground beneath your feet? What are you wearing? You get to your garden: more questions about its appearance, composition, and state, your feelings about these things. Who else is there: goddesses, friends, plant spirits? Do they have a message for you? Eventually you do the journey in reverse, come back through yourself. You say your name out loud and then clap three times to make sure you're truly back.

We returned to the standing circle on the flat ground to create a wish web. The purpose is to make a big web held between everyone in the circle containing wishes. River started by fastening one end of the string to her wrist. As usually performed, the ritual involves verbalizing a wish and then tossing the ball of yarn to someone else in the circle, but we had Heidi's daughter and son carry the balls of yarn across the circle instead. They skipped and danced around the inside of the circle, laughing delightedly each time they granted the yarn to someone.

People wished for a variety of things, social justice oriented, environmental, political, and personal: Holly Jones and her family;[21] health and safety for children; good leaders; patience; self-control; success for Starhawk's San Francisco Reclaiming group in the direct action the next day around agricultural issues; homes for everyone; clean air and water;

an end to poverty; no speedboats so that being outside wouldn't be about conspicuous consumption; self-love; guidance; a strong and healthy African continent; "Africa to resist genetically modified so-called aid"; for the Yarrow Collective itself to become more culturally diverse.

After all the wishes were done, we walked around clockwise and sang the weaving song we had learned earlier: "Weaving wishes . . . weaving life . . . weaving what we hope to be." As we walked, we raised the web up and down. We sang and walked faster and faster, finally dissolving into quick hums and finally giggles. River said we should ground the web, so we touched it to the ground and touched our hands to the ground with it for a few moments.

We got back up to finish the ritual. We held hands again and each said something about the work that was done here, then we thanked the Goddess with the traditional words: "Stay if you will. Go if you must." "Let the circle be open but never broken." Then, swinging arms, we said, "Merry meet and merry part and merry meet again," a common Pagan closing, breaking hands on the last line. The ritual was followed by announcements and a potluck picnic on the beach.

Yarrow Collective: Samhain

Pagan communities often hold big rituals for Samhain. Starhawk's Reclaiming Collective in San Francisco has been holding large events for the public for several decades. The Yarrow Collective, with its many Reclaiming members, decided to plan a ritual for its own members but to make it an "open" ritual—that is, to advertise it as open to the public, especially Pagans who may not have a place to go for the holiday. This open ritual was intended as a holiday gift to the larger Toronto Pagan community.[22] To this end the group distributed flyers to local bookstores and cafés and made them available at an academic conference on motherhood and spirituality held at York University in northern Toronto.

This was one of few open holiday rituals that actually took place during my fieldwork, the Summer Solstice ritual discussed earlier being the other. Lammas and Spring Equinox, planned to be held at parks, were rained out. Many members attended the River of Light, a multi-faith Winter Solstice celebration held in the hip Kensington Market, as their Winter Solstice activity. Smaller rituals, such as those conducted in the reading groups, happened more regularly.

With Yarrow the strain of organizing was more apparent than in the Christian groups with which I spent time. Because meetings were less regular, it was harder to get people to commit to come because of other obligations such as family, covens, ritual dance groups, political and other volunteer activities. With the Samhain ritual the conflict was WomynSpirit. The WomynSpirit Festival, an annual, ecumenical, celebration of women's spirituality, is always held on the weekend closest to Samhain. WomynSpirit has been going on for many years, and Yarrow members consider it an important Samhain tradition. In addition, Starhawk had attended a conference at York University the preceding week and announced the WomynSpirit Festival to the audience at her talk. Because of these factors, several regular Yarrow members did not attend the Toronto Samhain ritual.

However, it was still the largest turn out for any ritual that I observed and included more people from outside the immediate Yarrow circle than I saw anywhere else. Perhaps this was due to "Christmas and Easter syndrome." Halloween or Samhain is arguably the biggest holiday of the Pagan year. People who might not attend regular coven rituals either because they are "Solitaries," that is, they practice their religion alone, or because they don't make religion a big part of their daily lives may choose to participate in a group event at Halloween. In addition, the coverage of contemporary Paganism and Witchcraft in the media increases around this time of year, which may spur the curious to investigate Halloween rituals.

Yarrow held its open Samhain ritual in an Anglican church building downtown. The ritual was planned by members of the public ritual petal (working group), a small group of women within the collective, who then asked others to fulfill different roles for the night. River had asked me at reading group if I would help collect money. The group was asking for donations at the door, pay-what-you-can contributions of at least five dollars, but no one would be turned away. The money was mainly for renting the space. I arrived a bit early to help and approached a cluster of women, including River, Heidi, Bea, Ashley, and Kennedy, who were learning and rehearsing an elements song for the ritual.

Within the church the pews had been moved and pushed back along two walls. The room was aglow with indirect lighting that cast everything golden. There were altars set up at the front of the sanctuary, tables of varying heights covered in soft scarves and throws of luscious jewel tones. Participants were encouraged to place upon them pictures of loved ones who had been born or died in the past year, along with pictures of "ancestors." People also brought sacred objects, like items from their home altars and images and symbols of deities. There were feathers, necklaces, and autumn leaves interspersed with bowls of incense and many framed pictures, both recent and old. Some of the ancestor photographs featured sepia-tinted grandmothers and great-grandparents. There were also recent photos of babies in brightly colored jumpers. Tea lights and tapers flickered throughout the displays. At the back of the room, near the kitchen, was a table of food for the potluck after the ritual. There were already many different kinds of bread and fruit spread out.

As they arrived, people milled around a bit, moving to the altars to place their personal items, back to the food tables to add their contributions, and to the middle of the sanctuary to greet one another. Ashley, a free spirit barely in her twenties, had brought her parents, which was unusual. She introduced me to them and was clearly very happy to have them attend. They seemed a bit out of their element but interested. I helped another member at the door with greeting and collecting money. Most people were happy to donate more than the required amount when asked. A few people, not knowing what the event was, came in, drawn by the activity, but left after we explained the purpose of the event. Those who left, however, seemed amused, rather than disturbed or hostile.

Eventually we were called to the circle, and the door was closed. There were about seventy people in attendance. Looking around, I recognized most people from Yarrow or Shapeshifters, a Pagan women's group predating Yarrow and with overlapping membership, which organizes an annual Autumn Equinox women's retreat. But there were new people there, too, and some men interspersed with the women. This was not unheard of but was less common for Yarrow events, as there was only one male regular at Yarrow meetings, though a few more participated on the group's Listserv. Members of the larger Pagan community had come, drawn by flyers and word of mouth.

Most collective members were festively dressed in flowing, feminine, witchy clothes, some with pointed hats. Kennedy had added sparkles to her face. I wore a spooky T-shirt with jeans and paled my face, a generic dead thing. There was a beautiful Caribbean woman in bright red, orange, and yellow with her baby boy. Some of the "members of the public" had actual costumes. I remember a skull mask and an alien with glowy head bobbles, in particular.

The ritual itself began with a standard grounding, casting the circle, and calling in the directions. For the grounding we were asked to sit, concentrate on our breathing, and slowly feel our breath and attention drop into the earth, like roots, through the layers of the earth, through soil and rock and bedrock, past the ancestors and animals that have come before us, asking them permission to share the space. Then we envisioned reaching into the core, the warm center of the earth. There we were to leave all our negative thoughts and things we don't need and gather things we do need, bringing them and ourselves slowly back up through the layers and into our centers, up through our bodies and out the top of our heads, like branches, reaching up into the sky until the stars and the earth's core were connected through our bodies and our breathing. We were grounded.

Next the organizers cast the circle and called in the directions with the elements song they had been practicing when I arrived. This was all fairly normal, if a bit more formal than smaller, closed rituals, in which there was more random participation, for example, in calling the directions or deciding which deities to invoke. The grounding, casting, and calling were followed by a planned, deliberate, and formal invocation. Different women called in the deities that the organizers had chosen to invite to the ritual. River called on the Celtic goddess Cerridwen, with her cauldron of life and mysteries, and asked her to stir us in our circle as she stirs the potions of her cauldron. As she called on Cerridwen, River moved around the inside of our circle in her dark, flowing dress, stirring the air in the center of the circle with a large staff. Next Bea called in the Stag as an aspect of the Horned God, specifically male and fated to die, to join us as she danced lightly around the inside of the circle. Lastly, Kennedy called in the Greek goddess Hecate to be with us on this night especially suited to her as Crone, keeper of the crossroads and dark of the moon.

This was the only ritual in which I participated with the collective that a male deity was specifically invoked. I was even a bit surprised that the Stag was called, though it made sense, given the holiday and its place in the yearly myth cycle. The God dies on Samhain to be reborn to the Goddess at the Winter Solstice. In other rituals in which I participated with Yarrow, groups of deities or spirits that presumably include males, like "the Little People" fairies, were invoked, and occasionally animal spirits of indeterminate gender would be called, but Samhain was the only time a specifically male deity was invited.

After the invocation Bea led a guided trance to the Isle of Apples, an afterlife in Pagan tradition, to visit loved ones who had passed. People were given the opportunity to speak the names of loved ones or personal heroes who had died in the past year. Then there was an opportunity to name babies born in the past year, welcoming them as new spirits. There is also a tradition among certain collective members of being given a gift, fruit or a special object, during the trance to the Isle of Apples to bring back upon one's return. The story is that three women each had a spirit gift experience at WomynSpirit two years earlier and by the next Samhain each had a new baby. This story was related to me by Star, one of those new mothers.[23]

After the naming, Bea then asked the Otherworld to help us raise energy to heal the earth and grant visions for how to improve the world, to make change for the better. Guiding the trance, she encouraged everyone to go off on their own and meet and talk with spirits and deities on the Isle of Apples whom they wanted to visit. After a while she warned everyone that it would soon be time to leave again until next year.

The trance culminated in a spiral dance with the Dead, led by Bea, in which we all whipped around, passing each other with flushed faces, huge smiles, and much laughter. As the spiral dance unfolded itself back into a circle, we stood, holding hands and swaying, sort of basking in the moment, the glow of energy raised by the trance and dancing, the "cone of power." This is a culmination of the energy raised during a ritual, energy that is then directed toward specific group goals. Bea asked everyone to take what energy they needed and to release the rest to the earth to help Her heal. After a moment we all broke slowly from the circle and placed our hands on the ground.

Then there was guided de-trancing, or "coming back," leaving the Isle of Apples and the loved ones and deities we had met there. The same women who had called in Cerridwen, the Stag, and Hecate thanked each one in turn for joining us in the ritual and told them that they could leave: "Go if you must, stay if you will." The circle was opened with each of us holding hands and swinging them in and out while saying the traditional "Merry meet and merry part and merry meet again." Then we each participated in grounding any excess energy by again touching the ground.

Everyone gravitated to the back of the room, where the food was. There were soups and breads, muffins and cakes, with juice to drink. Everyone munched and chatted. Most people talked about what a good ritual it had been. In looking around, I didn't notice anyone looking dissatisfied. I only saw big smiles.

I left after about a half hour of snacking and talking. There were still a number of people who remained after I had gone. At the next reading group meeting, River told me that later a belligerent homeless man had wandered in and that the group had called the police to get rid of him, but they never showed. It struck me as contradictory that on a night celebrating community and positive change, a group of progressive activists would call the police on a homeless man. But again, I did not have the opportunity to find out the full context of what happened.

Catholic Worker: Easter

The Catholic Worker Easter service was planned for the lakeshore at dawn.[24] The community coordinated rides from the house, so I got up at 3:30 a.m. and took a city night bus down. Walking up to Zacchaeus House in the quiet dark, the first thing I saw were a few tea light candles glowing on the steps. They were all over the main floor of the house and were the only lights, casting a dreamy glow on everything. There were piles of shoes by the door. Coming in, I noticed about seven sleeping bags in the living room, their occupants just waking up. Everyone was bleary-eyed and exhausted, but they seemed happily excited. Someone said they were going to get a nap afterward. "No, you can't go back to sleep! If you go back to sleep Jesus dies again!" We all laughed really hard.

I wandered toward the kitchen and greeted Regina, one of the two coordinators of the main house. She and another woman, a community member from Costa Rica, were scooping muffin batter into baking tins. There was already maple French toast in the oven. A couple of boys were just standing around. Regina explained that the coffee had just run out. Francis, a Zacchaeus House resident from Tanzania, helped me make more.

Waiting for the coffee to brew, I hung around in the dining room. There was more shuffling, and more Catholic Worker regulars showed up from the different houses. Sophie came by to say they had an extra seat in the car "for a very skinny person." Regina said she had the seating worked out, so they could go on ahead and we'd see them there. Neil, the other Zacchaeus House coordinator, was already at our meeting site setting up and building the bonfire.

Regina went upstairs to check one more time on her sisters. They were finally awake and up. After they came down, we all went around blowing out the candles.

We were assigned to cars. I went with two people I knew from Wednesday night liturgies, Jesse, a Catholic Worker in her late thirties, and Jim, a Christian Peacemaker Team (CPT) activist in his early thirties who was home between assignments in Iraq. We did not know it at the time, but Jim's next trip was to be a difficult one. He was one of four CPT members taken hostage in Iraq in November 2005. Much to the relief of the Toronto Catholic Worker community, Jim was among the three who were rescued in March 2006 and able to return home, though the community mourned Tom Fox, the CPT member who did not return.[25]

Jesse, Jim, and I traveled with two visiting young men in their car. Other folks piled into a big van. There was a caravan of about five or six cars on the way down the highway. We went to a water treatment park, just west of downtown Toronto. There were two or three tea lights in jars under the park sign.

When we got to the parking lot, there were quite a few cars. More people arrived on bicycles. By the time we started the ritual, there were about fifty people. The moon hung bright and big in the eastern sky, rising late above the surrounding trees. Aside from the moonglow, it was dark all around. Neil had built a bonfire in a garbage can, and people followed tea lights in jars to form a loose circle.

I found Angel, in her midtwenties, whom I knew from other political projects and our university's Women's Center, and we hugged. Her partner, Rita, brother, Tim, and father, Bob, were there with her. "Do you celebrate Easter?" she asked me.

"Well, you can say 'Happy Easter,'" I told her.

"Happy Easter!"

"Happy Easter!"

Once everyone had settled, candles and programs, printed on purple paper with block print illustrations, were distributed, and the ritual began. The service was designed by Neil and Regina. They and other Catholic Workers read different parts as we went along. First, an opening prayer and a reading from Mark 16:1–3. Then everyone took a candle. We silently processed from the parking lot along a hilly path with trees and ponds to the edge of Lake Ontario. I walked with Angel and her partner and brother. Angel jostled and joked, though mostly everyone was quiet. There were swans sleeping on the ponds. The procession was a thread of flickering lights. The walk took about fifteen minutes, meandering around the marshy trails. The procession ended in a clearing by the lake, all scrubby with dry grass. The muted cityscape glowed in the distance, across the water to the east, with the moon above it. We re-formed the circle.

Next we were invited to break the circle and search in silence nearby for a stone while reflecting on the stone that was rolled away from the tomb of Jesus on Easter morning. As we searched for our rocks, we were to reflect on the question "What barriers have we let our culture put between us and our neighbors?" When we each had a stone, we returned to the circle.

We turned to the west. Someone read: "The following ritual is an ancient practice performed by the catechumens during the Easter Vigil. Just before the first light of dawn, they would face the west where the light dies each day and would renounce together that which was hardened and lifeless." We were invited to name something that we wanted to renounce.

Next, someone read: "After the catechumens had turned in renunci-ation to the west where the sun sinks, they would then turn towards the east, in expectation of the rising sun. Facing the east, they would profess their faith, embracing new life." Before we all turned, however, another speaker read: "The Hassidic teacher Rabbi Bunam said, 'The sins which we commit, these are not our great crime. Temptation is powerful, and our strength is slight. The great crime of humanity is that we can turn at every moment and do not do so.'" We turned together to the east and were invited to name something we wished to embrace in our lives.

We faced the circle again and were led in a prayer focusing on God's help in rolling away stones in our lives that lay between us and "resur-rection in our lives," such as "our privilege, our self-focus, our fearful-ness, our pride." The prayer ended with, "Help us to cast these stones into the crazy, healing, limitless waters of new life that you offer us this morning. Amen." Then we all went to the lake and threw our stones in "as a sign of our acceptance of new life!"

Returning to the circle, we read a prayer together, focused on the resurrection of Christ. Then we sang the hymn "As the Green Blade Rises," while Neil accompanied us on guitar. Next was a reading from Luke 24:1–12, followed by a moment of silence, which was eventually broken with loud "Alleluias" from everyone. Then we read together the Canticle of Zechariah.

As the service proceeded, the world around us became gradually lighter. Birds awoke and started calling. Seagulls dived and soared. Ducks flew past our assembly. It also seemed to get colder and colder from all the standing around. We were all stomping feet and breathing on gloved hands. My toes lost feeling for the last fifteen minutes or so. It really was *so* cold.

Next Jim led the spiral dance. People joked, "Jim is our 'Lord of the Spiral Dance!'" I mentioned to Angel that Sydney Carter had written "Lord of the Dance" after seeing a Nataraja depiction of Shiva, some-thing I'd heard the week before at the Clearwater Palm Sunday service. Carter had passed away recently, so we had talked about him and sung the hymn. "Cool!" she said.

We all wove ourselves into the center and out to the edge of the dance, whizzing past each other with shouts and laughter as the spiral got faster. When we were all back in the circle, the benediction was read, and we sang "Lord of the Dance" together. At the end of the song everyone shouted, "Amen!" The ritual was ended.

At this point it was fully morning, with the sun firmly up in the eastern sky. People wandered around and greeted one another with many "Happy Easter" greetings and hugs. Danny and Mike, Maggie's little boys, ran around with Jim. Jesse knocked Mike over a lot in his protective, puffy coat, eliciting his squeals of laughter.

Eventually we started to wander back along the path to the parking lot. I walked back with Angel and her group. They were headed back to her parents' house for breakfast. In the parking lot I found my ride back to Zacchaeus House, where we had a potluck brunch for participants and for other members and friends of the community.

Clearwater United Church: Easter

I arrived a bit early to Clearwater's Easter service because I was coming from a Catholic Worker ritual.[26] Sophie, a member originally from Germany, brought Easter egg ornaments from home and hung them on the flowers in a vase at the center of the room. I helped Beatrice fold programs. Rather than being the simple photocopied programs of other weeks, these Easter programs were United Church issued, featuring a black cover with a photograph of Easter lilies on the front and, on the back, a call to worship that we did not use.

Eventually Bill, the pastor, called us from the chapel to the gym to form a circle around a little table displaying a taper, a container of smaller candles, and some flowers and greenery. He taught us a new candle lighting song. Alexa, a young girl in pigtails and a bright red shirt, played it on the piano in the corner of the gym. Bill lit the central candle, and then different people approached it, lit smaller candles, and returned with them to the circle.

The plan was that Alexa would play "As the Green Blade Rises" on the recorder and lead us in circles into the chapel, "like the Pied Piper," as Bill explained it. But she got nervous and started to cry into her father's chest, so Bill suggested that we all hum the song instead. We went in a roundabout circle into the chapel and each placed our candles in the sand tray. In a previous service memorial candles for Tooker Gomberg, an activist and former mayoral candidate, had been placed in the same tray.

Bill called in the directions as the call to worship. We all got up and faced each cardinal direction. He held his hands in different ways for each direction and listed things associated with each one, such as the excitement of youth and the sun for the east and the wisdom of old age for the west. After the directions were called, Bill told us that Alexa had brought stickers for decorating Easter eggs and that people should, at any point during the service, come to the center table and decorate one. By the end of the service Annie, Marjorie, and Bill had each decorated an egg.

We sang "As the Green Blade Rises." Bill gave a Table Talk, a section of the service designed for children, in which the leader sits at the low table in the center of the chapel. The only little girl in attendance, Alexa, stayed with her parents and did not join him at the table, but Annie and Marjorie did. Bill reminded everyone that Easter Sunday is the beginning of the Easter season, not its culmination. "So if you don't get to sing your favorite Easter hymn today, you've still got seven more weeks," he chuckled. He talked about eggs as symbols of resurrection and seeds, too, with reference to the preceding hymn.

He revealed a tray full of dirt and a handful of grain. He intimated that it had been difficult for him to find wheat to buy the day before. That was particularly funny to him, being a farmer's son; its scarcity in the city seemed surreal. His idea was that we could plant the seeds today and watch them grow over the Easter season. He carried the tray around the sanctuary. As they planted their seeds in the dirt, people said things like "understanding," "peace," and "empathy." Once everyone had a turn, he said, "Now we have all planted these seeds, and we can watch them grow with what we have wished for."

We sang some hymns, and Joe, Alexa's father, read the Easter story from a children's book. It was very long and, in places, emphasized the perspective that Jews were to blame for Jesus's crucifixion. The congregation seemed to tolerate that he needed to read the book, but people seemed to tune in and out. The anti-Semitism made me uncomfortable, particularly because I felt that it wasn't coming from him. It was in the narrative of this children's book, and he had simply failed to screen it. If someone had pointed it out, I'm certain that he would have chosen something else to read.

Leah, Alexa's older sister and Joe's daughter, delivered the reflection. One of Annie's sons had done the same thing the week before as part of his confirmation as a young adult into the community. Leah was about fifteen and quiet. Bill introduced her talk by saying that she was often watching, rather than talking, and that he was excited to hear what she had to say.

She blew everyone away. She talked about the crucifixion story being based on humiliation and shame and revenge and how these things cycle in society, choosing examples from school: her friend's Jewish-themed artwork having been defaced with a swastika and another friend's bad interaction with a homophobic bully. She quoted the homophobe as saying: "I'm discriminated against because of my skin color, so I can discriminate against gays. It makes me feel good." As a woman of color, she felt particularly struck by this statement.

She pondered these tragic and infuriating things and came to the conclusion that she was glad that she had a Christian background and church community to support her in working through issues of shame and anger. She understands her Christian community as helping her to have compassion, rather than only anger or despair. Her talk was powerful, highlighted all the more because she was so young. Her father, the one who had read the Easter story, cried; he was so proud of her. Her mother beamed.

After the reflection we sang a hymn, and the offering basket was passed around. There were also announcements. Then there was a special blessing for Laura. She came to the front and talked about having been accepted for Canada World Youth, which meant that she would spend a year in Alberta and three months in India. She talked about how supportive she had found the church to be and how she would miss it while she was away. Franka and Sophie rose. Franka said a few words about what a joy it was to have Laura there and how they would think of her while she was away. Sophie thanked her for all her time and help, especially with the refugee family the church had sponsored. Laura just smiled and smiled at all the love and appreciation.

Bill got up and had everyone touch Laura or touch someone touching her, just as we had done for Annie's son's confirmation a week earlier. He told her that she was an important part of the community and that it was so nice to have her participate, that we would be thinking of her as she embarked on her new path and that we looked forward to her return.

We ended the service with a hymn and then moved to the gym to enjoy coffee and the many Easter treats people had brought. Back at the snack table, people chatted about the service and particularly about Leah's talk. After a while we had a short discussion about the service back in the chapel. Everyone told Leah that they were very impressed and appreciated her reflection. Joe, her father, talked about how proud he was. He also said that he had felt compelled to read his contribution, the Easter story, from a book because he did not trust his own words and that she had scolded him for not speaking for himself. He said that the next time he would probably write in his own words—"and it will also probably be a bit shorter," he chuckled.

Rites in Common

By drawing on a common ritual repertoire, each of these groups positions itself as part of a larger movement of social justice–oriented spirituality but chooses to express this orientation in denominationally specific ways. That is, each group still chooses to identify specifically as Catholic, United Church, or contemporary Pagan, rather than describing themselves as more generically "spiritual." Despite discrete religious identities, the common ritual elements that each group employs place their members within a larger progressive community. Even in their separate ceremonies, participants position themselves in relation to one another.

On a very basic level all three groups arrange themselves in circles during rites.[27] All three call in the directions. All three end with a common meal. However, the similarities go beyond the general, arguably coincidental, or "universal," ritual elements.[28] The Catholic Worker and the United Church Easter services use the same hymns. The Pagan Samhain celebration and the Catholic Worker Easter both use spiral dances as symbols of resurrection and rebirth. And the United Church Easter service includes the planting of seeds with prayers, an activity very similar to the weaving of wishes into a yarn web by the Pagan collective in its Summer Solstice celebration.

Just as the boundaries between individual, community and world are permeable for these groups, the boundaries between traditions are deliberately crossed, especially in the Catholic Worker and Clearwater United Church rites. In both, ritual elements associated with contemporary Paganism are incorporated into their Easter services. Perhaps this is because, as is often joked, contemporary Paganism is the "civil religion" of social justice activism or because contemporary Paganism is more consciously linked to nature and is therefore considered less institutionally limited. Through ritual borrowing of contemporary Paganism by Christian groups, contemporary Paganism comes to express a more general and accessible spirituality, rather than institutionalized religious tradition.[29]

All three groups turn to nature as a way to express connection to divinity. Yarrow holds its rites outside whenever weather and access to space permit. Ritualizing outside is the norm for them. Occasionally a member will wistfully raise the suggestion of purchasing land for a more permanent ritual space, but that requires more money and logistical planning than the group currently has at its disposal. Instead, particular spots around the city are considered each time a ritual is being planned. The Toronto Islands, accessible by public ferry, are popular in the warm months. Yarrow also takes advantage of spaces containing labyrinths, such as the city's High Park, the Anglican Church of the Holy Trinity courtyard, and Lavender's personal garden. Dufferin Grove Park, managed by a public collective of which several Yarrow women are also members,[30] is popular for colder months and less elaborate rites, such as equinoxes. In addition, Night of Dread, an inter-Pagan parade of costumes and puppets reminiscent of Dia de los Muertos celebrations and open to public participation,[31] takes place there near Halloween each year.

Because contemporary Paganism offers an abundant ritual repertoire relating to nature as sacred, contemporary Pagan elements become an appealing way to venerate this aspect of Christianity on Easter, a holiday linked in Christian theology and tradition with spring, growth, and birth. Clearwater and the Catholic Worker have regular meeting spaces indoors, so ritualizing outside is a special occasion for them. In their Easter rites the proximity of nature provides access to the sacred. In the Catholic Worker Easter service the sunrise serves as a natural expression of the Christ's resurrection. Compare this to Yarrow's celebration of Summer Solstice on Ward's Island Beach in the afternoon sun. Clearwater brings nature inside the sanctuary by incorporating soil and seeds into the service. The Clearwater congregation and the Catholic Worker community are comfortable turning to contemporary Pagan ritualizing in their services because they understand the sacredness of nature as crossing institutional religious boundaries.[32] In this perspective nature offers unmediated access to personal, spiritual experience of the sacred.[33]

The use of contemporary Pagan ritual elements by the Catholic and United Church groups also contain ludic elements of humor and fun. Bill chuckled about how strange it was to have one's relationship with agriculture mediated by the city. More to the point, the Catholic Workers laughed and played during the spiral dance, deliberately juxtaposing it to the Christian hymn "Lord of the Dance." They were aware of crossing institutional boundaries and enjoyed themselves while they did it.[34] The same lighthearted syncretism was indulged after the service, albeit with more explicitly secular culture, when Neil and his friend strummed the guitar and sang "I Wanna Rock 'n' Roll All Nite," a song by KISS, very solemnly in the style of a hymn, and got some laughs for it.

Despite the emphasis in contemporary Paganism on ritual experimentation and respectful borrowing from other religious traditions, and despite the "affinities" some Pagans might feel for Jesus or some aspects of Christian community,[35] the Pagan collective did not experiment with Christian rituals. However, the ritual year coordinates with Christian liturgical calendars, with the god dying at Samhain to be reborn at Winter Solstice. From a Pagan perspective this is evidence that the church built its holiday cycle on pre-Christian folk traditions.[36]

Moreover, Yarrow held its open Samhain ritual in an Anglican church building. The church building is in the courtyard of the biggest mall in Toronto, the Eaton Centre. The congregation of the church is known for being active with social justice work, for its ecumenical focus, and for giving its blessing to community groups and other faith traditions that may wish to use the building. Later I would attend a service here at the completion of the ecumenical Good Friday walk, in which members of Clearwater United Church participated. Even though Yarrow members did not use explicitly Christian elements in their group ritualizing, other types of border crossings were evident in their ritual practice.

The Personal Relevance of Ritual

Similar worldviews and understandings of ritual shared by the Catholic Worker, Clearwater United Church, and the Yarrow Collective not only provide possibilities for playing with ritual elements from other religious traditions but also incorporate personal preferences as legitimate components of ritual. In their emphasis on creativity and personal taste, the approaches of these groups contrast with popular ideas of ritual as staid, traditional, and constant. As Ronald Grimes writes, "The notion of experimenting ritually implies attitudes far more tentative than those we normally associate with religious rites, which we typically think of as relatively fixed and unquestionable."[37] As compared to formalized ritual in traditional Catholic congregations or Gardnerian Wiccan circles, the rites practiced by the three groups featured here are downright haphazard and anarchic. Not only are they are different every time, but they are designed to be that way.

Some participants, like United Church member Laura, value spontaneity and informality as more genuine than authoritative tradition. "I guess it's a casual kind of ritual that speaks to me," she explained, "and sometimes people can become too narrow about it perhaps. Or there can be too much and then it becomes less meaningful for me, less beautiful. It's like going from one to the other, formulistic maybe, and that's actually what I see in some other congregations, if I happen to go to another church somewhere. It seems to become rote sometimes, some of it, so that actually distracts me from what I'm there for, rather than helping."[38] For ritual to be successful for her, Laura must be emotionally engaged; the rite must "speak to her." Laura contrasts the spontaneity and personal relevance of ritual within Clearwater to other churches she has visited, in which the routinization of ritual action becomes and obstacle to the spiritual experiences she seeks.[39]

Laura's focus on personal experience emphasizes that ritual spontaneity provides opportunities to address individual concerns within the context of community. As Catherine Bell writes of contemporary approaches to ritual: "The new paradigm is directed more inward than outward, apt to define community and society in terms of the self, rather than the self in terms of the community. Metaphors of wholeness and attainment replace older ones of transcendence and deliverance."[40] By positioning the individual self as the center of community, such a worldview asserts that the health and happiness of the individual affects others. Each of the rites describe here reflect a cosmology in which both pain and healing move through interconnected aspects of self, community, society, and globe, a cosmology I discuss in chapter 4 as one of "social justice."

At its most solipsistic, however, an approach to ritual as "a self-enhancing, self-enriching activity" could mean exclusive focus on the self:[41] ritual is performed only to facilitate self-actualization, rather than to benefit other members of the group, to strengthen community, or to bring about improvements in the outside world. One of the major criticisms of religious engagement from nonreligious activists within social justice circles—one of the communities with which my participants identify—is that ritualizing is a frivolous and selfish waste of time, especially ritualizing with the goal of personal development. For example, Becky Thompson writes of anti-racist activists, "Those who . . . draw connections between spirituality and activism then come up against the stereotype that spiritual people are flaky, self-centered, and apolitical."[42] Philip Goodchild sums up this perspective: "When our most urgent concern is survival, what time and money remains for a consideration of religion?"[43]

Social critic Wendy Kaminer uses the phrase *magical thinking* to describe self-help ideologies and worries that therapeutic movements encourage people to seek personal coping strategies to problems caused by systemic injustice.[44] Sociologist Robert Wuthnow, in his study of small groups in the United States, writes: "They supply and revitalize the sacred. But . . . these communities can be manipulated for personal ends, and the sacred reduced to a magical formula for alleviating anxiety."[45] Certainly this potential cannot be exclusive to small groups and new religious movements.

Apparent in Wuthnow's and Kaminer's criticisms is not only a traditional Western suspicion of "magic" but also latent assumptions that there is a right and wrong way to be religious.[46] They share a cultural suspicion of long lineage: that ritual is emotional, irrational, not socially productive, associated with civilization's shadow. Charles Long writes, "Either religion was authentic to the extent that it constituted the past of Western culture or human culture at large or it was relegated to the peripheries of human existence, for example, the contemporary Western lower classes or women or in the peripheral areas of the world, among 'primitive' peoples or other cultures that were technologically inferior to the West."[47] Further, through associating ritual self-healing with self-service, critiques such as these produce a contrast between false or temporary self-change and lasting self-transformation brought on by hard personal labor, labor that feminist theorist Jacqui Alexander calls "the spiritual dimensions of work."[48]

Conflict over Ritual and Action

Concern about the effectiveness of ritual and whether it is a waste of energy better directed elsewhere is not exclusive to those outside religious traditions. In her work on women in the southern United States, Marla Frederick highlights a distinction, traced by Eric Lincoln and Lawrence Mamiya through the history of the Black Church, between "priestly" and "prophetic functions."[49] Priestly functions focus on "maintaining the spiritual life of members," whereas prophetic functions emphasize "political concerns and activities in the wider community."[50] Religious groups that engage in political activism must negotiate these different functions. Those negotiations do not always go smoothly.

Among the groups I studied, the place where conflicts over the purpose of group worship were most pronounced was the United Church congregation. This may reflect the suspicion of ritual inherent in Protestant reactions to Catholicism.[51] It may also be because the other two groups have had to address their relationship with ritual more directly. The Catholic Workers must deal with the same Protestant prejudices about the "empty ritual" of Catholicism from the other side. The contemporary Pagan collective faces stereotypes of "flaky white kids dancing in the woods," as one Catholic participant summed it up.[52]

In my interview with Deborah, a member of the worship planning committee at Clearwater, she mentioned that there were often conflicts within the group over how to balance ritual and explicit activism. Deborah said, "We have this debate all the time in my congregation about whether we can cut some of the ritual, some of the focusing, some of the stuff, because ritual, for some people, is empty ritual, or they don't even get what the rest of us are doing in those times."[53] The conflict is over how much ritual to do and how much time to devote to announcements about political issues and upcoming events.

As it stands now, a part of the service, about ten minutes or so in the middle, is devoted to announcements, both personal and political. During this time the group discusses many different subjects. People share news about members of the congregation who are ill and provide updates on friends and family and personal achievements. News directly related to the congregation itself is reported as well. For example, the congregation helps sponsor a street nurse who regularly administers to the neighborhood homeless population out of one of the participating churches. She may give a report during this time. Deborah, who keeps the financial books for the congregation, may give budget updates. Members like Marjorie and Joe, who are closely involved with the congregation's sponsorship of an immigrant family, may report on how things are going for the family.

Clearwater United Church gains many of its members from people who are specifically searching for a politically engaged church. My participants talked about actively seeking a congregation that would support their activism. Annie and Christine, for example, shared with me that they stayed at Clearwater, despite the allure of feminist Pagan groups, precisely because the congregation was so politically involved.[54]

Political interest is reflected in the fact that more general information about activism and community meetings makes up about half of the announcements time. During my participation an inquest was being conducted into the death of a homeless person from tuberculosis. Marjorie urged people to attend court if they could, to show solidarity with groups working to improve shelter conditions.

A petition to the provincial government for better public transit funding was announced several weeks in a row. An anti-war demonstration was announced one week, and many members enthusiastically planned to attend together and march with the congregation's banner.

They worked out where to meet for the march during announcements time. Christine shared information about purchasing Zatoun's Palestinian olive oil through her as part of a fair trade project modeled after Franka's early days of distributing fair trade coffee through Bridgehead Trading.[55] Clearwater members joined with the congregation of their host church after services once a month or so to write letters for Amnesty International and these dates were announced. In addition, many of these political events were printed on the back of the worship programs each week, with dates, places, and times.

Despite time dedicated to politics, some members express dissatisfaction with the current balance between ritual and political discussion in the service each week. One such member is Donna. She became involved in Christianity through a job at the World Council of Churches in Geneva thirty years ago. She and her partner joined Clearwater because they wanted an activist church, but she is not entirely satisfied with it. She said: "I'd like to see more enthusiasm on the political scene, you know, on the politics of life. But what can you do?"[56] She thinks that the congregation puts too much emphasis on ritual and not enough on political action.

For those, like Donna, who want to be more overtly involved in political activities through the church, there is the Justice, Peace and Environment Group, which meets monthly after worship. Bill, the pastor, encouraged me to attend the group meeting upstairs in his office after post-service coffee. He thought that it fit well with my project. He also mentioned that it would make the committee members happy to have me attend.[57] This meeting was to evaluate the previous Amnesty International letter writing day, plan for the next one, give personal reports about demonstrations and events, and figure out whether to try to revitalize the congregation's role in the ecumenical KAIROS project and, if so, how.

KAIROS, Canadian Ecumenical Justice Initiatives / Initiatives canadiennes oecuméniques pour la justice, is a network of Canadian churches founded on July 1, 2001. It focuses on social justice concerns. KAIROS is made up of former church groups that addressed specific issues. For example, many of the United Church and Catholic women with whom I spoke had previously been involved with Ten Days for Global Justice (formerly Ten Days for World Development), an organization that focused on structural development and global equity. KAIROS brought this and other groups together under one organization.[58]

There were four members in the meeting plus me—one man and the rest women. Bill was not a member of this committee and stayed downstairs at the post-service coffee while we met. Apparently Marjorie, a congregation member known to be very active with immigrant rights work and advocacy for Toronto's homeless population, had been expected to attend. However, there had been a kerfuffle after worship the week before with another member, Heather, over making Marjorie's contact lists available for a project. The disagreement was referred to several times during the meeting and met with grumbles and nervous laughter.

This meeting was the only time during my fieldwork in which I was intensely questioned about my own religious affiliation. At the beginning of the meeting, Kevin asked in several ways, but not directly, whether I was Christian. I told him I had been raised Presbyterian. I explained that my project was ethnographic rather than theological. These answers didn't seem to address his main concern of whether I currently identified as religious, and as I was searching for words that would satisfy him, our conversation was cut short by the official beginning of the meeting.

Donna talked about the various demonstrations and meetings she and her partner had attended recently. They were very active with the International Socialists (IS) political group, and she shared information about IS events that she had attended and those that were upcoming. Clearwater's host church provides office space for community and activist groups, such as the IS and another Marxist group, so as Donna announced events put on by different organizations, she gestured in various directions their offices were located in relation to the congregation's office. Donna expressed frustration that other members of the congregation did not network with these groups.[59] She was also upset because Clearwater's annual retreat always conflicted with the International Socialists' retreat.

Most members of the Justice, Peace and Environment Group had attended the major demonstration against the war in Iraq the week before. They discussed their experiences. Heather said she went but was unable to find the congregation with the banner. Donna and her partner had marched with the congregation. They talked about who else from the congregation had or had not attended.

The members expressed again and again that they felt frustrated that other people from the congregation did not support the projects they suggested and did not help them enough. At different times Heather and Donna would talk about how they didn't trust other people within the congregation, or in the other United Church congregations with whom they worked, to follow through on things they had asked them to do. The feeling seemed to be that no one took any of these tasks seriously enough, so anything that the group wanted done, they would have to do themselves. It was clear that everyone in the group felt overextended and underappreciated.

Organizing the next Amnesty International letter writing day was one of the things they worried about. When Heather said that she did not want to organize the next letter writing day because it was so much work, Donna offered to do it. However, Heather seemed to take this offer as a personal criticism and argued with Donna, saying that Donna was only willing to do it because she did not understand how much work it really was.

During this exchange Kevin leaned over and explained to me that the KAIROS project was a serious source of stress for the group and the cause for the coffee time argument between Heather and Marjorie the previous week. The Clearwater Justice, Peace, and Environment group was attempting to contact other activist groups and churches with which it had worked in the past to get them involved in the new KAIROS organization. It was for this purpose that Heather had expected access to Marjorie's contact lists the week before. Kevin said that this project was really frustrating and overwhelming for the group. The group was very small, yet members felt obligated to take the initiative in getting other churches involved. The discrepancy between what they felt they should do and what they were actually able to do was causing tension. He thought that things would go more smoothly in the group once they decided what to do about it.

The meeting was difficult. Members spent a good deal of time processing their concerns that no one did as much as they did and that the congregation did not appreciate how much effort they contributed. In fact, many of the names they brought up were members whom I knew to be very active and effective in their own spheres of organizing. I found it discomfiting to listen to harsh criticisms of people who did important work. Moreover, the Amnesty International letter writing, which the group took as such a monumental task, had originally been organized by Annie and Marjorie simply as a way of motivating themselves to write their own letters. It started as a relaxed drop-in activity to offer mutual encouragement, a way of simplifying the task and feeling less isolated.[60] The organization of the monthly meeting had been turned over to the Justice, Peace and Environment Group because they had wanted it, yet they clearly felt burdened by the responsibility.

Upon reflection, however, I realized that the group is useful in the larger context of the congregation. The group resolves some of the concerns repeatedly brought to the Worship Committee about the balance of ritual to political discussion in the service. Although I do not want to imply that this was a conscious strategy on the part of the congregation, the group also seemed to serve the purpose of making its participants feel important and validated. After all, they were put in charge of organizing activities that Clearwater and partner congregations put on, such as the letter writing and KAIROS networking. By setting aside special time for them to meet, those in the congregation who found interactions with them challenging could, for the most part, avoid engaging with them over these issues. This strategy did not isolate them entirely; they still sought out other members when they decided they needed something, as demonstrated by the incident between Heather and Marjorie a week earlier.

Group members seem to have internalized many of the criticisms of nonreligious activist groups about religion itself being a waste of time. They were annoyed that other congregation members did not want to so thoroughly extend themselves in the ways that they had chosen to. This meeting replicated much of the stress that many of my participants discussed as a problem in activist circles, a problem to which they found remedy in religious community. Yet here were people within not only a religious community but one supportive of anti-oppression values and political activism who clearly experienced the anxiety and distress that most of my participants ascribe to nonreligious political groups. I don't think it was entirely coincidental that several members strongly identified with the International Socialists, an explicitly Marxist organization.[61] Nonetheless, the Justice, Peace and Environment Group kept such worrying contained within a small circle. This left other congregation members free to pursue their own needs during church time, such as personal grounding, ritualizing, and providing mutual social support.

The difficulties of this working group demonstrate that the distinction between nonreligious activist groups and their own, which my participants often emphasize, is not always as stark as they perceive or at least hope for. Rather than being a problem, however, the group actually serves members of the congregation, both within and outside it, quite well. For those who are anxious that the worship service is not directly connected enough to activism, it supplies a space in which to process these anxieties with like minds and plan work to remedy that shortcoming. It is also a place where members who are newer to thinking about their religious and political identities as being connected can learn from longtime activists and discuss explicitly what other politically engaged members may take more for granted. In the end it is a space for participants to work out some of the emotional difficulties, acknowledged and otherwise, that come with intentional community.

Individual and Collective Change

While the ritualizing of my participants can be interpreted as at least partly self-focused, the desired self-improvements are not solely to bolster the self, as would be, for example, better public speaking skills, a lifting of depression, or attaining inner peace. Instead, the desired changes relate to moving from self-centeredness to better relationships with other people—for example, toward "empathy," "patience," and "compassion." These changes are framed as efforts that benefit people beyond the individual self. In the Catholic Worker service these others are identified as "neighbors." In the United Church service they are abstracted as "society." In the case of the Pagan collective they are sometimes named (Holly Jones and her family or Starhawk and her collective) and sometimes specified in different ways ("children and families," the "African continent," or homeless people). This approach is consistent with Lesley Northup's argument that personal change is connected to political engagement: "Ritual provides one way for humans to get more deeply in touch with their sense of self. Personal growth, however, can also be understood as the starting point for political awareness."[62] The connection between changing oneself and changing society is one that many of my participants articulate.

Ritualizing is also not their only activity. These groups are already working for concrete political change in other ways. Among them there is a strong sense that in order to continue to be effective activists, they must also continue to work on and care for themselves. In response to my question "What significance does ritual have for your politics?" Deborah, a United Church member, said, "It has a lot of significance for me religiously and because of that it nourishes me for the politics."[63] She understands ritual as fortifying her for political work. Camille, a contemporary Pagan, said something very similar about her sacred dance circle: "For people who are activists, it's a place to rest and ground, to come back to the earth and remember who they are."[64] Sue, another Pagan, said of ritual, "I get a sense of relief without having to escape."[65] Ritual supports activism by supporting activists.

In my participants' understanding of ritual, there is also an element of creating themselves as subjects with agency in the familiar liberal-progressivist sense of resisting disempowerment.[66] In response to my question "Do you see ritual, outside of political contexts, as having political significance?" River said: "Anything that says I have value as a human being is a political action. In a world, on a planet, where mainstream culture, especially for women and other disenfranchised groups, [if] you're not a millionaire, you don't have value unless you're way up there, so anything that encourages human value is a political act. And it's wonderful!"[67] Here River stresses the importance of asserting one's own value in the face of the negation she perceives in mainstream culture. For River enhancing personal esteem is a political act in and of itself not only because self-worth supports other political actions but because self-esteem has intrinsic value.[68]

This assertion of one's value depends on the possibility that ritual can affect reality.[69] Griffith writes of the ritual of prayer, "By making room for new ways of imagining a situation, such practices push at the walls of those boundaries, set them in motion, and stretch the range of options within that world."[70] Ritual can create new possibilities for action in the world. An expression of this perspective can be found in the Yarrow Collective's ritual of calling the directions. After calling the four cardinal directions and their elements, along with center, the fifth direction, the Witches say, "We are now between the worlds, and what is between the worlds can change the world!" What happens inside ritual space has implications outside it.

A further example of ritual creating social reality can be found in the Clearwater Easter service. Here the send-off ceremony for Laura can be understood as a concrete example of Leah's belief that Christian community supports individuals in improving the world. Members of the congregation came together to affirm Laura and give her support in her new endeavor.

Northup highlights ritual's ability to influence social relations, writing, "Ritualization can function as a powerful tool because of its ability not only to reflect but also to construct various aspects of social reality."[71] Through this understanding of ritual, what happens within ritual space has the power to change the external world. If, for example, River acts as an empowered subject within a ritual context, she becomes so outside of ritual space. Jonathan Z. Smith provides a slightly different perspective when he writes, "Ritual is a means of performing the way things ought to be in conscious tension with the way things are in such a way that this ritualized perfection is recollected in the ordinary, uncontrolled course of things."[72] When River feels devalued in everyday life, she can draw on her memories of experience in ritual space, her rehearsals of self-empowerment, and use them to shift her perspective and her behavior. As Grimes writes, "Rituals model actions into paradigms" through "the process of imaginative world making."[73]

In addition to sparking improvement through personal change, my participants believe that ritual affects their communities even more directly, bringing them into being by creating and sustaining connections between people.[74] Regina, a Catholic Worker leader, said of successful ritual, "It feels really unifying, and really strengthening."[75] Even Donna, a Clearwater member who is openly ambivalent about the role of ritual in her congregation, said, "I'm not really big on ritual, but I think it helps the groups to become something more cohesive."[76] Ritualizing together is a way to strengthen group solidarity.[77]

Emily, a Catholic, finds value in the creation of community beyond its usefulness for political work and social change. She said: "Maybe that's what sort of unites the political stuff and the religious stuff is the need for community. That is what going to a march or going to church or going to tea or being part of anything is about, because I have a really strong need for community. . . . The thing that makes fighting against injustice fun is the people that you get to do it with and the people that you get to meet in the process. That's good. That makes it almost like a ministry."[78] For Emily ritualizing brings people together, a worthy goal in and of itself.

River stresses community-building aspects of ritual within the context of creating social change. Discussing the importance of ritual for politics, she said: "It's about connection, to each other and to the issue and to the earth, and . . . being grounded so that you don't panic and having a community, being connected to a community of people you can trust. If something bad happens, you know you're going to be looked after, and it's about establishing community and knowing you're not alone and being part of a community and sending energy into the issue."[79] For River ritual grounds activists and creates connections between them. This connection to each other allows activists to take risks because they can take care of and be cared for by one another. Moreover, ritual can focus groups' energy for larger causes, taking the burden off individuals.

These feminist activists understand ritual to be politically important both for its own sake and for the support it offers to their work. Ritual helps individuals improve themselves and, within a broader cosmology of relationship, creates change for the better, through connections between individuals with each other, their communities, and the world. Ritualizing helps prevent burnout, which weakens political effectiveness. It helps focus groups for collective action. Lastly, it provides a sense of community more broadly, which in turn also helps individuals and prevents burnout. Ritual, personal change, and political work are intertwined.

Ritual Makes Things Happen

Simply because ritual is used to effect personal change does not mean it is not also perceived as helpful in facilitating change in other, more direct ways. Rites are also understood as instrumental, bringing about changes on more than a psychological level. Ritual is an important part of alleviating suffering in the world. As River said earlier of ritual, "It's what you bring to your spiritual practice and that you can send energy out, and that energy has an effect."[80]

Rituals performed by the Catholic Worker, the Clearwater congregation, and the Yarrow Collective focus on present concerns. Rites may emphasize healing a member of the group, rectifying a global problem, or de-escalating violence at protests, rather than emphasizing personal change. If one is moved or shifts one's attitudes toward the problem in the process of one of these rituals, then this is a happy side effect but not the focus and certainly not the exclusive goal.

Within each of the holiday rites there are elements of personal, group, and global transformation. In the Pagan collective Samhain ritual, guided trance offers opportunities for personal interactions with loved ones who have died, ancestors one may not have known personally, and deities in the Otherworld. The culmination of the trance is a spiral dance, meant to raise energy for both personal and ecological healing. In the Summer Solstice ritual, wishes for personal improvement are interspersed with wishes for more concrete political changes.

In the Catholic Worker Easter Dawning service, participants throw away aspects of personality or behavior that inhibit personal growth and connectedness with others. They then name things that they would like to bring into their lives. Self-healing is contextualized, however, as part of an effort to strengthen communities and society. Moreover, the language they use is that of anti-oppression, moving away from "privilege, self-focus, and pride" in order to connect with other people. The ritual, at least in terms of its intentional messages, has moral formation as one of its goals.[81]

In the Clearwater Easter service, members plant intentions with wheat seeds, creating an analogy between the sprouting of the seeds and the fulfillment of personal hopes. Self-improvements, such as "understanding," are combined with more outwardly focused intentions, such as "peace" and "compassion." Improvements of self and the world commingle. In the midst of this interconnection, where does change begin? As the center of the service, Leah's talk directly links the ability to work through personal issues of shame and anger to ending cycles of violence in society, abilities that are made possible through Christian community. Change starts within both self and community.

In each of their rites these groups link personal change to global change, but the specific nature of the links are different. The Pagan rites seek to raise positive energy and then direct it to self and world. The Catholic Worker rite, opening up "the places of death in our lives," endeavors to improve relationships and clear "barriers we have let our culture put between us and our neighbors," thus leading to a better world. In the Clearwater rite a healthy self is needed to improve the world, and community is required to maintain a healthy self. Setting oneself right enables right relationships with others. In each of these rituals, improvement ripples from self to others to the world.

One of the main ways that religiously motivated feminist activists engage with their religious traditions is through group ritual. Ideally ritual is creative and engages them emotionally, facilitating personal well-being and group solidarity. In addition, my participants understand ritual as instrumental, not only working socially but metaphysically to bring about change in the world. There is sometimes tension within their groups about the proper balance of ritual to overt political action and about the types of ritual that best meet group needs. Ritual nonetheless remains an important activity among those in the Clearwater congregation, the Toronto Catholic Worker, and the Yarrow Collective and a significant way that they understand themselves as members of religious communities.

A significant way my participants strive to improve the world is by participating in public demonstrations that call attention to injustices. Political protests provide opportunities for them to bring their religions into public spaces, challenging common assumptions about the relationship between religion and politics in North American society. In the next chapter I continue the discussion of ritual, exploring its use by religiously motivated activists within anti-globalization protests.

2 "The Shrine Was Human Rights"

PILGRIMAGE AND PROTEST

A statue of Mary presided from her palanquin, floating above the throngs of the Saturday mass march against the Free Trade Area of the Americas (FTAA) in Quebec City, April 19–22, 2001. The Holy Mother was resplendent in her cloak of dollar bills and a sash that read, "Our Lady of Consumption." She held a tiny toy camel in one hand and a giant needle in the other. Her attendants handed out prayer cards on which the McDonald's logo blazes across her chest—a cultural critique sardonically delivered in religious iconography (figs. 1–2).

Another Lady also moved among the protesters. Our Lady of Guadalupe, the patron saint of the Americas, smiled from hand-drawn prayer cards distributed to protesters by a Catholic activist. The cards depict no docile Mary; she is posed mid-kick and grinning. The petition on the back of the cards reads, "We offer you our prayers for the protection of all people of the Americas against the Global Capitalist Machine and its evils" (figs. 3–4). The cards earnestly call on the intercessory power of the saint to fight global injustice.

These two representations of Mary, found at the heart of an anti-globalization protest, discredit popular assumptions about an exclusive relationship between religion and conservative politics. Religiously motivated social justice activists negotiate roles for religion in public discourse,[1] incorporating religious and spiritual elements into political demonstrations and creating rituals to perform in civic spaces. Despite the suspicion with which it is sometimes met within activist communities, religion has nonetheless been present in global justice protests concurrent with international trade conferences, such as the demonstrations against the FTAA in Quebec City in April 2001, those against the World Trade Organization (WTO) in Seattle in November 1999 and in Cancun in September 2003, and against the G20 in Toronto in June 2010. Such protests represent significant elements of the political landscape in North America and around the world, expressing frustration about free trade policies and the global dominance of the United States, frustrations that also developed into the Occupy movement,[2] Standing Rock, and the Women's March movement.

Ritual is central to how religiously motivated feminist activists understand their religiosity. Anti-globalization demonstrations are ritualized in many ways. For example, activist Louise Leclair compares them to larger patterns of pre-Lenten Carnival in the West.[3] Geographer Steven Flusty draws on Mikhail Bakhtin's exploration of "carnival" to examine ways in which anti-globalization demonstrations create "temporary autonomous zone[s]" with alternative social orders.[4] Bakhtin's concept of carnival involves a ritualized reversal of social structures, akin to Victor Turner's notion of *communitas*, which I discuss later. For Bakhtin participants in carnival constitute a new social organization for the duration of the celebration.[5]

Rather than mapping a diffuse, implicit ritualization found throughout global justice demonstrations, I begin by exploring the "public religion" of explicit ritual performances within protest space. In addition, travel by religiously motivated activists to global justice demonstrations can be viewed as a form of pilgrimage—itself a very public performance of religion. An exploration of ritualizing by religiously motivated protesters contributes to understanding the political phenomenon of mass anti-globalization protests—in the West generally and in North America particularly—and its relationship with religious worldviews. Further, it augments scholarship concerned with how older patterns of ritual and pilgrimage may influence contemporary understandings of religious experience and their impact on political expression.

In *Ritual: Perspectives and Dimensions* Catherine Bell writes: "While ritual once stood for the status quo and the authority of the dominant social institutions, for many it has become anti-structural, revolutionary, and capable of deconstructing inhuman institutions and generating alternative structures. . . . The older conviction that increasing modernization, rational utilitarianism and individualism would inevitably do away with most forms of traditional ritual life has given way to a heroic championing of ritual as the way to remain human in an increasingly dehumanized world."[6]

Many of the feminist Catholic, United Church Protestant, and contemporary Pagan activists with whom I spoke express an affinity with Bell's contention that participants often experience engaging in ritual as a humanizing act. Through explicit ritual performances within anti-globalization demonstrations, they attempt to remind all participants in the event, other protesters as well as police, of the mutual humanity of all involved. They understand their use of religious ritual to be helpful in combating political and economic systems that oppress and dehumanize people around the world.

Setting the Stage

I began hearing about the Summit of the Americas, during which international political leaders were to discuss the FTAA, months in advance.[7] For Toronto social justice activists, the protest in Quebec City was exciting and important. It was the first major anti-globalization protest in Canada after the 1999 confrontation in Seattle, which, for many activists, marked a new era in global justice organizing.[8] Held in April 2001, the Quebec City protest was called to coincide with and disrupt the international meeting of world leaders to discuss the Free Trade Area of the Americas. In going to the Quebec City protest, I was joining activists who came from all over the world, but particularly from North and South America, to participate in the protest and alternative activities.

An estimated thirty thousand protesters participated in actions and counter-activities during the FTAA talks.[9] One such alternative activity was the People's Summit, named in contrast to the official gathering, the Summit of the Americas, and hosted by the Hemispheric Social Alliance.[10] It featured speakers on issues such as economic justice, environmental protection, and responsible development.[11] I attended talks by activists Naomi Klein and David Suzuki, among others. Another event in which a majority of protesters participated was an officially planned march on Saturday afternoon that began in a local park and led protesters through the streets away from the fenced-in summit center.[12] In addition to these centralized activities, various protesters engaged in a variety of small-group actions along the fence and around the cordoned-off downtown, everything from combat with police security forces through theater performance, art installations, singing, dancing, drumming, chanting, and chalking slogans or drawing and painting on the closed-off streets.

At the same time that this event was exciting to activists as the first major anti-globalization protest in Canada, it also marked a turn in Canadian police tactics for controlling crowds. Despite legal challenges, authorities erected a security fence of metal and concrete barricades around the downtown core to prevent protesters from entering the area of the city where the summit was taking place. This measure restricted not only activists; residents required special security passes to move into and out of the restricted zone.[13] During the protests police incorporated "nonlethal" weapons, such as tear gas, rubber bullets, and water cannons, into their crowd control tactics and did so on a scale that surprised protesters and many people watching news coverage at home.[14]

In some places Quebec City looked postapocalyptic: highways shut down; stores temporarily abandoned to the conflict; boards over windows; groups of protesters roaming about looking for shelter, water, lost friends—all surrounded by horizons of police in riot gear, helmets veiling their faces, and thick, toxic fog billows of tear gas. The traffic cameras now focused on the blocked-off streets. At night they showed clashes between police and a few lone protesters, often from the black bloc, that is, individuals and small groups that accept street combat as a legitimate protest tactic and who are often scapegoated in police statements and media coverage as simply agitators, not "real" protesters.[15] The two sides scrambled around in black outfits, shadows bathed in the sulfur of the streetlights, accompanied by the sounds of breaking glass as protesters lobbed bottles and police launched tear gas canisters and let loose water cannons. Helicopters constantly menaced the city from overhead, especially at night. Many protesters believed that the helicopters were used deliberately to harass activists and prevent them from sleeping.[16]

Organizing groups tried to provide information about which demonstration activities were less risky and which were more likely to involve confrontations with police. The geography around the fence and the marching routes were color coded: green for safe, orange for slight risk, and red for likelihood of confrontation with police and arrest (fig. 5).[17] As a person on a temporary visa to Canada and therefore at risk of deportation, I was anxious to stay out of areas where a confrontation with police was more likely. However, the color system quickly broke down as police and protesters confronted one another. There was no place in the heart of the city where activists could be sure the police would not rush and no place that tear gas did not taint.[18]

Every now and then, driven by strategies that protesters could rarely determine, the police would charge a street to recover it from demonstrators. It seemed arbitrary and terrifying. One minute I would be walking along, talking to people about their reasons for coming and their plans for later, and the next minute a wave of desperate people would stampede, yelling for everyone to run. About the last thing you really want to do in a situation like that is turn and run blindly down a highway ramp or bridge, so everyone would start yelling back, "Walk!" "Marché!" and we'd hurry as best we could away from the dangerous area. Over four hundred protesters were arrested during the summit.[19]

Along with the violence, confusion, and fear, however, there was also beauty, creativity, and fun. Many different groups brought their messages to the protest and chose to express them in both more conventional—placards and chants—and less conventional ways. Throughout the weekend activist groups engaged in sidewalk art, singing, guerrilla theater, dancing, and games, some planned by specific people in advance and rehearsed, others created spontaneously by people who had just met.

Get to Know Some Activists

A diversity of activist groups participated in the demonstrations, and the color coding of protest routes was paralleled by the use of color by different groups. One that received the most sensationalized media coverage is the black bloc,[20] composed of disparate groups and individuals who dress in black, often cover their faces to prevent identification by law enforcement agencies, and share a philosophy that street combat with police is a valid protest tactic. In contrast, the Pagan Living River is an international coalition of religious Pagans who "flowed" through the protest together, dressed in blue, to promote nonviolence and to raise awareness about water rights issues. Starhawk, one of the founders of Reclaiming Witchcraft and a well-respected global justice activist,[21] took part in the Living River actions. Also present were the Raging Grannies, an alliance of older women who regularly participate in demonstrations in the United States and Canada. They appear in bright and eccentric "granny" outfits, deliberately satirizing the stereotype of crazy old ladies, and sing witty political lyrics to popular tunes, usually resulting in much laughter and merriment among themselves and the crowds of other protesters.[22] In addition to these and other organized groups, including trade unions, religious communities, and nonprofit organizations, there were also thousands of individuals, alone or with informal groups of friends, relatives, or coworkers, who had come to register their opposition to the FTAA.

Angel, in her midtwenties, was among the protesters. She identifies as feminist and Catholic and has strong ties with the Toronto Catholic Worker, though she is not in residence there. Her activism focuses on anti-racism, anti-poverty, and global justice, and she often organizes with anarchist groups. At the time of the Quebec City protest, she was active in Organizing Autonomous Telecoms (OAT),[23] a collective that works to make computer communication technology accessible for grassroots activists and community organizations. A few weeks before the protest, she took the train to Quebec City and stayed with friends. While there, she did advance work setting up communication technologies for the protest marches and actions. During the protests she helped coordinate activists and spent time in the underpass area, the "anarchist village," where she helped distribute free vegetarian food for Food Not Bombs, an organization dedicated to redistributing military spending to end global violence, poverty, and hunger.[24] After the protest she waited until the people she knew who had been arrested were released from jail. Then she hitchhiked back to Toronto with several friends.[25]

River is in her early forties and works as an office administrator in a nonprofit organization that helps find housing for people dealing with mental illness. She is also a seasoned Pagan activist with many demonstrations and a few civil disobedience arrests under her belt. From the moment she heard about the protest, she knew she needed to go. She traveled from Toronto on a bus with activists from different progressive organizations, meeting up with the "Pagan Cluster" organizing group in Quebec City. Like many activists from all over North America, she slept on the floor at a local university.

Before the official summit began, River facilitated an activist training workshop with Starhawk, an intimidating task for her but one of which she is very proud. She also, like many of my participants from all three communities, participated in a special women's action, called for in advance by Starhawk,[26] on the Thursday night preceding the opening of FTAA negotiations. At this action women created webs of yarn, ribbons, string, and cloth, weaving together their magical intentions to stop the FTAA and to create more just systems of international economic relationships. River walked with her group during the official Saturday march and joined with the Living River throughout the weekend struggles between police and demonstrators. After the protests River returned home in a van that other members of the Pagan Cluster had rented to travel together to and from Quebec City.

Judy is in her early thirties and identifies as a feminist and a member of the United Church. She works with a group that advocates for justice in international economic development. She went to Quebec City in a car with friends and slept on a gym floor. While in Quebec, she met up with Catholic coworkers and walked with church coalitions in the official march. She also participated in vigils, an interfaith ceremony held at a downtown church that mourned global exploitation committed in the name of free trade, and protest actions at the fence that divided protesters from delegates to the FTAA meeting.[27]

Jenna, in her midtwenties, is also a Catholic whose activism is rooted in her faith. She works for a nongovernmental organization focused on justice in international development. She was able to attend the Quebec City protests because her work sent her with several of her coworkers to the People's Summit that preceded the FTAA negotiations. She traveled with her group by train, and they stayed in a retreat center just outside Quebec City, along with other groups funded by her NGO from across Canada, the United States, and Europe.

She arrived in Quebec City several days in advance and was able to watch the city core change from business as usual to one divided by the security fence and emptied of people. At the People's Summit Jenna attended sessions on agriculture because she was working on a campaign that deals with the patenting of seeds and the problems this raises for farmers. She and her coworkers went on the official march on Saturday. In the evening she attended an interfaith service in a downtown church. It was a candlelight vigil for peace and took place over twenty-four hours. Before they took the train back to Toronto, Jenna and her group walked around downtown, surveying the damage that a weekend of "security" had wrought.

Lavender is in her early sixties and identifies as a contemporary Pagan. She is a member of the Raging Grannies. She also belongs to other political organizations and does activist work around anti-homelessness and anti-poverty issues, especially focusing on older women, as well as environmentalism, anti-war, and global justice. She went to Quebec City with her Pagan affinity group in a rented van.

Affinity groups are consensus-based collectives of people who come to protest together. Activist Janet Conway describes their history: "Affinity group organizing has its roots in feminist, anarchist, and anti-nuclear movements in which small, autonomous groups decide on the nature of their participation in direct action, organizing independently of any centralized movement authority."[28] Affinity groups are intentional communities formed by activists to provide support and protection during protests. In forming an affinity group, activists agree to be responsible for each other. For example, affinity groups negotiate about when and where to participate in protests and what direct actions to perform. Ideally members of your affinity group help you if you are teargassed, call a lawyer if you are arrested, and are waiting to meet you when you are released from holding.

Like many activists from a variety of backgrounds and groups, Lavender slept on the floor in the cafeteria at Laval University. She participated in the women's action on Thursday and the official march on Saturday, flowing with the Pagan Living River. Although she decided to only go on green routes—those intended to avoid civil disobedience—she often found herself in the thick of confrontations between protesters and police.[29]

Performing Ritual

The Quebec City women's action took place on April 19, 2001, the Thursday night preceding the official opening of the FTAA summit. The call was written by Starhawk. Sent out to activist email lists and passed around on flyers in advance of the event, it describes the demonstration's purpose:

> We will, as women, weave together our hopes and dreams, our aspirations, our indictments, our testimony, our witnessing, our demands, our visions. We will write on ribbons, on strips, on cloth, on rags. We will draw, paint, knot cords, braid yarn, whisper into pieces of string. And from these materials we will weave our web.
>
> If they ignore our voices and continue their deliberations, the cries of women will haunt them and undo all their plans. Though they erect a fence to stop us, we will twine our web through its mesh to be the visible symbol of the power of women, of the revolution we weave. When they try to wall us out of their meetings, they will only wall themselves in. We claim all of the world beyond their wall.[30]

Groups were encouraged to bring webs from home to incorporate into the larger web or even to mail in web work if their group was unable to be physically present at the protest.[31] The demonstration centered on integrating materials into the fence that separated the summit space from the rest of the city and the official delegates from the protesters. The action was designed to incorporate different ritual actions within this larger frame of ritual weaving.

A ritual led by Starhawk culminated in a spiral dance. Lavender related:

> There was a huge puppet of the goddess Nemesis, which was really great, and there was a woman from the Mothers of the Plaza de Mayo, in Argentina, who spoke to us before we set off. That was really powerful. Then when we were chanting, we chanted also in Spanish, and there was just this feeling of unity as we were trudging up the hill. . . . I felt really good when we went on the Thursday night and we took a web from Toronto—we had done a WomynSpirit ritual. So we [her WomynSpirit group] did that for Quebec City, and we took

it, and we put it up on the fence. And then we created another one there with Starhawk, . . . and we put that up on the fence. And did a spiral dance and that was, that was really fabulous. The woman's action was wonderful.[32]

In addition to the ritual that Starhawk led, other rituals took place during the action. Jesse, a Catholic Worker and journalist, described her experience within the larger action:

A wail rose up from the five women huddled on the ground as the black cloth settled over them, a wail that grew until the street was filled with its resonant grief and anger. It . . . rang through the nearby security fence . . . and grew in my chest until Linzi and I raised up the six-meter swath of black cloth and pulled it taught between us, freeing the women beneath. Into the waiting silence, we ripped the cloth end from end and ran whooping to weave it into the chain-link fence, the final joyful crescendo of our dance of lament and resistance.[33]

The webs of yarn and cloth woven into the fence during the women's action remained on display throughout the protest weekend. Along with other artistic installations on the fence, like flowers, balloons, and bras decorated with anti-FTAA slogans, they contributed to the carnival mood of the protesters and, alternatively, offered stark contrast to the tear gas and police violence that began with the official commencement of the summit.

Why Ritualize?

Democratic protest has often taken ritual form. Reflecting on the Civil Rights movement and the struggle for same-sex marriage equality, David M. Craig writes: "Ritual can contribute to these broader debates because it is a special type of social practice that makes explicit the proper channeling of participants' desires toward the formative goals and commitments, virtues and relationships, accepted by some group of people. This means that the use of ritual in public reasoning will often be asymmetrically geared toward a partially shared vision of good desire."[34] Within global justice protests religious ritual may serve several functions for the ritual participants themselves, for different audiences, and for others who may not witness the ritual, but these functions revolve around creating shared values. Activists may use ritual theater to encourage other activists and create a safer and more comfortable social environment. Jenna, the Catholic who works for a nonprofit focused on justice in economic development, explained that part of what made the experience positive and exciting for her companions was the art, color, and ritual.[35]

Lavender, a contemporary Pagan, said that she always tries to get a spiral dance going in areas where violence might break out. "Everyone likes to feel included," she said, explaining that she understands violence as resulting from protesters not knowing what else to do.[36] She sees the ritual of spiral dancing—a common Pagan practice in which a circle of people holding hands weaves inward in a spiral and back out again, causing each dancer to face all others as they pass—as providing a positive way to channel anxious group energy. Spiral dances are lighthearted and sometimes rambunctious affairs; the spiral gets faster and faster until it whips back out into a circle, an activity frequently accompanied by breathless laughter and feelings of camaraderie. Lavender consciously uses spiral dances to create communities out of motley groups of strangers.

Protesters may employ ritual to signal peaceful intentions to other protesters and to police. In the Quebec City protest, for example, radical Catholics sat down in front of a line of riot police and sang hymns with their hands held open in front of them.[37] Abby, a Catholic Worker in her twenties, relates a story from that action:

What we did is we went to the top of the hill and we followed a group of police in riot squad down the hill toward the fence, and we were singing the song "Freedom" and dancing. And then we stopped, the police stopped us, they turned around, and we sang for an hour. Every once in a while the police would come up to our backs, and it was really amazing because I could feel this police person, his legs touching my back, sitting on the ground, and I'm like, "Oh my God." And we were singing this song, the words kept changing, and we said, "Our hands were made for peace," and we all raised our hands at the same time, and the police just backed two feet away from our backs. It was amazing, you know, I was like, "That's just great," because, you know, we all raised our hands, we were all sitting on the ground . . . and we did that for about two hours and then we got a little bit sore in the voice, and then we left. . . . It was just really powerful to see how quickly the song and the prayer just calmed everybody down, including the cops.[38]

Pagan attendees participated in a very similar action in which they drummed and read "The Cochabamba Declaration," a treatise on the sacredness of water, to a line of riot police.[39]

Religiously motivated activists may also use ritual to diffuse tension more generally. Pagan, United Church, and Catholic women use ritual to help them stay calm and focused within chaotic environments. At Quebec City one of the downtown churches held an Ecumenical candle-light vigil for peace that was described to me by several United Church and Catholic activists as a moving and important element in their protest experience.[40] It provided a sense of calm and safety in the midst of a chaotic and often violent environment. Jenna told me, for example: "Going to the church and having some kind of service, that was really neat. And they were open twenty-four hours, and it was just kind of nice to feel like there was some safe place there. Still, it wasn't a safe space that was denying the political reality of the day, not like the mall. It was still recognizing that and trying to find a centering there."[41]

Many women of all three traditions recounted stories of contemporary Pagan activists arriving at dangerous protest scenes and using ritual to "shift the energy" in order to create an environment in which peace and safety are more possible.[42] The Pagan Living River deliberately went to areas of conflict and worked rituals to calm both sides. Catholic activists also referred to moments in which they turned to prayer or meditation to calm themselves in difficult interactions during protests. Angel, for example, said: "I've stood in front of riot cops and very quietly said something to myself. . . . I will admit that in really scary situations, to center myself, I will speak the name of God, but it's sort of under my breath or silently."[43] Contemporary Pagan, United Church, and Catholic anti-globalization activists with whom I spoke referred to the concept of "grounding" themselves in the midst of the fear and turmoil that protests can generate. For example, Sue, a contemporary Pagan peace activist, told me: "Religion is really grounding. [It's about] shifting the energy, instead of the agenda being set by the police."[44]

Performing ritual may also be experienced as helping to alleviate danger for others who are not around to see the performance happen. Camille, a contemporary Pagan, environmentalist and member of a sacred dance troupe, related her experience with her Pagan activist group:

> So it played out like that, that we marched, and we weren't in any great danger, and we did some ritual at times, and we were not where the real action was. And we were clear that there were people who were being teargassed at the center of it, so we formed a circle and did some visualization and sent energy to people in the thick of it. We also said, "There needs to be"—it was so grim, it was feeling so grim—we said, "There also needs to be vision and life in this," and so we also really were evoking the positive, and other women had flowers, and just invoking a sense of wonder and gratitude and bringing some positive images and offering those up.[45]

Assessments of the usefulness, or futility, of ritual actions outside the heart of demonstrations vary widely.[46] Nonetheless, Camille's group understood itself to be using ritual to help specific people in crisis, those getting teargassed at the center of the protest. The group's members also believed that their use of ritual helped people more generally by working to change the emotional environment of the city.

Rituals of Pilgrimage

So far we have been investigating public performances that protesters themselves define explicitly as rituals. In this section I would like to shift attention to the act of traveling to protests itself. Such a move allows us to explore broader understandings how religious ritual plays into protest activism. Could travel to anti-globalization protests by activists be considered an act of pilgrimage? Pursuing this question illuminates broader ways that religious ritual interacts with protest activism. While there are enough differences between traveling to mass demonstrations and undertaking pilgrimages to sacred sites to warrant care in using the analogy, there are evocative similarities, especially for those protesters who are motivated to go because of religious commitments.

Anthropological theory on pilgrimage suggests several aspects of the practice that distinguish it from other forms of travel.[47] Pilgrimages are normally understood as journeys to specific geographic locations that are central within particular religious cosmologies: a shrine to a saint, a place where an important event took place within the sacred history of a tradition, a main temple within a geographically diffuse community. These journeys may be undertaken out of obligation—either collective, such as the hajj, or personal, the result of a vow to Our Lady of Lourdes, for example—in order to gain merit, or to "see for oneself," to be close to supernatural power. Pilgrimage also implies self-sacrifice and hardship, rather than the luxury and relaxation one might associate with a vacation. Anthropologists argue about whether pilgrimages are characterized by shared feelings of camaraderie among travelers or whether they are instead the focus of power struggles over defining true meanings within religious and political systems.

In the case of global justice protests, like more traditional sacred journeys, travel to a specific site is undertaken with specific goals for change in mind. Like some contemporary pilgrims to Santiago de Compostela who travel to counteract a perceived ethical decline of society, anti-globalization protesters in North America may ask the divine to intercede in the world on behalf of the marginalized.[48] Moreover, they may ask world leaders to change their ways in favor of religiously inspired values. In some sense both traditional pilgrims and anti-globalization activists are looking for miracles and understand their petitions as such.

Many of the women with whom I spoke expressed feelings of obligation compelling them to go to the protest. For example, Lavender, a contemporary Pagan, said: "How could I not go? . . . I had to be there."[49] Angel, a Catholic, said: "Well you have to believe that what you're involved in is right and good. But to keep going back is hard. So it does require some level of faith to keep convincing yourself to keep going out on the streets, to keep facing the police. Like, it's not pleasant; it's not fun. . . . I don't go for fun; I don't go to see people; I don't go for a social event. Like, it's miserable. I don't like going to demos anymore, but it's still that idea that I can't stop. So yeah, there is a level of faith. You have to tell yourself that this is what you're being called to do and do it."[50]

River, a contemporary Pagan, said: "I felt a real pull, a need to be there. I felt it was really important that people who had a commitment to nonviolence were going to be there and had some skill. From the moment I started hearing about it, I wanted to go."[51]

Travel to protest can also serve to initiate religiously motivated activists, not into a particular religion, but into a particular way of being religious. In fact, one of the women with whom I spoke was annoyed that participation in protests, or lack thereof, seemed to divide activists into hierarchal relationships. Betty pointed out some of the factors, such as work, financial constraints (or, others might add, childcare responsibilities) that prevent people from being able to participate in protests, resulting in a lack of authority within their activist communities.[52] She concluded: "Although in some ways I see myself involved in anti-globalization stuff, in other ways I feel much more removed from it, too, because there seems to be a real kind of stress on people traveling to particular places, you know? And I can't travel. So I work locally, I guess is what I'm saying. I can't, you know, fly to the next country, or whatever, to do that kind of work, and I'm not sure that's my priority really."[53]

Jenna, the Catholic activist who was able to attend Quebec City because her work sent her, expressed a similar sentiment, saying: "I mean, I'm concerned about the FTAA, but [I'm unsure about the] effectiveness of one trip spending X amount of money and X amount of time, but then saying I could have done X here [in Toronto] and it would have been more effective or more for the common good or something? I'm a little cynical about how we spend all this time to get somewhere and then we go home and nothing changes."[54] Both Betty and Jenna are concerned that a focus on traveling to protests detracts from work within local communities and may mean that local issues and the activists who focus on them are not given the attention or authority they deserve.

While aspects of obligation and initiation are present in the attendance at anti-globalization protests by religiously motivated activists, these journeys fit most fully under the rubric of instrumental sacred journey. Anthropologist Alan Morinis lists examples of instrumental pilgrimages, which include goals such as personal healing or fertility, and are based in individual problems.[55] By comparison, the instrumental goals of religiously motivated anti-globalization protesters are broader in their focus: achieving universal human rights and eliminating poverty, economic exploitation, neocolonialism, and environmental destruction.

Time and Place

Traditional pilgrimages are very site focused: pilgrims travel to a specific place that has established religious associations. The entrenchment of custom and ritual serves to link current pilgrims with those of the past.[56] Even in discussions of "secular pilgrimages," it is the travel to and participation in activities at specific sites that lead scholars to define these journeys as pilgrimages.[57]

In contrast, anti-globalization protests take place in different major cities where world economic leaders choose to meet. Because there is not a link to the place but rather to the event, rituals and customs result from people who have "done this before."[58] It is the event itself that creates continuity, not the space. While traditional pilgrimage is geographically bounded, the religious travel and associated customs of anti-globalization protests are temporally bounded. In this sense these events have much in common with experience-centered travel, such as Grateful Dead concerts formerly or,[59] in a different way, academic conferences.

Several anthropologists suggest broadening considerations of pilgrimage to include journeys with nongeographical centers. Jennifer Porter turns to Alan Morinis's definition of *pilgrimage*, "a journey undertaken by a person in quest of a place or state that he or she believes to embody a valued ideal,"[60] in her investigation of participation in *Star Trek* conventions. Despite the fact that *Star Trek* conventions, like anti-globalization protests, take place at different times and in varying locations all over North America, participants understand going to conventions as a way to experience their ideals and commune with others who share them.[61] Sarah Pike and Lee Gilmore suggest that attendance at Pagan festivals and participation in the annual Burning Man performance art community, respectively, are worth considering as pilgrimages for similar reasons.[62]

Centers and Margins

Sociologist Erik Cohen, following Victor Turner,[63] argues that a pilgrim journeys to the cosmological "Center" of his or her world from the periphery, whereas a tourist travels from the Center to the periphery.[64] In the case of anti-globalization protesters, they are often traveling to a Center, in that they go not only to a major city but also to a seat of international power in the form of a global conference of world leaders. Upon arrival, however, they are not allowed into the actual Center— that is, the conference—and instead spend their time on the periphery. Jenna describes this boundary:

> I was able to be there [in Quebec City] a couple days ahead [of the FTAA meeting] and walk around old Quebec and see them finishing the building of the fence. It was really weird . . . to see all this construction going to building the fence. And then anticipating, well, what's going to happen around this fence. And then, on the Sunday . . . we went back downtown and sort of walked around the perimeter, and it felt like what I would assume the . . . the Gaza Strip or Hebron or something would look like because it just looked like a war zone. I mean, you had like all this dirt and . . . everything was just so like something terrible, like a huge conflict had happened there, and it went right through people's backyards and playgrounds.[65]

The fence and police in riot gear demarcated the conference and protest (fig. 6). In addition, the clouds of tear gas and the helicopters menacing overhead contributed to a feeling of unease among activists in Quebec City.

The official Center, as the reason for the calls to protest, represents the very opposite of the ideals activists hold. Said Lavender: "The fence was just so awful, you know, that it was there, separating the ordinary people from these politicians who think they're so special. I mean, what are they but flesh and blood like the rest of us, and yet they are so terrified that people are out to get them."[66] As another Pagan activist at the WTO protest in September 2003 explained, "I am writing from Cancun where I have been the past 10 days as a 'diplomat' for those who cannot attend and are not represented, one of many definitions for an activist."[67] The inaccessibility of the trade talks, of the Center, draws protesters. In this way religiously motivated activists journeying to anti-globalization protests are moving toward the opposite of their cultural and religious ideals. They are traveling to seats of international power—power that they understand to be invalid and unethically wielded.

Through one lens this is the opposite of a journey to a landscape that reflects sacred values.[68] Of this kind of travel to opposites, James Bielo writes that "atheist groups will visit creation museums to confront an ideological Other and take pleasure in mocking the site and the worldview it presents."[69] Reflecting on her experience in Quebec City, Vinci Daro writes, "This shared experience of exclusion and criminalization added meaning and intensity to struggles against the neo-liberal project for so many of us there."[70] Protesters physically counterpose themselves against that with which they deeply disagree.

Yet through another lens the protesters travel to join with one another in asserting alternatives to these other values, a mobilization that protesters have called "alter-globalization," following the World Social Forum,[71] emphasizing that activists promote many forms of transnational solidarity and connection as deliberate alternatives to those relationships of exploitation offered by *neoliberal economic* globalization. Wayne Fife argues that scholarly analysis of pilgrimage should broaden its focus to include the process of creating sacred space, rather than limit pilgrimage to specific geographical locations. He defines the pilgrimage sites of British missionaries in New Guinea not as specific locales related to holy people or things: "Instead these sites are shrines to an activity—the activity of evangelism itself."[72] Fife posits that what is being commemorated in these places is the *process* of missionizing, rather than a specific person or event. Travel by religiously motivated activists to anti-globalization protests can be read in a similar way: anti-globalization protests become "shrines to an activity," the activity of struggling for global justice. The community of protesters and the resistance activities in which they engage are ways activists transform protest spaces.

The missionizing aspect of pilgrimage that Fife introduces is also not out of place in investigating protest pilgrimage; protesters go to spread messages alternative to those of the conference holders. In a very real sense they are witnessing for others. Protesters feel marginalized by those in power and hope to redefine cultural values through their actions. This explains why, as Lavender put it, "The fence was just such a focus."[73] At the Quebec City protests activists took both physical and symbolic actions against the fence (fig. 7). One way to interpret the passion behind these actions is that if the protesters could break through the fence and into the conference, then their worldviews and values would symbolically redefine the Center.

At the boundary that separates official conference delegates from protesters, police and other armed officials enforce specific behavior toward and geographical distance from world leaders. Activists are not only journeying toward centers of international influence, however. They also join other protesters who feel similarly about the illegitimacy of corporate power and who envision alternatives to its hegemony. The communities of activists that form in the protest spaces can be said to embody the ideals to which protesters are traveling. Within the temporary communities set up outside these contested boundaries, there is no official authority or infrastructure in place to ensure specific behavior. Many diffuse, smaller centers of organization may form in this periphery, such as first aid tents, squats, free food areas, and informational events.

The "anarchist village," a space beneath a blocked-off highway overpass, became one such gathering place. Food Not Bombs set up a soup dispensary and provided portable toilets. There were bonfires and music. This space offered a small sense of safety in the midst of the chaos of the protests. There were enough people that it was unlikely to be raided by police; it was in a fixed location, making it possible to plan to meet comrades from whom one might become separated; and there was also a palpable feeling of solidarity among activists in this space.[74] People offered suggestions on where one might sleep that night and gave directions around the city, and activists came together in spontaneous collectives to plan actions that they then went up to the fence to perform—for example, sitting down in front of the main gate to block delegates' exit from the fenced-in summit space in the evening.[75]

Rather than geographical space representing the goal of the experience, it is the enactment of solidarity that does so. The created community of protesters and the resistance activities in which they engage are ways that activists transform protest spaces. Similar to Porter's *Star Trek* conventions or Pike's Pagan festivals, the protest experience includes the opportunity to express worldviews and embody ideals, in this case ideals that differ from those represented by the governments and corporate interests that have the international summit as their focus. In Quebec City collective aims and actions, in response to the fence and otherwise, served to re-center the event for the protesters themselves on the enactment of alternative communities.

Communitas

The lens of pilgrimage also allows opportunity to investigate ways that Victor Turner's controversial notion of *communitas* can be found in aspects of the protest experience.[76] *Communitas*, for Turner, is a state of coexistence among people in which aspects of identity that would normally divide individuals—such as socioeconomic class, gender, race, and sexual orientation—become inconsequential. People experience a sense of commonality that is in contrast to everyday, structured social hierarchies.[77] Together with Edith Turner, he applies this concept of *communitas* to Christian pilgrims, arguing that the act of traveling together toward a shared sacred goal temporarily disrupts social hierarchies and replaces them with a new sense of community.[78]

In his study of Marian devotion in Santa Fe, anthropologist Ronald Grimes argues that one of the distinguishing features of pilgrimages, in contrast to other modes of sacred and public movement, such as processions and parades, is this element of *communitas*. Whereas processions maintain hierarchies of status and parades, as "secularized processions," enforce normative social values, only pilgrimages offer the potential for liminality and social shake-up that result in *communitas*.[79] I would argue that a crucial addition to this categorization is the Bakhtinian carnival parade.[80] Public marches embodying hierarchal reversal, such as Gay Pride parades, Mardi Gras, and global justice protest marches, have more in common with pilgrimage than with normative parades due to their creation of a sense of newly structured community among participants and observers.

Communitas can be found in some aspects of the protest experience: like pilgrims on more traditional journeys, anti-globalization activists may travel together to the site of the protest, they may spend time together in created communities for the duration of the protest, and they may visit with people with whom they would not normally interact in their daily lives. Often they rely on help from strangers for transportation, housing, and food.[81] Lavender said, "I didn't find anybody, not one resident of Quebec City, who was not welcoming and really supportive, and people told me—I didn't have the need—but people told me about how residents came out and dragged them in their house to wash out their eyes and gave them water."[82]

Jenna made a further point about the *communitas* experienced within the protests themselves:

> For people who were involved [politically] in the '60s and '70s and '80s, [Quebec City] was a hugely, phenomenally empowering experience. . . . The people I was with were people who got involved in feminism rallies and then queer politics and then would be involved in liberation struggles of Africa and, in those moments it was always just a very one-focused gathering. So for them to be somewhere with environment and politics, social, political, every single group under the sun coming together unified, to an extent, compared to that normal life of people in politics, was such an amazing experience. . . . Their experience was walking with . . . thousands of people and seeing puppets and a lot of creativity and a lot of amazing coalitions and committees among, not just Canadians but all across the Americas, an incredible international organizing.[83]

Jenna emphasizes that the solidarity of the anti-globalization movement as expressed in the Quebec City protest was especially exciting for activists from other movements who were accustomed to divisions based on identity politics and competing factions among demonstrators. Lavender also described the feeling of inclusion and solidarity during the march: "It was a very powerful experience to be with sixty thousand who all cared about human rights. I really felt part of a huge movement."[84]

Imagining Global Community

Benedict Anderson writes that "all communities larger than primordial villages of face-to-face contact (and perhaps even these) are imagined.

Communities are to be distinguished, not by their falsity/genuineness, but by the style in which they are imagined."[85] In their identification with each other and with marginalized people around the world, anti-globalization protesters establish alternative communities to those of "nation." Within the "portable temporary autonomous zones" of protest space,[86] activists fashion new models of community based on international resistance to economic abuse, or, as geographer Steven Flusty writes, "globalization against globalization."[87]

In Anderson's invocation, the nation "is imagined because members of even the smallest nation will never know most of their fellow-members, meet them, or even hear of them, yet in the minds of each lives the image of their communion."[88] In understanding themselves to share common interests, values, and goals with diverse individuals in far-flung places and in identifying with an alternative global community that transcends national boundaries, protesters challenge nation-states and corporate institutions that allow international economic exploitation to go unchecked.[89]

The language of "human rights" appeals to a global *communitas*, of which the camaraderie of the protest environment is understood as a manifestation. As Talal Asad argues, however, the current universal definition of human rights is not only ethnocentric, but it invokes an ideal of global community that it cannot pragmatically achieve. By leaving enforcement of the United Nations standard to individual nations, international human rights requirements cannot curb economic exploitation of one nation or region by another, as is clearly the ongoing case in this age of global capitalism.[90] It is difficult for economically unstable countries to guarantee and protect human rights, yet members of struggling African nations often make up the most high-profile cases before the International Criminal Court at The Hague.[91] In addition, sanctions against despotic leaders often further harm their already exploited people.

Moreover, human rights derive from not only Western but explicitly Christian-centered values. Saba Mahmood, drawing on Linde Lindkvist, delineates the manner through which the Universal Declaration of Human Rights was directly influenced by Evangelical Christian missionary concerns, especially in article 18, "Right to freedom of thought and religion."[92] Acknowledging such a heritage reveals the otherwise obscured cultural specificity of all three pieces of "universal human rights." Tellingly, at least in the case of decisions by the European Court of Human Rights, state regulation of citizens in the name of latently Christian values are upheld by human rights enforcers as state prerogative, through decisions hinging on "wide margins of appreciation" and "legitimate interests," over and against both women's rights and Islam.[93]

While protesters generally do not question the Christocentric foundation of the concept of human rights, they do see vividly the obstacles to sustainable and equitable enforcement. Shifting their own "imagined community" from the limitations of nation to an international community, global justice protesters attempt to replace formulations of human rights that do not account for transnational economic abuse and therefore cannot prohibit or punish it. Protesters use their investment in an alternative global community to put pressure on exploiting nations—in the case of my participants, *their* nation and its allies—to change their domineering practices, make reparations, and put checks in place to prevent further degradations. Global justice activists struggle to repair the shortcomings that Asad criticizes as inherent in the language of human rights and its structure of global cooperation. The *communitas* created and experienced by activists in global justice demonstrations offers cosmological models of and for an alternative global community.[94]

The temporary autonomous zones of protest environments serve as embodiments of such communities. The Quebec City anarchist village under the highway, for example, served as a space in which economic exchange was not the basis of interaction among participants but rather mutual engagement around sharing resources (food, access to toilets, information) and creativity (dancing, music, ideas for direct actions). More broadly, however, the larger political projects in which activists engage—such as anti-corporate campaigns, fair trade relationships, and anti-war work—offer alternatives to structures of nation-state and economy that define individuals' interests primarily in terms of citizenship and class. These alternatives become the basis for an ethics of social justice (which I discuss in more detail in chapter 4).

Conflicts and Tensions

At the same time that protesters may experience a feeling of unity and identify as part of an alternative community, religiously motivated activists also travel and protest alongside people with very different motivations and ideals. In this sense John Eade and Michael Sallnow's counter-theory to *communitas* is helpful. They argue that contrary to claims that pilgrimage is best described in overarching rubrics of universality, pilgrimages are grounds for competing discourses. They maintain that pilgrimages are sites of conflicting interpretations and confrontations over meaning.[95] Pilgrimage is part of a struggle for narrative dominance.[96]

An excellent example of conscious wrestling with conflicting discourses can be found in discussions of protest tactics, or, to use a different narrative discourse, nonviolence versus violence. In her essay "Quebec City: Beyond Violence and Non-Violence" Starhawk writes, "In the lead-up to the action it often seemed that every single group involved was either actively disagreeing with some other group or ignoring their existence."[97]

One area of disagreement among activists was the planned route of the official protest march. It was divided up into levels of safety—green, orange, red—in a way that was supposed to offer activists choices about how much confrontation with police and possibility of getting teargassed they were willing to risk. As mentioned earlier, the safety assessments turned out to be overly optimistic. However, the most serious source of conflict among activists was that the main route of the march, designated green, led protesters in the opposite direction from the center of the city and the summit; it was designed to march all the demonstrators away from the FTAA meeting and its delegates. Those who disagreed with the route felt that it sent a message of capitulation.[98]

Another major area of contention among protesters, as the title of Starhawk's "Quebec City" essay suggests and media reports emphasize,[99] is the issue of violent and nonviolent strategies of protest. Many protesters dedicated to nonviolence are alienated by other activists engaging in property destruction or physically responding to police violence.[100] River, a Pagan, discussed her personal limits within protest situations: "My bottom line for actions that I will participate in is that I won't participate in anything that puts a living being at risk of injury, which would include horses that are underneath policemen. Nobody goes to the horse and asks, 'Hey, so you want to be a cop today?' I have this crazy theory that nobody should be beaten up, and that includes the cops [*laughs*]."[101] Many activists share River's opinion that violence in any form is unacceptable in the protest environment.

However, some protesters are concerned that the emphasis on nonviolent action reinforces hierarchies of power and privilege within activist communities. Angel, a Catholic, described her perspective on the divisions that arise in relation to protest tactics: "It's mostly the older, Christian activists that I find are really domineering and totally inconsiderate of how much privilege that they wield. So there's a consistent song of, you know, 'nonviolent actions.' And how divisive their language has been within the activist community! Sort of offering kids up to the police and that kind of thing."[102] Angel sees a generational divide in understanding the issue of combative protest. To her the exclusive prioritizing of nonviolence has served to turn activists against each other. She does not make a clear distinction around nonviolence and combat as inherently good or bad; instead, she bases decisions around the context of particular situations.

Even within conflicts over street combat and nonviolence, however, we can see points in which those with divergent opinions on the subject of tactics can come together. For example, many global justice activists happily recount stories of cooperation, solidarity, even mutual protection, between black bloc factions and explicitly nonviolent groups such as the Pagan Living River groups and the Raging Grannies.[103] As Lavender related: "The Raging Grannies rescued some people from the police at one point. . . . They were at an alley . . . during the fiercest time on Saturday of the teargassing, and they accidentally ended up in this dead-end alley. The police were there, and it was blocked, and the Raging Grannies went to the front . . . basically the Raging Grannies stood between the young people and the police. And they've done that in a lot of places."[104]

Moreover, activist communities have "agreed to disagree" to some extent about nonviolence and street combat. This position is usually described as respecting "a diversity of tactics." Many of the women with whom I spoke distance themselves personally from combative forms of protest but are also quick to acknowledge that people in different situations will make different choices around these issues. They suggested that some people may have fewer options than others. In contrast to the exclusionary and dichotomous understanding that Angel described earlier, both nonviolence and street combat were interpreted by women with whom I spoke in terms of privilege, class, and race; that is, people who feel most disempowered by the North American social structure and political processes are most likely to engage in property destruction or rock throwing.[105]

There are often implicit value judgments in such assessments. For example, River sees combat tactics as strategically naive, explaining: "It just reminds me of the ultimate stupidity of rocks versus guns. Rocks, guns, rocks, guns [*weighing her hands*] . . . hmm, you're not going to win this!"[106] To Lavender the use of combat tactics are the result of inexperience; she said of the black bloc, "These are just kids who haven't learned the skills of other ways."[107] This belief has inspired her to develop in-depth nonviolence training for young people with fellow Raging Grannies.

Protesters most well-known for engaging in property destruction and street combat with police, those participating in the black bloc, are also widely recognized as predominantly young, white, and male.[108] This characterization contradicts assumptions that it is the most marginalized and vulnerable people who engage in property destruction and fight with police. Angel gave an example from the anti-G8 protests in Ottawa in June 2002:

> There was one day that was sort of "anti-capitalist day" with all the kids in the black bloc running around, and then the next day, with the Palestinian Solidarity movement, in part of our negotiations, we'd agreed to not throw rocks, basically to not engage in combat, which was a big step for the anarchist movement, putting aside their own privilege. Like, "Okay, we're working with a group of people that are people of color, and they're at higher risk of arrest and they're marginalized by the police force, and that's who's going to be out on the streets, so we're going to negotiate"—that was part of negotiations. And it felt really good. The day was really good. It was amazing to go

to a demo that was half people of color. And I'm willing to make those kind of negotiations if it means that we are respecting the people.[109]

In Angel's example activists negotiated with each other to establish standards of conduct to follow during the protest. This negotiation explicitly acknowledged that people of color cannot afford to engage in street combat because they are especially vulnerable to being targeted by police for violence and arrest.

Such negotiation among protesters highlights conflicting elements in debates about the legitimacy of street combat. On one hand, those who support a diversity of tactics argue that more socially privileged protesters must respect the right of more socially disadvantaged people to engage in combat. On the other hand, it is the less socially privileged protesters who can least afford to engage in combat because they are profiled as the most likely to by police.

Within the protest space of Quebec City, activists used a plethora of protest techniques and overall understand themselves to have coexisted constructively. Lavender said:

You'll have debates, but I think that most people feel really good about people from many, many backgrounds coming together. And the people who are activist, I think there is a strong sense that we're . . . all climbing the same mountain reaching for the same mountaintop, but they're just coming from different sides . . . and ways of looking at the world, but I get really excited when I see people from many, many religious and philosophical backgrounds working together. I mean, that's the way it ought to be, and we should celebrate our diversity and our strength in diversity and not say we have to get somebody to think like we do. No, we can all support each other, and there's more strength when we're all supporting each other.[110]

About this kind of coming together in Quebec City, Starhawk writes: "My sense [is] that something was unleashed that can't be put back, that underlying the chaos, the confusion, the real differences among us, and the danger we were in was something so tender, exuberant and wild that I don't want to let it go. . . . How we achieved this sense of sweet unity is a mystery to me."[111]

Eade and Sallnow's interpretation of pilgrimage as encompassing conflict, like the Turnerian blanket of *communitas*, becomes overly simplistic when applied to religiously motivated protesters or even protesters in general. As anthropologist Simon Coleman asks, "Why should we assume that pilgrimage must be 'about' any one thing, whether it be heightened conflict or the heightened absence of it?"[112] The activists with whom I spoke are not only conscious of but also take pride in the varying backgrounds and political goals that others bring to protest spaces, and they engage in a conscious effort among themselves to create community out of conflicting discourses. There is a purposeful celebration of diversity among protesters. The travel to and participation in anti-globalization protests involve different discourses and meanings for different travelers; however, many religiously motivated activists understand these differences of discourse to coexist within community. Nonetheless, this sense of community and shared purpose comes as a result of common opponents, namely, the corporate and political interests promoting free trade and economic globalization, as represented by the delegates in the summit and the police mobilized to insulate them.

The Authority of Danger

An important element in discussions of more traditional pilgrimage is the potential danger associated with the journey. Indeed, Pagan theologian Michael York suggests, "It is perhaps this very risk of danger that distinguishes the pilgrim's sacred journey from that of the twentieth-century tourist."[113] The distinction between pilgrim and tourist is one that scholars of pilgrimage scrutinize for analytical clarity but that pilgrims and pilgrimage authorities engage as a demarcation of authenticity.[114] The potential to face not only discomfort but also danger can provide a clear line between otherwise fuzzily similar experiences. Nancy Frey relates, for example, how pilgrims on the road to Santiago de Compostela in Spain tell stories of nasty encounters with threatening feral dogs as part of their narratives about hardships overcome during the Camino.[115] In a similar way anti-globalization protesters may relate stories—their own or their friends'—about run-ins with police, chaotic situations, or being arrested.[116] This discourse implies that in order to be a "real" activist, you must put yourself at risk, at least occasionally.

Linda, a Catholic activist originally from El Salvador and now living in Toronto, discussed reasons why not all activists might feel safe going to large-scale protests. She explained why she did not attend the Quebec City protests, despite many invitations from friends and coworkers and despite her strong desire to go:

> I'm going to tell you why. English is my second language. What happens if, suddenly they say, like in El Salvador, "Run!" and I cannot understand? Do you understand? I already have my own experience. And what I decided, at this point, is that right now I am not ready until I understand English, until I know exactly what I am going to do. . . . If I have to give money for something that they need, for the bus or to stay to hotel or whatever, I provide the money. You know, I am not going, but I am doing my part.[117]

The dangers Linda references are real. Police tactics toward protesters are often harsh and indiscriminant, responding to great numbers of people for the behavior of particular individuals. For example, police reprisal to a thrown rock can take the form of teargassing an entire crowd, sometimes with a long delay between provocation and retaliation, which means that people who arrive on the scene after the affront take the brunt of the response.[118] Moreover, the use of water cannons, rubber bullets, and tear gas is intended to be dangerous: these tools are favored by riot police as nonlethal; however, they are far from harmless.[119] Crowd control weapons are purposefully punitive.

While I managed to avoid any direct experience of water hoses or rubber bullets, I, like most Quebec City residents and demonstrators, spent days in clouds of tear gas.[120] My second night in Quebec City I returned to the room I was sharing with eight other activists. After being there for a few minutes, one of my roommates told me that tear gas was fuming off of me.[121] I couldn't even smell it anymore because I had been soaking in it all day. She urged me to put my clothes into a plastic bag and to shower with Dr. Bronner's castile soap to stop the worst of the smell.

Later that night one of our companions started bleeding in the middle of her menstrual cycle. "Should I be worried?" she asked. We all assured her that it was probably just the stress of the protest, but we shared concerned looks. I later heard from several activists that one of the many effects of tear gas is that it causes early menstrual bleeding. The charitable organization Science for Peace received widespread reports of early menstruation from women who had attended Quebec City.[122] My first menstrual period after Quebec City was especially painful, with cramps like I hadn't suffered since my teens. I happened to mention this to Angel over coffee one day. "Well, yeah," she said, "probably every woman who was in Quebec City is feeling it. Tear gas does that." My cycle continued to be affected for about a year after the protest.

After Toronto activists returned from the protest, rumors circulated that a woman suffered a miscarriage at Quebec City resulting from exposure to the gas. Because of a disturbing dearth of scholarship on the effects of exposure to tear gas for humans in general, a scientific basis for concerns that tear gas harms women's reproductive systems is difficult to establish definitively. However, the information that does exist indicates a likely connection between tear gas and miscarriage, based on its "potential for genotoxicity" and its metabolization in the body as hydrogen cyanide, which blocks the use of oxygen.[123] There is also speculation among scientists that components of the gas may act as hormone blockers, accounting for both premature menstruation and miscarriage.[124]

These understudied effects of tear gas demonstrate that there are dangers of protest environments that are specific to women. Everyone hates getting teargassed: it stings, blinds you, makes it very hard to breathe, induces asthma, causes vision damage if you're wearing contact lenses, burns skin, disorients you, and you can get struck by the canisters as they are fired by police into the crowd.[125] Tear gas is not good for anyone. Nonetheless, given the evidence of its effects on women's reproductive systems, the use of tear gas is especially detrimental to women. This is a gender-specific danger of the protest environment.

Activists prefer calm and collected riot police who do not use gas or physical force, and de-escalating conflict with police is an important focus of ritual in protest situations. Yet some of my participants expressed ambivalence about the relaxed demeanors the police showed during the women's ritual action. They did not encounter this relaxed attitude in mixed-gender actions once the summit was officially under way. As one Pagan activist, Lavender, said: "It was . . . interesting to see that they didn't have the huge security for the women's action. I guess they figured we weren't going to climb the fence, but the black bloc might, so I thought we weren't taken seriously in a way. And yet, you know, it's not that I wanted the cops there."[126]

Concern with lack of police attention engages debates among activists about attitudes toward protest. Native American sovereignty activist Ward Churchill criticizes leftist veneration of personal martyrdom at the hands of the state as complacent and strategically flawed. In *Pacifism as Pathology* he ridicules protest models that culminate in arrests or beatings by police and calls for more directly militant forms of engagement, including armed struggle.[127] In contrast, Starhawk urges fellow activists to find new and creative ways to "tighten the web of restraint" that prevents both police and protesters from committing violent acts in tense situations, making nonviolent tactics more viable and powerful.[128] Lastly, Saba Mahmood has argued against the Western feminist tendency, shared by the Left in general, of limiting understandings of personal agency solely to those found in acts of resistance,[129] assumptions implicit in using police response and degree of personal danger as measurements of the success of a demonstration.

The ambivalence that Lavender expressed about the presence of police and their attitudes toward protesters engaged in ritual results, at least in part, from the clear distance of the protesters from those with whom they would like to communicate their messages. Judith Butler writes: "The public sphere is constituted in part by what cannot be said and what cannot be shown. The limits of the sayable, the limits of what can appear, circumscribe the domain in which political speech operates and certain kinds of subjects appear as viable actors."[130] When protesters feel ignored by political leaders and the mainstream media, then even negative attention from riot police can come to serve as validation of their subjectivity, visible proof that their actions are not worthless, not without value or impact. This is part of a larger frame of activist discourse in which repression becomes equated with a type of success: activists caused enough trouble to get noticed. Nevertheless, Lavender recognized the contradictory elements within her complaint. Just as stories of dangers encountered during pilgrimage serve to frame travel as part of a narrative of cosmological significance, so, too, stories of dangers encountered in the protest environment serve to lend importance to protesters' actions and experiences.

Words and Actions

Pilgrimage has traditionally involved notions of religiously motivated travel. In exploring the applicability of the concept of pilgrimage to emerging forms of ritual and political action, I am conscious of the fact that this exploration stretches established ideas of pilgrimage and at the same time defines certain contemporary religious expressions in ways that practitioners may find artificial. Because I knew in advance that this was an issue I wanted to explore in my work, I had the opportunity to ask participants whether they would in fact describe their journeys to anti-globalization protests in a city where they do not reside as pilgrimages. I received a wide variety of answers.

Antonia, a contemporary Pagan, would not characterize her trip to the Quebec City protest as a pilgrimage. "At that moment," she said, "it wasn't really because I didn't go with people who are the same [religion]. I don't want to say it wasn't, [just] because they weren't the same religion as me, but I wasn't actively involved in the Witchcraft community at that time. I was practicing [as a] Solitary, but I wasn't as connected [to the Pagan community]. . . . So I just more went because of politics. My religion is always part of that, but it wasn't a defining factor."[131] Although her religion influenced her political choices and actions, Antonia did not regard her travel to Quebec City primarily as a sacred journey.

Judy, a United Church member, was more willing to acknowledge a potential applicability of the term but also didn't feel that pilgrimage was a concept she would organically associate with her protest experience:

> Well, in the United Church tradition there isn't really a tradition of pilgrimage, so it's a little bit difficult to answer that as fully as someone who's Catholic might be able to. I mean, yes, in the wider definition of it. I guess in a pilgrimage you're going to experience, but also to bear witness, and that was what it was about. I certainly didn't think of it in those terms at that time, but I wouldn't be against casting it

in those terms. But truly there is not that tradition in the United Church, for all the increasing numbers of Catholics in the church, that has not really permeated how we see ourselves, so I wouldn't think in those terms naturally, no.[132]

Judy cited a lack of pilgrimage ritual in Protestant tradition to determine that she did not consider her experience in Quebec City as primarily a pilgrimage. In doing so, she positioned herself in relation to the tradition of her own denomination and in contrast to Catholicism. We see in her response a balancing between personal experience, institutional historical narrative, and ideas of difference.

Angel, a Catholic, and Sue, a Pagan, both felt that the term *pilgrimage* was somewhat appropriate for them; however, they preferred it as a metaphor for their lives and political learning rather that for their actual journeys to Quebec City and other global justice protests.[133] Angel articulated this theme of life as pilgrimage, saying: "I think my journey into the world of activism can be considered a pilgrimage. I'm trying to figure out how to be. I guess it's that idea of the Christian in the world; how to be the Christian in the world around you that is not necessarily in agreement with your theology, or even the way you see the world. How to exist, how to maintain your integrity, and yet still be involved."[134]

Sue responded similarly, saying: "I think in terms of always seeking, yes, yes it is [a pilgrimage]. Gandhi said, you know, our life stories are experiments with truth, and it is. I really aspire to that. I'm on kind of a path. And I'm trying to define my place, what it is I can uniquely do."[135] Both activists use pilgrimage as an allegory for finding ethical ways to be in the world.

River, a Pagan, felt pilgrimage was a reasonable description of her trip to the anti-FTAA protest in Quebec City. However, her ideas about pilgrimage involved a strong element of personal healing, an aspect that she felt was lacking from the experience. She said:

> In some ways I'd say yes, because when I did the [Living] River action, I really felt like here is a group of people who combine this sort of belief and this spiritual life, and it's like, "Oh, I'm home." Because I really did [combine belief and spirituality into the action], and the affinity group I was with didn't, and I was really trying to find the

[the Living River activists]. I went to Pagan Cluster meetings, and I spent time talking, and I had a good relationship with some of the people from other stuff. But coming home is not pilgrimage. Pilgrimage is when you go somewhere for healing, and tear gas never healed anybody! But in some ways it was [a pilgrimage] because it was coming to a spiritual home, and that's what pilgrimages were traditionally about.[136]

Lastly, Lavender was enthusiastic about defining her trip to Quebec City in terms of pilgrimage. She said: "Yes, yes, for sure! Marching in that crowd was like marching with a bunch of pilgrims. . . . I get all choked up about it. Yes, we weren't going to some shrine. The shrine was human rights. And so, yes, it was a pilgrimage. That's why I had to be there."[137]

I am not particularly surprised to find that United Church participants did not associate their protest experiences with pilgrimage. Protestant Christianity has traditionally not used this term for journeys of faith. Protestant theologian Graham Tomlin writes, somewhat condescendingly: "Protestants do not go on Pilgrimages—at least that is the common perception. In fact, many Protestants go on pilgrimage, although they tend not to call it that." He goes on to trace this reticence to critiques of medieval Catholic pilgrimage set forth by Luther and Calvin.[138] Protestants shifted from venerating icons and relics as particularly holy to understanding the entire world as holy, establishing the metaphor articulated in John Bunyan's *Pilgrim's Progress*,[139] and mentioned by Angel and Sue, that one's whole life is a pilgrimage. To put it another way, Mary Lee Nolan and Sidney Nolan write that Protestants may have "little personal awareness of pilgrimage as a part of their religious backgrounds."[140] Yet it is important to keep in mind that there is a long history of English Protestant journeys to the Holy Land as well as the "recent invention" of traditions of Anglican pilgrimage to shrines within the United Kingdom, such as Walsingham.[141]

Catholic participants, in contrast to United Church members, do have an explicit tradition of pilgrimage from which to draw. However, because these rituals have been officially defined by the church, extending the definition to encompass travel to anti-globalization protests may be stretching the term too far for Catholic activists. Nonetheless, as we see in Angel's response, understanding pilgrimage as a metaphor for one's personal spiritual journey might (somewhat ironically, given its Protestant origin) fit better within traditional Catholic theological frameworks.

The group that seems most comfortable expressing members' travel to anti-globalization protests as pilgrimage is the contemporary Pagan.[142] This fits with their patterns of religious innovation, experimentation, and borrowing. Sabina Magliocco writes: "Contemporary Pagan ritual artists are adept at combining and adapting materials from widely divergent sources, cultures, historical periods, and media into a harmonious whole." She concludes that "the invention of tradition by contemporary Pagans can be seen as tactic, a *bricolage* of disparate forms from the academic and mass continuum to create a folk culture whose ultimate end is to offer an alternative to a consumer culture that can be sterile and numbing."[143] There is an established acceptance of borrowing or adopting concepts from outside contemporary Pagan tradition. The adaptation of the term *pilgrimage* may be seen as part of a familiar process. In addition, as both Christian theologian Martin Robinson and Pagan theologian Michael York comment,[144] the practice of pilgrimage can be found in many different religious traditions throughout the world and also predates not only Catholicism but Christianity itself. Because of this history, Pagan practitioners may perceive pilgrimage as more eligible for "borrowing" than, for example, elements from Indigenous cultures around the world today.[145]

Evaluating Success and Infelicity

Ritual plays many roles for religiously motivated activists within anti-globalization demonstrations. Protesters may use ritual to express peaceful intentions, influence police and other protesters, create community, communicate with those in power, and provide personal focus. How is the "success" or "infelicity" of these rituals, to use the terms of Ronald Grimes,[146] assessed by activists?

In relating their experiences of ritualizing at the Quebec City protest, a majority of the women with whom I spoke from each of the three traditions discussed the performance of ritual within that space as a positive thing in and of itself. They understand ritual within protests to bring variety and creativity to protest actions.[147] They feel good about letting other protesters know that it is because of their religious motivation that they are part of the global justice movement.[148] They understand religious ritual as signaling to police that protesters are not just out of control and mis-socialized, as activists feel they are sometimes stereotyped.[149] Ritual in protest space provides opportunities for media coverage to depict positive, nonviolent action, in contrast to sensationalized violence.[150] Moreover, these women understand explicit religious ritual as lending legitimacy to their demands for global justice, not only for police and media but also for world leaders.[151]

Aside from Lavender's disappointment with the lack of attention that the women's action garnered, I did not receive many reports of infelicitous performance—that is, rituals that did not succeed in their social or metaphysical aims. There may be several reasons for this. First, global justice activists are very sensitive to their portrayal in the mainstream media and so, when given an opportunity to represent themselves, may be less likely to report actions that were inconsequential or unsuccessful.[152] Jenna, a Catholic, said that when she returned from Quebec City, there was not a lot of room even within the Catholic activist community to critique what had happened there.[153] Second, religiously motivated activists often feel invisible or disrespected within the larger, more secularly oriented global justice movement, so the very performance of ritual at all is understood as positive. Assessing ritual efficacy, especially discussing situations of inefficacy, becomes particularly loaded within a context of dismissal from other activists, who, in a Marxist vein, may see religion as wasting resources better put toward direct action.[154] Third, many of the goals for which rituals are performed are long-term and somewhat abstract. How, for example, can a group assess whether it has helped shift the global attitude toward ecological concern or increased the energy available in the world for positive change? How does one determine a baseline for comparison prior to and following such a shift?

On the other hand, there were rituals that could be assessed on more concrete terms. Camille, for example, explained that her group did ritual work to help those in the center of the protest violence. She did not assess whether her ritualizing had a concrete effect for them because that was not part of her stated motivation for being at the protest: "I just needed to be really grounded in the fact that I was there for myself, not to cause an effect, which is what the universe told me—that I wouldn't be doing it in order to save the world; I'd be doing it because I needed to do that."[155] So, although Camille could have investigated whether her ritual aided other protesters in need by asking friends and colleagues who were in the places where she directed her energy, this was less important to her than that she attempt to help. Her performance of ritual was more powerful as making change for her personally than any effects it might have, or not have, on others, and she determined ritual success accordingly. An analysis of ritual success or infelicity based on the help and comfort experienced by those at whom the rites were ostensibly aimed, activists in the midst of the protest, might reach different conclusions.

A further example of ritual that could be assessed as successful or unsuccessful is Abby's sing-in before a line of riot police. Not only did the police back off, but all of their attempts to teargas the singers were unsuccessful because of the direction of the wind.[156] More abstract is the reporting of ritual used in various conflicts to diffuse the tension between police and protesters, a diffusion described as successful.[157]

Interpretations of Ritual in Protest Space

There are striking similarities in the ways that feminist Catholic, United Church, and contemporary Pagan activists understand and use ritual within protest environments. While activists of different religious affiliations did participate in separate planned actions, they also came together, both in the larger milieu of protests at the fence and in specific actions. I spoke with members of all three groups who participated in the women's action and the rituals that it incorporated, such as web weaving and the spiral dance. When you also consider, for example, that the women in Jesse's dance troupe, who did the performance ripping the black cloth, were inspired by the Women in Black, Israeli peace activists,[158] then the spiral of influence swirls even wider. Both United Church and Catholic groups took part in church vigils.[159] Both Catholic and Pagan groups engaged in explicit, though spontaneous, group rituals in front of lines of police.[160] All three groups grounded their discussions of activism in the context of their religions.

Nevertheless, there are also clear differences in their understandings of ritual in protest space. Many of the United Church women with whom I spoke do not consider themselves to have engaged in explicit ritualizing while at the Quebec City protest. Contemporary Pagan women, on the other hand, are more likely to describe the whole experience as ritualized: actions were purposefully planned around specific rituals or incorporated ritual elements, such as passing out water to other protesters with the blessing "May you never thirst."[161] Stories of their Quebec City experiences incorporate discussions of working to shift energy. The Catholic women with whom I spoke did refer to specific rituals in which they participated but were less likely to describe the entire experience as ritualized.

Another difference between the three groups is concern about explicit ritualization within protest space. The contemporary Pagan women were very comfortable with creating and performing rituals in the midst of other protesters. As Lavender's earlier comment about people appreciating inclusion indicates, there is a sense that other protesters will welcome an opportunity to participate in contemporary Pagan ritual.

Catholic and United Church women, in contrast, expressed concern about engaging in explicit rituals in the midst of other protesters. As Angel said:

> Different Christians will pray or whatever, and I don't really want to knock it, but, at the same time, it *is* alienating. It is an alienating thing to be doing on the street. . . . I mean, I don't want that to infringe on my ability to organize with a diversity of communities, so I wouldn't do that. . . . I think that when it comes out onto the street, you have to be very careful because Christianity is an incredibly privileged religion. It's not the same as if Muslims decide to pray on the street in North America. They're an underprivileged religion, so it's a very different thing to be doing. . . . Also, the Christian Church has caused so much pain to so many people. It's only reminding people of that. So I think it's okay, I mean if a church identifies itself and marches in the PRIDE parade . . . but it does get sort of iffy when you're at an antiglobalization thing.[162]

Angel was very uneasy with overt Christian practice in public because of the social privilege that Christianity enjoys and the trauma it may cause to non-Christians. Judy, a United Church member, expressed similar concerns: "Christianity has drowned out other spiritual traditions for so long. . . . And I didn't see a lot of other religious groups self-identifying at all in that time in Quebec."[163] As uncomfortable with public Christian ritualizing as Angel is, she can think of situations in which it would be appropriate to support causes traditionally condemned by churches, such as Gay Pride. She and Judy also maintain, however, that public religious expression by religions other than Christianity would be appropriate.

As Angel and Judy point out, performing ritual publicly is not without counterproductive risks, risks that are especially acute for Christian activists. The very institutional power and privilege that make them and their churches persuasive to government, police, and media organizations are the same influences that Christian social justice activists desperately want to work against in North American culture more broadly. They do not want to force their religious privilege on other activists or on non-Christians in general. The quandary becomes one of wielding the power of religious institution against the state but not, in the same blunt stroke, reinforcing the oppression of those not sharing the advantage of being Christian in a Christian-normative culture.

Contemporary Pagans, on the other hand, are happy to pray and ritualize in public. Because they do not understand themselves as a culturally dominant religious tradition, contemporary Pagans do not share Christians' concerns about oppressing others through the performance of public rituals. In fact, through proudly and explicitly engaging in religious ritual in public, Pagans may hope to establish their tradition as a serious and authoritative religion, thereby gaining the moral influence they observe other religious groups as enjoying.

Religiously motivated global justice activists bring their traditions with them into the public space of anti-globalization demonstrations. In the chaos of Quebec City, Catholic, United Church, and contemporary Pagan feminist activists used ritual to manage space, forge community, communicate their political messages, and mitigate environments fraught with conflict, tension, and confusion. Just as they turn to ritual within their religious groups in order to change themselves, their communities, and the world, they turn to ritual in protest environments to express alternative visions to the industrial globalization and economic exploitation that international trade summits have come to represent. Like the two images of Mary with which we began, ritualizing in protest space engages a cultural dialogue about relationships between religion and the politics of globalization, a dialogue in which travel by religiously motivated activists to global justice protests plays a further part.

Moreover, exploring travel to global justice protests as a form of pilgrimage ritual provides insight into new ways practitioners are "religious" in public. Does traveling with one's religion automatically mean that one is engaged in religious travel? Clearly not in every case, or the term *pilgrimage* would lose all meaning and usefulness, describing any kind of movement undertaken by religious individuals. Yet just as the two Marys interacted with other symbols in the Quebec City protest environment, so, too, circulating among the multitudes who gather together in anti-globalization demonstrations, are people of faith who bring their religious convictions along with them, not incidentally but as an integral part of why they come.

Religiously motivated protesters going to these demonstrations can be understood as engaging in sacred travel and very public performances of religion. But is it pilgrimage? As this chapter has explored, there are many reasons to consider it so. This kind of travel is undertaken out of moral obligation, a journey to a kind of sacred center, that of an alternative social world in which commitments to global justice contest with unfair state and economic systems in metaphoric and, in the case of clashes with police, literal ways. Anti-globalization protesters can be understood to experience both the camaraderie of Turnerian *communitas* and the struggles for dominance inherent in Eade and Sallnow's concept of competing discourses. This travel also involves personal discomfort and varying degrees of danger. Like more traditional pilgrims, religiously motivated anti-globalization activists interface sacred ideals with the shortcomings of an imperfect world. Re-centering the focus of trade summits through counterdemonstration, activists juxtapose their aspirations of global community with the inadequacies of international economic policies, national limitations on democratic expression, and local policing practices.

Mobilizing the moral authority of religion in the service of progressive political causes, as religiously motivated social justice protesters do, implicates them in relationships of hierarchy and power. For Christians, more so than contemporary Pagans, finding a balance between rejecting religious institution and authority and using the social and legal power of these institutions toward just ends is a painful challenge. They do not want to exacerbate Christian dominance and therefore worry about unintended consequences of ritualizing in protest space. Because contemporary Pagans understand themselves to be outside culturally privileged religious structures, they do not face the same kinds of dilemmas in bringing their religion into civic spaces. In the next chapter I investigate more closely tensions around the place of religion in public space and politics.

FIGS. 1 & 2. Our Lady of Consumption prayer card leaflet, received by author, People's March against the FTAA, April 21, 2001. Artist unknown.

FIGS. 3 & 4. Our Lady of Guadalupe prayer card, received by author, People's March against the FTAA, April 21, 2001. Gabe Thirlwall / Fish on Fridays.

FIG. 5. The People's March against the FTAA, Quebec City, April 21, 2001.
Photograph by David Ferris.

FIG. 6. Protesters observe police in riot gear through the temporary fencing, Quebec City, April 21, 2001. Photograph by David Ferris.

FIG. 7. Anti-FTAA activists discuss tactics while meeting delegates talk with a police officer on opposite sides of the temporary fencing, April 21, 2001. The protest sign reads in part, "They keep us OUT. Let's keep them IN. PROVINCIAL PENITENTIARY for POLITICIANS." Photograph by David Ferris.

FIG. 8. Ward's Island Beach, June 2004. Photograph by author.

3 "Spirituality" as Feminist Third Choice

GENDERING RELIGION AND THE SECULAR

Whether it evokes nods of identification or spurs furrows of distaste, the statement "I am spiritual but not religious" is by now familiar to most North Americans. In such declarations *religion* is associated with institution and societal pressure, whereas *spirituality* relates to personal experience, privacy, and individuality.[1] The contradictory dynamics of spirituality's role in secular worldviews is well illustrated by Bruno Latour in *We Have Never Been Modern* when he writes, "You are indignant that the world is being mechanized? The modern critique will tell you about the creator God to whom everything belongs and who gave man everything. You are indignant that society is secular? The modern critique will show you that spirituality is thereby liberated, and that wholly spiritual religion is far superior. You call yourself religious? The modern critique will have a hearty laugh at your expense!"[2]

At their heart discussions of religion and spirituality engage cultural concerns about public and private space, secularization, gender, and the appropriate roles of religious institutions in the public sphere. The previous chapter examined ways in which religiously motivated feminist activists weigh the consequences of wielding social power rooted in their religious traditions against concerns that doing so tacitly supports unfair privilege. By embracing the concept of private spirituality, as opposed to public religion, activists negotiate with their political communities, and North American culture more broadly, for the inclusion of religion in public space.

The flexibility of the term *spirituality*, its "protean" nature, facilitates communication across boundaries of religious institution, constructing commonalities out of disparate, deeply personal experiences. Under the rubric of a more universal spirituality, my participants emphasize connections to those of other religions or of no religious affiliations. Using popularly accepted distinctions between *religion* and *spirituality*, they defend their religious affiliation through a discourse of authenticity, in which they distinguish between institutional expressions of faith and their own spirituality, which may or may not be found in combination with institutional religion.[3] This gives religiously motivated social justice activists an opportunity to emphasize that real, powerful personal experiences underlie their identification with religious traditions and that this identification is not arbitrary, the result of ignorance or intellectual laziness. It also allows them to gain critical distance from right-wing activists, onto whom they pass many of these same criticisms. Further, the manner in which all of these categories—religion, politics, spirituality—are gendered, and the ways in which this gendering is instantiated, particularly impact my participants, as women and as feminists.

Semantics: Spirituality *and* Religion

I did not begin my fieldwork with an assumption that the distinction between *spirituality* and *religion* would be an important one for religiously motivated feminist activists. In my interview question template, I exclusively used the word *religion*, phrasing questions, for example, "How do you understand the relationship between your religion and your feminism?" Yet in responding to my use of the term *religion*, many of my participants articulated an explicit distinction between *religion*, from which they distanced themselves, and *spirituality*, with which they allied themselves. In doing so, they used these terms to position themselves politically and socially, communicating important information about their relationships to particular institutions, communities, and worldviews.

One participant who sees a particularly sharp dichotomy between religion and spirituality is Sarah, a contemporary Pagan of Greek descent in her early twenties who grew up in an anarchist, atheist home. Explaining the distinction between spirituality and religion that she introduced into our conversation, she said:

Spirituality, I feel, is the spirit of the law, definitely, and that religion is the letter of the law. And I truly think there's a place for both. But I think . . . what's so screwed up and why there's such a backlash against religion is because the balance has been lost so long ago. . . . I think if we lived in a world that had been dominated for thousands of years by just the spirit and not the letter, people would be craving structure and order and a physical manifestation of things, you know, in the forms of collective ritualization. But because we have an abundance of that and have been drowned in that for thousands of years, I think, therefore, there's such a huge resurgence of reclaiming our individual spirituality.[4]

Sarah's definition, in which religion and spirituality are opposite ends of a spectrum, throws into relief a distinction articulated by many of my participants. However, they do not always express these terms as part of such a stark dichotomy. Often spirituality and religion are entwined within participants' narratives. In dividing spirituality and formal structure, United Church member Laura expresses something similar to Sarah. She said: "In a way spirituality is central to me, it's very important. I think it probably always has been. And the church itself wasn't important for many, many, many years. Now it is. It's a sense of community, and whenever I have found a church I like, it's always been the minister and the sermons. If they can say something to me, they have me. I'm there. It's nourishing, it's enriching, and if not, then there's no point for me."[5] *Spirituality* is separate from *the church* in her discussion. What is different in Laura's language, however, is that the terms are complementary, rather than competing, as *spirituality* and *religion* appear to be for Sarah.

Most participants differentiate between more social and more personal aspects within religion. Angel, a Catholic, said, for example: "What does religion mean to me? Well . . . it's both a cultural thing and a personal belief system. Culturally I was raised Catholic. My family's Catholic, all their friends are Catholic, all of the feast days we celebrate together are all Catholic, and so those are all significant to me, so that's a big part of it. And then the other part of it is just adopting the belief for myself and believing in God and believing in Jesus."[6] Here Angel distinguishes between social or cultural aspects of the tradition and individual relationship to the divine, a distinction other women also recognize.

For example, Grace, a United Church member in her sixties who is very active with the peace movement, engages in this dialogue in a different way from Sarah, treating *religion* and *spirituality* as synonyms for the same genuine personal experience. She said: "I happen to be a bit of a contemplative person. Spirituality is very important, mysticism. I'm just always conscious of it. . . . Religion I don't think is going to church, the formalities of church, the structures, the doctrines, and all of that. I find that interesting, but I think it's because of [my] contemplativeness."[7] If we understand Grace's comments within the context of the popular distinction between religion and spirituality, she seems to be reclaiming religion as something personally meaningful. Yet a distinction between personal experience and institution is still very present in her response.

Spirituality *and Protestant Anti-Catholicism*

While the semantic shift may be relatively recent in popular culture, the ideas represented in the language of freeing spirituality versus constraining religion have a long history in Protestant Christian theology, particularly in rhetoric designed to emphasize the distinctions between Protestantism and Catholicism. Among scholars the interconnections between Protestant Christianity, the "free" market, and the ideology of secularism are well established. These Protestant ideologies require others against whom to construct superior purity and authenticity.[8] As historian John Wolffe observes, "Antagonism to Catholics was fueled as much by the internal dynamics in Protestantism as by any direct response to Catholics themselves."[9] Starting with the Reformation, Protestants have often presented their Christianity as a living, engaged faith, over and against empty, magical rituals of Catholicism.[10] The criticisms of religion that we find in the language of spirituality mesh well with the criticisms of Catholicism we find in Protestant anti-Catholicism.[11] Wolffe writes, "In the Protestant-Catholic conflicts of the past are to be found significant roots of the broader religious-secular divide of the present, and illuminating evidence that secularity itself has had a long and complex history."[12]

There are historical traditions of anti-Catholicism in both English and North American culture.[13] The early English colonies in North America were concerned with "popish" encroachment by both High Church Anglicanism from England as well as Catholicism from France in the colonies, particularly Quebec, where Aboriginal peoples were converting.[14] The usurpation of Canada from the French made Anglo Protestants breathe a sigh of relief and envision a wondrous new start for the land; "freed from the shackles of popery, Canada would flourish under Protestantism just as New England had. . . . Protestant Enlightenment would supplant popish ignorance."[15] These early concerns still echo in the tensions between Quebec and the rest of Canada.[16]

Raymond Tumbleson, in his analysis of anti-Catholicism in early modern English literature, lays out the main concern: that Catholicism is perceived by Protestant Christians as a tyrannical anachronism incompatible with modern rationality.[17] Anti-Catholic rhetoric presents "those poor fools deluded by Romish subtlety" against a Protestantism linked with independence and autonomy.[18] In fact, political scientist Clement Fatovic argues that fearful stereotypes about Catholicism directly contributed to the development of theories of liberty upon which North American ideas of democracy continue to be based.[19]

Turning to a later historical period, Jody Roy argues that Evangelical revivalists continued rhetorical representations of Catholicism as "unchristian, authoritarian, and immoral." "In the early nineteenth century revivalism eroded lingering commitments to both high-church clergy and theology. During the wave of change in religion in America, individuals and their English Bibles were the only necessary components of Christianity." Believers presented Protestant revivalism as the religion of the autonomous individualist, "an egalitarian faith which seemed at home in America's democracy."[20]

Jesuit Mark Massa argues that this emphasis on individuality is a key component in current versions of North American, anti-Catholic rhetoric. He contends that contemporary anti-Catholicism is responding to a real difference in Catholic and Protestant, or veiled Protestant, worldviews.[21] Robert Orsi supports the position that there has been a fundamental difference between Protestant nation-building myths and Catholic worldviews, writing, "Catholics lived in the United States with values, religious practices and imaginings, political views, experiences of family life and of the social world, and historical memories and stories that were all deeply incongruous with mainstream American values, religious imaginings, and memories."[22] In a nation built at least partly in ideological opposition to them, Catholics had to work that much harder to write themselves into patriotic narratives.

Massa specifies some of these cultural differences, arguing that "the analogical, or Catholic, impulse—which emphasizes mediation, community, sacrament, and respect for tradition—really does represent a different set of cultural emphases than the dialectical, or Protestant, one of unmediated experience, individualism, and communal restraint."[23] In mainstream North American, tacitly Protestant worldviews, the emphasis on community and tradition in Catholicism is set in opposition to ideals of individualism and autonomy.[24] Reflecting on historical constructions, Elizabeth Fenton argues, "'Protestantism' does not operate in early-national tests as a cohesive identity formation but rather appears as a system that—unlike 'Catholicism'—can accommodate a plurality of beliefs, *including Catholicism*, because of its commitment to privacy."[25] This assumption of opposing values—individuality, privacy, personal choice versus community, family, tradition—echoes in current discourses about spirituality. Contemporary society has inherited this complex of ideas from the Reformation, carried through the "anti-popery" of early modern England and the North American colonies and continuing into the Protestant revivals of the nineteenth century.

The Study of Religion

Concerns about individual agency also wend their way into religious studies scholarship. Jonathan Z. Smith bemoans the problem of "traditional Protestant bugaboos of 'habit,' 'dogma,' and 'magic,' which has resulted in the vast majority of religious phenomena remaining unintelligible to modern western scholarship."[26] Scholars attribute such "bugaboos" not only to Catholicism. Orsi, criticizing the exclusionary formation of the discipline of religious studies in North America, writes, "The embedded, hidden others against whom the religion in Religious Studies is constituted are the religions on the American landscape that appeared so terrifying and un-American to the guardians of the culture—

Mormonism, Catholicism, evangelicalism, Pentecostalism, among others."[27] We can see the implicit maintenance of mainstream Protestantism as a norm against which other religious traditions deviate, with their suspicious rituals, hierarchies, and immanent deities. Talal Asad demonstrates that this is no coincidence because the very concept of religion and the categories into which it is subdivided are products of Western Christian thought.[28]

Steven Wasserstrom has also discussed the tendency of certain schools of religious studies scholars to try to abstract essential religious experience from the rules and dictates of particular religious traditions, that is, to find "religion after religion." Wasserstrom argues that in searching for a universal essence of religion, Jung-influenced scholars ignored institutional and cultural particularities, such as doctrine and ritual, finding commonality in myth and mysticism. He writes: "The dominance of mysticism in the History of Religions, more generally, remains regnant (not only genealogically) throughout the study of religion. . . . What is 'really' religious, what is a 'religious reality,' what is distinctively and essentially 'religious,' as opposed to, say, economic or psychological, is something that turns out to fall under the rubric of mysticism."[29] Here we have "true" religion defined, by religious studies scholars, as personal experience over and against the doctrine, rituals, and practices of particular religious traditions. In this school of the history of religions, personal experience trumps history, tradition, and community.

The tension between individual freedom and communal authority is one that is central to the Reformation ideal of individual experience as forming the heart of religion in contrast to sacerdotalism. The dichotomy reinforces the colonial story of leaving the oppressions of Europe for independence in the "new world" and the North American emphasis on independence and self-reliance.[30] Leigh Schmidt traces the implications of these worldviews in traditions of mysticism among transcendentalists and other spiritual seekers in North America.[31] In his discussion of the North American intellectuals at the heart of the secularization project, sociologist Christian Smith adds another dimension to this tension, writing, "Intellectuals' love of autonomy easily disposes them against the historical religious traditions of the West, for these traditions make it impossible to escape that which violates autonomy, namely dependence and authority with regard to things beyond and above oneself—on God at least, if not also on Scriptures, bishops, church teachings, moral commands, and clergy."[32] Contemporary North American society—and perhaps more important, the academic study of religion—has inherited ideals of individualism, autonomy, and rebellion against authority and dependence.[33]

I agree with Smith that while scholars too often blame exclusively religious causes for secularization, it is more than an ironic coincidence that the charges laid by Protestant Christianity against Catholicism have become those invoked by secularists against religion in general, including Protestantism.[34] Protestants depicted Catholicism as tyrannical, just as secularists now depict religion as a whole. My participants, women who self-identify as part of religious traditions—Protestant, contemporary Pagan, as well as Catholic—insist that they are not blindly submitting to religious authority. They contrast their personal spiritualities with religion in general, just as earlier Protestants distinguished their "independent" Christianity from "slavish" Catholicism.

There is a long history of forcing Catholics and other marginalized religious movements in North America to defend themselves against charges of authoritarianism. What is new is that anti-Catholicism is now also couched in secular, rather than exclusively Protestant, terms and that Protestants now find themselves criticized as well. By leveling denunciations of domineering social control against Catholicism, Protestant Christianity embraced and promoted rationalizations that can be used to position it, too, on the margins.[35] Moreover, both Catholicism and Protestantism become implicitly subsumed under the label of "religion,"[36] largely criticized currently among advocates of secularism, and popular discourse influenced by them, through using extreme examples of repressive versions of Islam. Unfortunately, Western feminists have also actively contributed to this Islamophobic discourse.[37]

Secular Citizens

Proponents of secularization alternately present it as either inevitable—the natural result of cultural evolution into modernity—or, conversely, as a fragile, precarious state in need of defense against the incursions of conservative traditionalism.[38] Both historically and in the contemporary world, women serve as metonyms for their national, ethnic, and religious communities.[39] As a result of their objectification, in the conflict between religion and the secular, women often become the focus of anxious boundary keeping: what they are allowed or required to wear; with whom they are allowed or required to be in relationships; how much control they are given or subjected to over their sexuality and reproductive roles. If we approach the "secular versus religious" dichotomy as a contestation between political and religious institutions for control of public space, then it is logical that social categories, such as women and LGBTQ people, historically denied access to public power in either arena yet policed by both, would not easily fit themselves into such a divide.[40]

The Enlightenment separation of the social world into separate spheres of politics, religion, and domestic life is inseparable from the emergence of market capitalism, itself deeply dependent on state violence and colonial expansion.[41] With the religious-secular divide resulting from the creation of modern capitalism, spirituality, in refusing the dualism, could offer a rare position from which to challenge not only the division but the system itself. There is no guarantee, however, that interest in spirituality will coincide with such political commitments.

Much of the criticism of people who identify as spiritual but not religious has focused on commodification, cultural appropriation, and the concern that tools for and trappings of spiritual achievement are too easily accessible for simple purchase, rather than through personal labor.[42] An intertwined strand of criticism emphasizes the personalized nature of spiritual practices, which may focus on personal healing or achievement over and against cultural change,[43] discourses that may actually denigrate engagement with public politics. Viewing these criticisms alongside historical Christian concerns reveals ways in which they align with gendered suspicions: women are perhaps too involved in the world, in this case through flippant consumerism; they are self-focused, better confined to the private domestic sphere than the tough work of politics. In fact, Eeva Sointu and Linda Woodhead argue that part of the popular backlash against spirituality movements is that they encourage women to direct care to themselves, in contrast to traditional messages that women must sacrifice themselves in the care of others.[44]

It is often an aspect of male privilege in androcentric societies to expect to see oneself reflected and one's experiences recognized in public space and discourse.[45] This right to expectation is not as common for women, as they have historically been relegated to representing the private sphere, with all its irrationalities of emotion, sexuality, attachment, and bodily needs. In fact, as secular formations construct religion as existing within the realm of "the private," religion becomes more closely associated with women.[46]

Anecdotally, reflect on the famous secular humanists and missionizing atheists active over the last decade or so: Richard Dawkins, Christopher Hitchens, Sam Harris, even the entertaining Ricky Gervais and Stephen Fry. The main players are men, and they present a public face for the movement. Moreover, certainly the scandal itself but even more so the reactions and negative comments in response to "elevator-gate"—the community meltdown resulting from the public naming by a female atheist, Rebecca Watson, of sexual harassment at a skepticism conference—point to an unwillingness on the part of this particular community to take seriously the ways their "equal-opportunity" public space is not only centered on male experience but is self-righteously so.[47]

My point is not to conflate secularization processes with humanist/ atheist ideals but to use the secular humanist community as a particular example of ways in which secularist ideals and women's experience, at least Western-facing feminism, may be constructed in opposition. Because secular humanists deliberately engage debates about human rights and the public sphere, they influence political communities with which my participants come in contact, and sometimes form coalitions with, around particular social justice issues.

Of course, the tendency to see struggles for gender equality as conflicting with more pressing political oppressions is not a new one. Such fights have been constructed in struggles for full emancipation and suffrage for people of color and women in the United States. Similar conflicts played out in the social movements of the 1960s and 1970s, especially constructed between Civil Rights and feminism.[48] Equally habitual is the pitting of feminist concerns at home with stereotypes of gender oppression abroad. It is worth noting that one of the main strategies for discrediting Watson was to compare her complaint to Orientalist stereotypes of Muslim women's oppression, thereby trivializing her concerns as a woman in the Western world.[49] In the historically Islamophobic West, Muslim women are frequently objectified to this purpose.[50]

Naming the power struggles inherent in secularizing projects brings to the surface the violence for which it is meant to provide cover. From colonial repressions through anti-Catholic and anti-Mormon sentiment to current Islamophobia, secularism in the West has served not to empty public space of religious values but to unmark *dominant* religious values, making them if not invisible, then impossible to name and thus impossible to subject to the justice apparatuses of legislation and courts.[51] These dominant religious values encode male and heterosexual privilege.

Such unacknowledged assumptions frame the terms of debate for our every political and social concern. Recent gendered controversies in North America provide examples. Women's freedoms, frequently reduced to sexuality, are popularly understood as being tied to the secular trajectory, and examples of sexism in other cultures, even in one's own historically, are used to silence women's critiques of the here and now. Yet in the United States currently, in the very bastions of the secular state, such as higher education, the military, and the free market, sexual violence and exploitation continue at crisis proportions, women cannot rely with any security on the government to guarantee their right to make their own decisions about pregnancy and parenthood, and it remains both legal and common practice to pay women less than men for the same work.

This last point lays bare ties between secular ideologies and global capitalism, especially in their impact on women. The gendered pay gap clearly contradicts democratic claims to equity, but this injustice pales in comparison to global income inequality, running down the same grooves set by colonial relationships over the centuries. The triumvirate of Secularism-Democracy-Capitalism, promoted as the guarantee of fairness and flourishing—worth any short-term cost of human life or liberty—enshrines contradictions, as the United States in particular seems stubbornly intent on proving. For example, the Supreme Court's *Hobby Lobby* decision restricting women's right to birth control in the face of the religious objections of their employers—along with aggressive restrictions on women's abortion choices and the confused impossibility of legal justice for survivors of sexual assault—coexist with the *Citizens United* decision, granting political personhood to corporations. Corporations are citizens, but women might not be. Similarly, how do we reconcile expanding, though clearly contested, federal marriage and employment rights for LGBTQ people evolving concurrently with crackdowns on immigration, police lynchings of black men, and criminal profiling of Muslims?[52]

In their conflict both religion and secularism cast the other as feminine. Religious authorities, in the Western case this generally means church institutions, equate secularism with relaxed sexual rules, especially the uncoupling of intercourse from procreation in the form of popularized birth control, non-heteronormative relationships, and legitimized access to abortion, the latter painted as the ultimate illegitimate exercise of self above other. This focus on sexuality is really a focus on *women's* sexuality because women traditionally bear the burdens of representing both human embodiment and culture.[53]

On the other hand, proponents of secularism depict religion as irrational, tribal, emotional, and credulous, all states traditionally associated with women, to their detriment.[54] As Janet Jakobsen and Ann Pellegrini write, "Some bodies cannot win (women, for example, or homosexuals), no matter which side of the religion-secular divide they come to occupy."[55] And finally, in the venerable tradition of collapsing sexual difference onto racial and religious otherness in the Orientalist imaginary, both sides of the Evangelical Christian–secularist "resonance machine" accuse the other of protecting inherently violent Islam from rational scrutiny.[56] In jointly framing the debate for public space in bifurcated terms, Evangelicals and secularists collude in foreclosing any other options for religious configurations.[57]

The Privileged Secular

Given this framing, in addition to feeling marginalized within their religious institutions, religiously motivated activists often feel invisible or disrespected within the larger, more secularly oriented global justice movement. Even though the secularization thesis is supposed to be objective and value neutral, simply a description of empirical data,[58] people both inside and outside academe interpret this change as positive. Peter

Berger links positive assessments of secularization to Enlightenment ideals, writing, "Most Enlightenment thinkers and most progressive-minded people ever since have tended towards the idea that secularization is a good thing, at least as far as it does away with religious phenomena that are 'backward,' 'superstitious,' or 'reactionary' (a religious residue purged of these negative characteristics may still be deemed acceptable)."[59] Shedding cultural hang-ups related to tradition is key, and if the social power of religion must be eradicated in the process, then it is not much of a loss.

Assumptions that secularity is inevitable and inherently positive are subverted when we see it as just one among many responses to modernization.[60] Yet my participants are struggling with precisely these assumptions within larger activist communities, which they understand as denying any legitimate role for religion in public discourse. Religiously motivated social justice activists understand that other members of their wider communities hold worldviews in which secularization is to be valued as both evidence of and a requirement for social progress. As Jakobsen and Pellegrini explain: "Even though intellectuals and activists on the Left know the problems with the secularization narrative, secularism remains hard to relinquish in part because it appears to be a defense against the dominations ascribed to religion. Religion appears to be a threat to secular, liberal society, a threat to women, and a source of violence. Secularism is rarely subjected to critique in the academy and in progressive politics because it appears to be the only answer to these problems, the only safeguard against the dominations inscribed in religion."[61] In discussing the roles that religion plays in their lives and their activism, my participants are mindful that fellow activists may be very resistant to its presence.

Talking about religion or spirituality, especially identifying as part of a dominant tradition, such as Catholicism, becomes particularly loaded within a context of dismissal from other activists who, following Marx,[62] may see religion as wasting resources better put towards direct action or, worse, as actively regressive. Rhetoric equating religion with ignorance can be found throughout social justice activist communities. While such open hostility may be curbed when face-to-face with actual people who openly identify as religious, tensions and disapproval still simmer.

Regina, a Catholic participant quoted earlier, explains how some of these tensions can be felt at public demonstrations:

I think people, because of the history of the church, will be a lot more judgmental, and understandably so. A lot of people . . . their own lives have been affected by different actions of the Catholic Church, and by, in general, repression, the ways in which Christianity is used to oppress. . . . I do feel like a lot of times when we go as [Catholics], there's no direct confrontation, but there's also a lot of noticeable silence, like, "Oh, what is your community doing here?" There's this distance between us, not discussed often. . . . I feel a lot of judgment from them, activist folks.[63]

She is aware of the suspicion with which she is received in protest space as a Catholic, but she also understands that the Catholic Church has fostered that suspicion by alienating many people.

Judy, a United Church member, related a story about participating in an interfaith vigil outside a church during the protests in Quebec City in April 2001 against the Fair Trade Area of the Americas. At the point in the ceremony in which First Nations members were smudging the space, a few young, white activists passed by and laughed and swore at the gathering. Judy said, "And I just thought to myself, 'Do you even know what you're doing?'"[64] To her their derision of the vigil was inappropriate because she felt they were conflating their ideas about certain types of Christianity with all religion.

That their disrespect was expressed during the First Nations part of the ceremony only reinforced for Judy the racism and chauvinism for which the larger activist community often criticizes Christianity. She said: "I still have some questions around that. I mean, if I, as a Christian, am invisible to the larger justice movement, does that mean that there are Jewish and Muslim activists who are invisible to me as a Christian? And I think, 'What else is below everybody else's horizons?'"[65] Judy suggests that assumptions about religion, especially that it has no place in social justice movements, blind activists to diversity within their ranks and reinforce the omissions and stereotypes of the mainstream culture they wish to challenge.

Public and Private

Conflict and confusion about *visible* religion in public space hinges on traditional understandings of separate social spheres.[66] A common way, in both scholarship and everyday conversation, of distinguishing between spirituality and religion is to say that spirituality is a private experience, whereas religion is a more public expression of that experience. Yet one main problem with this formulation is that we do not always have a very good sense of what these terms mean. *Public* and *private* are far from clear.

As Jeff Weintraub demonstrates, a liberal economic theorist is apt to treat governmental/state institutions as "public" and the market economy as "private." Alternatively, some feminist work treats as public everything that is outside the private household unit, making the state, popular culture, and market economy all public.[67] Philosopher Philip Goodchild argues that these distinctions are actually arbitrary because in capitalist modernity, economic activity takes over all other spheres.[68] Confusion over what is public and what is private relates to attempts to map contemporary worldviews onto a dichotomy inherited from ancient Greek city-states and the Roman Empire, both of which also offered different versions of what constituted public and private.[69]

With so many different conceptions of public and private aspects of our worlds, it follows that trying to divide religion and spirituality between these two should leave that distinction indeterminate. Sociologist José Casanova suggests that what makes mapping ourselves into a public-private dichotomy especially difficult is the experience of modernity, which has resulted in a three-sided worldview—state, civil society, and family.[70] This third piece is the social realm that mediates between public and private, between state and household. It is the public sphere of civil discourse, as discussed by Jürgen Habermas and Nancy Fraser, among others.[71]

The distinction between religion and spirituality has implications for theorizing about the role of religion within this public sphere. Paul Heelas argues, for example, that while institutionalized religion is obviously declining, spirituality is actually becoming more important among individuals and the public as a whole; he refers to an increase in New Age spiritualities and language as evidence.[72] However, Steve Bruce concludes that this diffusion and diversity are instead part and parcel of the process of secularization.[73] He defines secularization not as a negation of religion in its entirety but as the specific decline of the influence of religion and religious institutions in the state, economy, and public sphere. The very individualizing inherent in Heelas's discussion of spirituality means, to Bruce, that such a movement will never actually challenge the decline of religion in Western culture. The strength of religion is not in whether individuals remain interested in religious or spiritual matters but whether that interest can be expressed collectively in a unified and influential manner.[74] In fact, Bruce's argument can be reduced to one that equates religious pluralism with the cultural impotence of all religions, one shared by Evangelical Christians.[75]

Indeed, if an increased interest in spirituality discourages people from interacting with each other ritually, then it could follow that religion will decline in political significance. Rituals are important means of forging meaningful bonds between individuals within a group. In her study of women's religious expression, Lesley Northup explains, "One of the most effective political aspects of ritualization is its ability to draw people together into a group, to create community, to communicate common grievances, values and goals, and to forge the group into a unified source for change."[76] If as both Heelas and Bruce tell us, people are drifting away from collective ritualization, even if they are maintaining a personal interest in spiritual matters, this leads to a decline in political unity and efficacy.

This pattern does not hold, however, among my participants. Women who have disassociated themselves from formal religious structures still participate in marginal religious communities and rituals. For example, many women in the contemporary Pagan collective, whom both Heelas and Bruce would place within the New Age rubric but who would not choose that designation for themselves,[77] purposely create community rituals. Even more applicable to this problem, some of the women living in the Catholic Worker community choose not to attend Mass or formal confession yet enthusiastically participate in the community's Wednesday night liturgies. Because I see ritual activity in places that Bruce and other scholars focused on traditional, institutional, and often androcentric power do not look, my participants demonstrate that the relationship between stable community and consolidated institution requires a more nuanced formulation. Lack of institutional interaction does not mean lack of collective, religious ritualization for my participants.[78]

Moreover, the number of people attending a particular church is less indicative of its potential political influence than the numbers of people it can reach on a particular political issue.[79] Those with a personal interest in religion may not lend directly measurable political clout to religious institutions as reflected in the numbers of their adherents; churches lose the opportunity to count these individuals among those for whom they speak. However, the same people may be more easily persuaded to support the political positions of religious institutions on specific issues. In this way religious institutions may significantly influence public opinion and governmental policy beyond the official census of their adherents.

It is in this role of moral guidance, as anchors of public conscience, that the activists with whom I spoke want to influence the public, to reshape social consensus on what counts as "good desire," as David Craig has phrased it, the desires that orient the individual toward productive community engagement and just morality.[80] My participants hope that corporations and governments will see them as expressing the opinion of larger numbers of people. In their actions they are both calling on and representing others.

Distancing Conservative Activists

In addition to their religious communities, my participants belong to activist communities engaged with social justice work. Inside and outside both kinds of groups, they may be too liberal for some members of their religious traditions and too religious for some members of their political communities.[81] The distinction between religion and spirituality made by my participants illuminates some of the particular facets of identity that religiously affiliated social justice activists negotiate. Utilizing the language of spirituality, over and against religion, my participants attempt both to distinguish themselves from and to engage in dialogue with more conservative members of their religious communities as well as with strongly, secularly oriented members of their activist communities.

The women with whom I spoke are concerned with conceptualizing themselves in relation to conservative activists, who also claim religious faith as inspiration for action. For example, Deborah responded to my question about the relationship between her religious work and her political work: "How [is it that] we, in our congregation can be so sure that calling ourselves 'Christians' makes it imperative that we be social and political activists? . . . there are many people in North America who feel that their religion compels them to be right-wing activists. I guess the common thread [between us] is that we feel our Christianity compels us to be involved . . . in social and political affairs."[82] She clearly sees a connection between Christian faith and political activism, her own and that of those on the other side of the political spectrum, that is, "right wing." Yet she sees herself as engaged in activism with goals that differ significantly from those of conservatives.

There are several reasons why differentiating themselves from more conservative religious activists may be especially important to religiously motivated social justice activists. There is the concern that people outside of their traditions—mostly mainstream secular culture, but also other activists oriented toward secular humanism—will not understand the differences between their political orientation and that of traditionalists. There are also real similarities between progressive and conservative Christian movements, as Deborah points out.

The ideal of Christian as activist in the world can be traced to the nineteenth century, in the common roots of these now diametrically opposed groups.[83] Moreover, as Grant Wacker explains, both Evangelical and liberal activists historically have shared belief in the power of the Holy Spirit in their personal lives and in history. This shared cosmology continues into the present.[84] Even Heelas, champion of the shift from formal religion to New Age spirituality, sees connections between contemporary Evangelical Christianity and the New Age movement in the role of immanence that the Holy Spirit plays in Evangelical churches.[85] Catherine Albanese argues that both conservative Protestant Christianity and the New Age movement have a "series of convergences" around metaphysical experience and mysticism: "Personal transformation and direct spiritual experience are at the heart of one's life project, and for both, private transformation must find its twin in the transformation of society."[86] These similarities, particularly in the motivation to work for change in the world, may invoke especially vehement rejections from both sides of the political progressive-conservative divide, as can be seen in the clash among North American Protestants over who gets included within the terms *Fundamentalist* and *Evangelical*.[87]

In addition to religious similarities between traditionalist and progressive activists, there is also overlap in some political concerns, particularly with regard to women's well-being. Judith Stacey and Susan Elizabeth Gerrard find ways in which feminist ideas about gender roles and relationships have entered into Evangelical Christian discourse on relationships and the family, and similarly Sara Moslener discusses feminist discourses of empowerment and choice within Evangelical Christian sexual purity culture.[88] In her ethnographic study of the conservative Women Aglow movement, R. Marie Griffith also writes, "Both conservative evangelical women and feminists . . . want to see women's cultural and social labor revalued, celebrated, and elevated in status; the basic difference between their images is that they ascribe contrary meanings to the substance of womanhood."[89] Pamela Klassen finds that both traditionalist and feminist women actively choose homebirth to respond to the ways that they understand the biomedical model of birth to disempower women. Although they give very different reasons for their critiques and alternatives, they nonetheless share common ground.[90] Lastly, Faye Ginsberg demonstrates that women on both sides of the abortion debate agree that women are oppressed in contemporary society.[91] As these examples illustrate, though their proposed solutions to these common concerns are radically different, both traditionalist activists and feminist activists often address the same perceived problems, in this case gender-based oppressions.

Lavender, the contemporary Pagan who attended Quebec City as a Raging Granny, is more blunt than Deborah about the contrast between herself and more conservative activists. At the end of our interview, when I asked if she had any last thoughts or comments about her "relationship with religion and politics," she said:

Just that it's all one. You can't take one and separate it out. I don't see how anybody can be spiritual without having it come in action. And I'm appalled at some of the actions that right-wing people come out with, like quoting the Bible as a reason to oppose gay marriage. You know, come on! What about poverty, what about homelessness, what about violence, what about, you now, landmines and bombs in space? For heaven's sake, pick your issues. This is ridiculous, to use religion as an excuse to try to prevent other people from having the same human rights as you do.[92]

For Lavender religion and politics are inextricable from one another, but she clearly feels that there is a very important difference between her political work and that of conservative Christians.

In distinguishing themselves from religious conservatives, many of my participants feel tension with their own religious institutions. This sentiment was most pronounced with, though certainly not exclusive to, Catholic participants. Winter, Lummis, and Stokes arrive at similar conclusions in *Defecting in Place*.[93] They found that more women feel alienated in the Catholic Church than in any other denomination they studied.

One participant who has struggled for a place within Catholicism is Agatha, who runs the Catholic Worker house for international refugees. She feels called to a religious life in the fullest sense of the Catholic Church. Considering herself a "female religious," she has taken personal vows and lives in an intentional community with other people of faith. She is dedicated to a life of service, helping refugees who come to Canada from all over the world. Yet she is unable to become a nun in the official sense. She divorced an abusive husband many years ago and is not willing to simply "say the right things" to get the marriage annulled, a required step for joining a Catholic order. Instead, she lives on the border of the church, following a call from her God to monasticism yet restricted by institutional requirements.[94]

A second participant, Emily, a woman in her early twenties finishing her undergraduate degree in religious studies, experienced conflict between her Catholic community and her own values in a very literal way. A conservative Catholic speaker was brought in by the anti-abortion group at her university to speak against same-sex marriage. Although she felt that his theology was shoddy and strongly disagreed with his homophobia, Emily found herself in an awkward position, sitting with more conservative Catholics but with her non-Catholic activist friends attending the lecture in order to express opposition to the speaker. She said:

> It was deeply upsetting for me because, here I was, with half of my community on one side of the room, half of my community on the other side of the room. And I did probably a thing that I feel more guilty for than anything I've ever done, which was, at the end, I'm sitting with my parents' friends, and they're all standing up around me [to applaud], and I stood up. And I felt like, "How can I stand up and be counted for this guy who is such a creep? And I'm hurting people right on the other side of the room!"[95]

This experience affected Emily significantly. She debriefed with friends about it and ended up writing a piece for the school paper about the inappropriateness of having invited the speaker. While she takes personal responsibility for expressing solidarity with views she does not hold, she is also resentful that through its conservative positions on many issues, the Catholic Church creates situations in which she must choose between her two communities, between the church's doctrines and her understandings of social justice.

Regina, the co-coordinator of the Zacchaeus House in the Catholic Worker community, explained her own marginal position within Catholicism:

> With the question how do I see myself in relationship with the institutional church as a group, I think that it's an interesting position because on one side, I feel more in a position to be able to challenge it, but on the other hand I also have the luxury, I feel very outside of it in one way. I feel comfortable in speaking the challenges and forcing them to not see me as an outsider because, even though I don't go to mass every weekend, or whatever, I'm still in some way committed to living a life where faith is central. It's fun sometimes, because they can't turn me off, the way they turn other people off, but then they'll just, I mean if they want to turn you off, they will anyway. . . . I think

I'm still working on how convinced I am that keeping anything of this institution is worthwhile, so for me, I don't know.[96]

For Regina her liminal position provides both an opportunity to exercise power as well as a sense of disenfranchisement from the institutional power.

United Church member Donna, who was upset about the balance of ritual to political action, voiced a similar uneasiness in discussing her relationship with her institutional church. "I guess I'm on the fringe of the United Church," she said. "I think it's fair to say that I'm on the fringes of it because I really don't like the institutional, the emphasis on the institution."[97] Although Regina and Donna expressed similar feelings of alienation from their respective religious institutions, the frustrations that Donna noted refer to issues such as how much time of the worship service should be devoted to political announcements. By contrast, priests have felt compelled to tell Regina that the Catholic Worker is very wrong and anti-church. Nevertheless, though the levels of authority expected and exercised by the Vatican and the administrative hierarchy of the United Church are very different, both Regina and Donna described feeling marginalized from these centers of authority within their traditions.

Even among the contemporary Pagans with whom I spoke, there was an emphasis on being on the margins of tradition. The contemporary Pagan collective, in which I did participant-observation, was formed by people who felt alienated by some of the other Toronto Pagan groups, which were explicitly disinterested in politics and social justice issues. This collective defines itself as a group in which members can combine contemporary Paganism and political activism, in contrast to what members perceive to be a general ethos of divorcing Pagan spirituality from social justice concerns.[98]

In telling their stories of religion, my participants emphasize personal experience, as distinct from authoritarian institutions. This is consistent with cultural trends in which authority and authenticity are sought through outsider status.[99] Laurence Moore argues that identifying as outside institutions of power gives people opportunities to "express their most cherished convictions in the language of dissent."[100] My participants enact authenticity by articulating distance from, even opposition to, their religious institutions through using the language of spirituality.

Third Choice

Given the exclusionary agendas at the core of identification as religious or secular, it may be difficult for those disempowered by such assumptions to feel fully at home in either category. For example, when I asked Judy, a United Church member in her late twenties studying in seminary, "What does religion mean to you?" she responded immediately: "Repression." "Yeah?" I asked.

> At its worst, repression. I think religion is just taking spirituality and putting a structure of control around it. . . . I mean, really, that's what it is. I think that one of the greatest sins in Christianity today is just how far away from the teaching of Jesus we've allowed a bunch of guys, largely, to take us. And to allow us to be led around by the nose by this huge structure that's claiming all of this power and authority that we've handed to it and is nothing but a human construct. It's got nothing to do with spirituality, I don't think. So that's what I'd say about religion.

I asked her to explain the distinction between spirituality and religion, and she said:

> Spirituality is about being in relationship with the whole of creation and however one finds God at work within that. So I suppose that kind of implies that there is a dimension beyond what your five senses can detect, if you want to put it that way. Or a dimension that kind of binds us to everything going on around us and everything that happened before and everything that will happen. That's one way of looking at it maybe. But, yeah, I'm still trying to get at how you can define the collective nature of spirituality without that conversation immediately taking you into religion, because I'm tired of the collective nature of it being defined by patriarchal religions.[101]

Bea, a Pagan in her early thirties and single mother of a toddler, left a little more room for religion to be a positive force, a collective of individual spiritualities coming together:

Well, religion and spirituality I tend to define differently. Religion I tend to see as more an organized thing. And spirituality is a more personalized connection with the universe . . . a good way of making sense of the universe and connecting with the divine in whatever way that people think of that mystery. And religion is a more formalized community that together has that commonality. So in terms of being Pagan or Wiccan, I kind of think of it as like spirituality and to a certain degree religion because there is sort of like a set order of that spirituality. There's like a whole common language and common practice, and so I guess religion for me is people coming together to, not formalize, but collectivizing their spirituality.

Yet she qualified her remarks: "I have a feminist critique of mainstream religions and the institutionalization of religions and the patriarchal, male-dominated images within religion, so that's there [too]."[102]

Despite their distancing from religion as patriarchal, my participants were also cautious not to cede to leftists the dismissal of religion entirely. Angel, a Catholic university student in her early twenties, said, for example:

How am I going to exist as a Christian within the world, a Christian within the anarchist community? You do get a lot of flack for that, where people will tell me, "But you can't be a real anarchist." You know it's like, "No gods, no masters," and then you go, "First Nations solidarity?" So I think, you know, although I don't believe in the church hierarchy or the hierarchy of grace or any of those sort of things, I don't think it's constructive to discount religion altogether, especially if you're going to try to do solidarity work, because religion is such an important part of so many people's existence.

For Angel rejecting religion entirely is poor politics because it dismisses the worldviews of marginalized others, such as Native Canadian groups, and denies a basis for human solidarity, which she calls "the soul": "There is a lot about Marx[ism] that I'm like, 'Oh, yeah, that makes sense,' but it denies that humans exist beyond the physical realm, beyond the realm of work. It denies that there's something innate in humanity that is, I don't know, the soul. . . . My experience of the world is different than a woman of color's. I'm gonna admit that, but I'm also gonna say that there is something that any person in the world has in common with me and that would be our souls."[103] For her the notion of something transcendent, the soul, is important for recognizing mutual humanity across difference but is left out of purely materialist politics.

Judy, the United Church member, also expressed feeling caught between her political commitment to feminism and her spiritual commitment, which she understands the church to have co-opted or misrepresented. "It's difficult because I think a lot of feminism has been fairly anti-religion and has, therefore, become fairly anti-spirituality. . . . Spirituality is often perceived and defined in terms of religion, which is really unfortunate. It's giving religion way too much power. So, I'm still figuring out how to deprogram myself from some of that, right? There's kind of two negative messages right there. There's the religion saying feminism has no place. And then feminism saying religion has no place."[104]

Naming their own positions as distinct from both religion and secularly constructed politics, set in explicit opposition to religion, may be particularly powerful for feminists who critique structural inequalities, such as gender-based violence, homophobia, and Islamophobia, that they understand as jointly perpetuated by both religious and political institutions.

Facilitating Communication

My participants convey a sense that spirituality transcends the boundaries of particular religions. One of the major criticisms of the language of spirituality, as distinct from religion, is that the term is vague to the point of meaningless.[105] Yet the vagueness of the term can be deliberate, allowing communication across institutional and social boundaries.[106] By using the term *spirituality* to describe something that can exist within and transcend particular religious traditions, my participants attempt to communicate their experiences in ways to which people of different religious affiliations, or lack thereof, will relate.

For example, several of my participants explained that they consider their spiritualities or personal theologies to be more in line with other faith groups than what is traditionally associated with their own. Angel said:

If you pushed, you'd probably find that I'm not, that I don't tow the Catholic line. That probably a lot of my theology is more Protestant because I do believe in personal interpretation of the Gospel and, you know, the priesthood of many, instead of, you know, some guy getting to be the priest and having a direct line to God. So if you pushed it you'd find that, yeah, I do fall more into the Protestant category, but, like I was saying, Catholicism is my culture. I also really get a lot out of the ritual of Catholicism, and you don't necessarily find that in all the Protestant churches.[107]

Angel disagrees with many of the formal teachings of the Catholic Church and leads a lifestyle that differs from officially sanctioned Catholic ideals. In explaining the ways in which her beliefs differ from traditional Catholic theology, Angel draws on the language of Protestantism. Yet she maintains her Catholicism as an important part of her identity, noting aspects of the religion that she is unable to get elsewhere, such as satisfying ritual and "culture," which for her includes her community of family and friends and their common celebrations.

Deborah, the United Church member who facilitated my fieldwork with Clearwater, also understands herself to go beyond the boundaries of her tradition. As she explained:

I'm a United Church person, but I'm also the sort of United Church person who's also contemporary Pagan in my theology. My theology is closer to contemporary Pagan than to a lot of Christian theology, although I'm very involved in Christian theology, and I'm studying it. . . . My experience of the divine is an immanent one. It's related to my reactions to the world, to my observations of the world, the created world, nature especially, but I don't, you know, exclude bricks. So I think, you know, that a lot of traditional Jews and Christians would call that a contemporary Pagan perspective or a Pagan perspective if you don't have that transcendent element of the divine.[108]

Deborah's theology encompasses both Christian and contemporary Pagan aspects. Like Angel, her understanding of herself as transcending traditional categories hinges on her assumptions about the interpretation of her personal theology by others. While she understands herself to be

Christian, she is conscious that others may view her as outside the fold. Nonetheless, this is a place she is happy to inhabit.

Maxine, a contemporary Pagan in her late twenties and manager of a popular yoga studio, finds important similarities between her experiences and other religious traditions:

> I feel a really strong affinity toward, not Christianity in the sense of how we understand the church today, but toward the values and ideals of the life of Christ. I also participated in a beautiful Easter workshop a couple of years ago. It was so beautiful. . . . So, I feel a huge affinity toward Christianity. I've, you know, been reading the New Testament and looking at that and going, "There's something in here for me." Same with Judaism. I feel a huge kinship, and it's the same way with people I talk to on the yogic path who are really serious. They're right on.[109]

Maxine expressed feelings of connection to Christianity, yet Christian culture, which encourages Angel to maintain her self-identification as Catholic, distances Maxine from self-identifying as Christian. On the other hand, both women described personal readings of the New Testament as being important to their practice.

For Angel, Deborah, and Maxine, relationship takes on important functions in their descriptions of spirituality. Angel's relationships with family and friends support her continued membership in the Catholic community, despite her theological differences with it. Also, these theological differences revolve around her relationship to God and Jesus and her personal ability to negotiate that relationship. Deborah said that it is her relationship to the world around her that informs her theology and her experience of the deity as immanent. Differently for Maxine, relationships with people outside of her faith tradition are made possible by similarities between their personal spiritualities. Significantly, she used terms like *affinity* and *kinship* to describe her feelings of connection to those people with whom, despite institutional differences, she understands herself to share common spiritual experiences. The boundaries between traditions blur dramatically as these speakers emphasize what they perceive to be similarities between faiths. Clearly, there is a difference for them between particular religious traditions and more universal, yet personal, experiences of the divine, which may be found across and between institutional boundaries.

At the same time, perhaps precisely because of these perceived similarities, participants may feel the need to explain or justify their adherence to one tradition and not another. Angel noted that she gets things out of Catholicism that she feels are unavailable in Protestantism, such as cultural connection and satisfying ritual. She also explained that she doesn't have much interest in contemporary Paganism:

> I understand some of the people I've talked to who are part of that community are people who formerly identified as Catholics or who call themselves recovering Catholics or whatever, and it's recognizing, like, "The Christian Church caused me so much pain, but I still want to identify with some religious experience, but not that way." And that I can totally understand: oh yeah, you're just looking for something that's not going to—like I find it hard to go to church. Church sucks. You get treated like dirt [laughs]. So, I get it. I just don't want to do it [laughs].[110]

Similarly, as Maxine explained, besides feeling an "affinity" for the Christian New Testament, she does not like "how we understand the church today."

A further example involves two of my United Church participants. During after-service coffee I was approached by Annie, a law professor who attended Clearwater with her youngest son, a teenager who was in the process of completing requirements to be welcomed into the community as a full adult member. Annie said that she'd been thinking about me because during Wednesday night Bible study, the group had been talking about how much unhelpful and upsetting material there is to wade through in Scripture to find things that are helpful and affirming, "So why do it?" she asked herself. She related that she had almost gotten into Goddess spirituality and contemporary Paganism but that she had gone to this United Church congregation first, at the suggestion of one of her graduate students. Referring to our interview session, she said, "But I realized during our discussion how much the United Church really makes our space possible." She felt like the Pagan groups that she had been involved with lacked a feeling of tradition and continuity, which she found important in her congregation. At this point another participant, Christine, joined our discussion and was eager to talk about how she, too, had been attracted to Goddess groups. Annie and Christine asked me about my research experiences in the contemporary Pagan community and how they could get information about upcoming events.[111]

Then Annie returned to her original question: "Anyway, why deal with these scriptural stories when they require so much work, unlike [a Native American story that Laura read in the worship service], in which the teachings about justice are so clear and in these scriptural passages so unclear? Why struggle like this?" She answered her question, "Because you are part of a community through space and time that is doing this work—it's worth it." For her the United Church has provided her and the other congregants with important support and space, along with the connection to past communities. "Look at this," she said. She and Christine led me over to the coffee table and pointed to the plates on which our cookies and snacks were being served. I hadn't noticed it before—each plate displayed the stamp of CLEARWATER METHODIST CHURCH, the original church from which the current United Church congregation was formed. The three of us stood there together pondering history and continuity.

Two decades ago this congregation relinquished its own building to donate the money to social ministry projects. The members chose to meet in another church's space, in contrast to many congregations that work very hard and take on serious debts for the privilege of owning their own church building. This decision is a point of pride for the congregation, even those who were not yet members at the time. Nevertheless, somewhere in the shuffle of leaving the old building and what it signified—financial stresses, unequal distribution of wealth, reified institutionalism—someone packed up those plates and made sure they moved to the new space, and now people pull them out every Sunday to serve food to the congregation.

One might ask if this can really be the same group, changed as it is through time, place, and composition of members. Yet people within the congregation do understand important consistencies between the Methodist church that bought those plates and the group of people eating off them today. That perceived continuity gives members like Annie and Christine hope that the oppressions they perceive, even within their own Scriptures, can be transformed through collective effort. They take heart in the knowledge that others have also struggled. As Annie put it, they are part of a community that is doing the work. It is this sense of historical community that keeps Annie and Christine in the United Church, despite the attractive alternative of contemporary Paganism, of which they are aware and to which they also feel drawn.

Although they understand spirituality to transcend boundaries, my participants do feel strong connections to their own religious traditions. Different aspects of relationships with family and friends, ritual, and continuity of tradition encourage my participants to maintain identification as Catholic, United Church, or contemporary Pagan. These connections are important enough to keep them within their specific traditions, despite affinities they might feel for other religions.

Spirituality as Pragmatic Method

Feminists interested in transcendent spirituality draw on an alternative secularizing tradition that runs parallel to that of critical denunciations of religion, one that instead promotes openness to religious exploration and celebrates public space as a meeting place for diverse religious ideas. In North America there is a historical link between movements for social progress and interest in alternatives to religious traditionalism. In the United States, for example, the first popularized swell of interest in Eastern traditions such as Buddhism and Hinduism, European occult sciences that feature ritual magic and alchemy, and hybrids of the two, such as Theosophy, coincided with the Progressive Era, roughly 1880–1920, a period of political agitation for universal voting rights for both women and people of color.[112] A second great surge of interest occurred in the 1960s and 1970s, another time of social upheaval focused on the Civil Rights movement against institutionalized racism and on what is referred to as the second wave of feminism.[113] As I write, we are in the throes of another wave of occult interest, at least in popular culture, even as debates about secularization rage on. This interest seems to coincide both with great agitation around income disparity, racism, and anti-immigration, as well as moral panic, in some sectors at least, over increasing legitimacy for LGBTQ civil rights.

The language of spirituality is especially compatible with the questioning of religious authority inherent in the search for alternatives.[114] Further, for my participants, who, in spite of general disdain for religion within their political milieu, continue to identify with their religious communities, spirituality discourse provides tools with which to position themselves between religious institutions and secular activist communities.

Angel, who is Catholic, explained the difference between invoking Christianity in protests against hurtful policies of the Catholic Church and openly mobilizing Christianity in more general public protest spaces:

> It's very appropriate to use Christian dialogue and to use prayer and to use all of that [in the first case] because what you're doing is you're up against the institutional Catholic Church. So, I [don't] find that that inappropriate. [For example], we did a lot of prayer services with survivors of abuse by clergy, and we had a service for queer Christians and those sorts of things, and that's a very fine use of it. . . . [But] I think Christians need to be careful, because they've pissed enough people off. . . . There's this feeling that it's just alienating people and making people angry.[115]

For Angel the traditional privileging of Christianity as morally superior and the ease with which practitioners are often able to dominate public space to the detriment of others means that overt Christian practices should only be mobilized for internal critique, not for problems that go beyond the church itself. Christian-specific ritual practices are too particular to be useful in the context of broader political protest, an environment in which more generic and therefore accessible practice would be more appropriate.

Judy, the United Church seminary student, talked about spirituality, in this case ecofeminist spirituality, as providing a needed corrective to both her Christianity and her politics: "I think where I've arrived is that linkage between feminism and spirituality has very much come from the ecofeminist work, right? It comes from introducing a really strong earth element into the religion because, you see, I think a lot of our spirituality has been corrupted by the religious paradigm. . . . I've had to do a lot of work to figure out what it means to be, for example, ridding myself of the notion that humans are kind of first in the creative order." Bea, contemporary Pagan, said something similar, stressing "the importance of the emphasis within spiritual feminism on just the feminine, images of women, the Goddess, and just the feminist work that's been done on that."[116]

In their usage spirituality can be interpreted as an orientation or practice that may supplement participation in particular religious or political communities but is not limited to them.[117] In this sense of being a pragmatic method, participants treat spirituality similarly to the way that ritual magic was treated by Victorian practitioners in England. Shared magical techniques were able to be practiced within differing cosmologies. Practitioners might be interested in connecting with ancient Greek or Egyptian gods, or they might, as was more commonly the fact, understand their mysticism in strictly Christian terms, the goal being to draw closer to Jesus and the Christian God.[118] Magical work could nonetheless be shared between practitioners with different worldviews, and techniques could be successfully taught across theological divides.[119] The language of spirituality transcends institutional boundaries in a similar way, especially in the caveats my participants added to their descriptions of their own experiences.

Religiously motivated social justice activists are in a liminal position between more conservative members of their religious traditions and those within their activist communities who dislike religion. In the current political climate they also balance between cultural discussions of "traditional values" pitted against secular social progress as well as assumptions about the positive value of secularization. Both of these paradigms link "liberal" values to secularity and "conservative" values to religion.

In continuing to identify with their religious institutions, my participants refuse to relinquish religion to conservatism. They also assert the right to continue to draw on their religions as resources in their social justice work. Sometimes, however, as in Emily's experience with the homophobic lecturer, they find it difficult to achieve balance and simply slip between the cracks of the discourse, conceding to a division of their worlds into separate religious and political areas.

A strategy among my participants for avoiding such a division can be found in separating personal spirituality from religious institutions. By drawing on this popular distinction between spiritual and religious, my participants attempt to signal to other social justice activists that they are not suffering from false consciousness. The language of spirituality becomes especially important to my participants in communicating that they are familiar with critiques of religion and that they do not continue to participate in their religious traditions due to lack of exposure to the paradigm that secularization and social progress require of one another. It also helps to clarify that they do not want to force their religious interpretations onto the spiritual experiences of others.

Within social justice activist circles, the language of spirituality also becomes useful in talking across institutional and ideological boundaries. While religion is too limited, ideologically linked to public behavior and institutionalization, spirituality becomes the common language. Religion, as already too public, becomes unacceptable in public discourse, whereas spirituality, as personal, becomes acceptable to talk about in public. This usage completely reverses the distinctions that most scholars, popular culture in general, and my participants in particular would make between religion and spirituality. With this reversal spirituality can be welcome in public space in a way that religion, as a personal variation on a more generally accessible spirituality, cannot.

Ultimately, while my participants' political engagements and religious practices do not allow them to ignore struggles between religion and secularism as inapplicable to their concerns, their active choice in articulating their own worldviews as spiritual creates a third alternative that allows them to escape the dichotomy. Further, such choice may be an especially appealing option for feminists because of the ways both religion and the secular have been gendered to the exclusion of women and other sexual minorities. Therefore, the concept of spirituality can often be more readily adapted to their personal and community needs.

Despite anxieties about bringing religion into the public sphere, religiously motivated activists integrate religious rituals and concepts into public demonstrations, as we saw in chapter 2. They also describe their religious communities as places from which they draw strength for their work. Through experiences of community and cooperation in their religious groups, these women model a cosmology of interconnection and mutual responsibility, an ethical worldview I discuss in the next chapter as that of social justice.

4   Self, Community, and Social Justice

Feminist scholars of religion, especially those focusing on women in conservative movements, insist that it is overly simplistic to understand personal agency exclusively in terms of resistance.[1] Saba Mahmood, in particular, emphasizes the importance of expanding notions of personal agency to include the enactment of norms and ideals, not only changing oneself in spite of social norms.[2] Agency solely realized through resistance reflects an understanding of power as transcendent and the individual's interaction with it as a "zero-sum" game.[3] From this perspective personal empowerment is understood in terms of the individual versus systems of power. Every accomplishment of the self, or "resistance," comes at the expense of transcendent power.

Narratives of resistance rely on the Enlightenment value of individual freedom, the fantasy of a total lack of connection and obligation to others.[4] Philip Goodchild has argued that this image of the isolated, self-sustaining subject is, ironically, enmeshed in the emergence of free market capitalism, which promises freedom from traditional obligations—familial, social, and religious—through economic autonomy.[5] The Canadian Lotto 649 advertises with the slogan "Imagine the Freedom!" But this "myth of autonomy" from relational responsibilities is a con. Older constructive relationships are replaced in the contemporary world by *economic* obligations—in other words, debts.[6] Within modern capitalism the dream of autonomy from social and moral obligation, which money is supposed to deliver, actually derives from the dehumanizing experience of debt. Debt is our hounding constraint, yet the obfuscations of the system make all other relationships come to look like debt and bear its weight, convincing us that the problems with the world are really our obligations to others, rather than our all-consuming, newly primary relationship to the market.

As political activists, my participants subscribe to resistance against mainstream culture and values as an important axis of social and religious identity; however, their sense of self is also based on embeddedness in social relationships and systems of power. They articulate a cosmology of relationship—an understanding of the universe, its workings, and the place of human beings within it—in which the well-being of the individual impacts the world more broadly. This worldview coexists with competing cosmologies offered by mainstream society and the implicit Marxism of their activist communities.

The Enlightenment's public-private split, also taken for granted in certain Marxist praxis, is an important factor in liberal feminist understandings of agency as resistance. Within this dichotomous framework of subject pitted against power, care of the self competes with social change. Through their incorporation of both feminist care ethics and justice ethics into a cosmology of relationship they call "social justice," my participants help disrupt the easy dichotomy of self versus society upon which the exclusive equation of agency and resistance is predicated.

Worldview of Relationship

Despite their different institutional affiliations as Catholics, United Church members, or contemporary Pagans, each group understands itself to be part of a larger movement of spiritually engaged activists for social justice. This movement transcends particular religions and emphasizes the explicitly political interconnectedness of individuals, communities, and world. For example, Regina co-facilitates the drop-in Zacchaeus House in the Catholic Worker community, a space in the community that is always open to those in need. In describing her role, she said: "It doesn't sound like much, but it's actually humungous, just hanging out with folks, cooking with people, chatting and going for walks, being at a birth, and translating. All this crazy stuff is really relationship building. In that context I feel it is activism because they're not people that my society encourages me to build relationships with. I really value hanging out with folks, so that's a big part of what I do."[7]

As a co-facilitator, Regina provides a wide range of services depending on what new people and more regular visitors to the community might require. In addition, she helps organize the community's common meals and liturgies and plans special events. As a result of these multiple roles, she interacts with many different kinds of people, including economically disadvantaged families from the neighborhood, recent immigrants, and homeless people. Building relationships across social divisions is a political act for Regina and one upon which the Catholic Worker movement is based.

Another Catholic participant, Tiffany, a legal researcher in her early twenties and originally from the Philippines, emphasized the consciousness of other people and their experiences: "What does it mean to be political? It means being aware. It means not just being centered on your own life or what's going on with you. It's knowing that there are other people around you and there are other realities around you, that there are other people with different experiences than you and to act on that." In response to my question "Do you think it takes a particular kind of faith to engage in activism?" Tiffany said, "I was brought up to respect people and to empathize with them."[8] Both Regina and Tiffany understand interacting with other people, moving beyond self-interest, as political engagement.

For Franka, formerly pastor of the Clearwater congregation, this connectedness to others is manifested through the presence of the Holy Spirit: "As the pastor I became much more conscious of building community and came to understand the importance of community and the relationship of connectedness. I began to see the Holy Spirit as that which connects us with each other and with the world, with all people, and so to nourish that connectedness within the congregation and, at the same time, the connections of the congregation to the world was what I would say I was about. And so, to me, social activism is based really on solidarity, connectedness with people all over the world."[9] Franka bases her activism in connections to other people. She understands these connections to preexist in the immanence of the Holy Spirit.

Grace, the United Church member active with the peace movement, responding to my question "Do you think it takes a particular kind of faith to engage in activism?" said: "Somehow, having the innate consciousness of other people's lives and the extent to which they are hurt, deprived, suffering injustice, in any other culture, having been made aware of that, then, somehow, you can't help but always be aware of that. The connection with your faith, it's incredibly important to have that awareness, to have someone make you aware of those situations."[10] For Grace, like Franka, the connections to others are already there but need to be acknowledged and sustained through interaction.

Discussing the relationship of politics and religion, Lavender, the contemporary Pagan Raging Granny, said:

> Even when I identified as Christian, I felt that you couldn't be Christian without being an activist. And even though I no longer would define myself as Christian, I would say Jesus was a feminist . . . and so I still feel that a lot of the roots of the activism come from that aspect of Christianity. . . . How can you not care for the earth and advocate for the earth and its creatures, people, plants, animals, whatever, to preserve and facilitate it when it involves spirituality? So it's just part and parcel of all that for me.[11]

Lavender draws a further line of relationship between her current religious identity and her past. Her description of moral responsibility links into a discourse of divine connection she first encountered in Christianity and resonates with that of Franka and Grace.

From the perspective of this worldview of relationship, change in one person's consciousness can have global repercussions because they are part of a web of influence. Each person is connected to every other through relationship to society, and self-improvement can ripple out into community. For example, Tiffany talked about coming to political consciousness via criticism of a charity project she took part in through her high school:[12]

> In Catholic school we were giving help and food, and the next week we would have to go back and give more help and give more food, and I was thinking, "Well, this is kind of crazy, you know. We just keep coming back here, and this is all we do." We'd get our pictures taken, and what is that? So, it made me realize how change has to come both ways because political change, economic change, it doesn't come quickly. It's a long process. So I think that the two perspectives,

from a grassroots basis—also from feminism, right—it comes from the self, so one person is empowered, and it's contagious and so on.[13]

Her new critiques of a system based on charity, rather than political change addressing underlying issues of inequality, enabled her to become involved in new projects to eliminate global poverty. Through her personal transformation, the global justice movement grew.

In this perspective once a person begins expressing new worldviews, they may find that there are many others who are also dissatisfied and desire change, as River suggested: "I think it's sort of the hundredth monkey theory, I think that's what they call it, that if enough people work at it and if enough people are influenced to think about it, that society's consciousness changes and that comes because enough people work at it, people talk about it, people take risks for it. And sometimes taking risks helps people find out they're not alone."[14] River roots social change in the self but also in connections between multiple selves and in their interactions with each other.

Regina expresses a similar perspective that sets personal transformation at the heart of global justice. She said:

I think right now change comes about when people find someone with a vision that can draw them out of the place of comfort or apathy where they are at that point, and be concrete enough for them to feel like they can go there with other people. I think that, it's so hard to talk about this without feeling clichéd, but I think it's the balance of doing your own inner work and following that up with being conscious of what you do with your privilege and how that plays out in your life and what you're going to do about that.[15]

For Regina self-change and social changes are inextricable. Role modeling is an important aspect of her view because "someone with a vision" can move others to new understandings of the world and their relationships to other people.

In J. Z. Smith's theory of social "conversion," " social change is preeminently symbol or symbolic change. . . . To change stance is to totally alter one's symbols and to inhabit a different world."[16] In other words, shift perspective and thereby shift the world order. My participants insist that changing their own perspectives and offering others alternative visions of social possibilities can bring about such change.

Cosmology on the Ground: The Fair Trade Movement

I turn now to an activist project in which interconnection between people is central, Franka's involvement with the fair trade movement as a remedy to global economic exploitation. Goodchild argues that part of the power of free market capitalism is that it remakes morality in its own image, replacing personal responsibility with economic rationality, "the theology of money."[17] In doing so, it creates a system in which the connections between economic choices and their consequences for other people and the planet are obscured and impossible to name. How many horrors are perpetuated in the name of "responsibility to shareholders"? How did such a constrained notion of responsibility come to dominate?

Global capitalism creates ever expanding networks of exploitation yet directs attention away from the consequences of those connections between people. According to Goodchild, "A consumer's knowledge and experience of eating chocolate does not encompass the experience of a slave who tended the cocoa plantations from which it derives."[18] What would the world look like if the exploitations of production were suddenly assimilatable into consumer experience? What if we no longer conceded to money's ideological "political and ethical neutrality" but instead identified its role as a medium of moral transmission?[19] The fair trade movement is one effort to attract attention to ethical connections produced through the global market and, by doing so, to change consumer practice.

Franka grew up in Texas and came to Canada as a young adult. After her ordination in the United Church in the late 1970s, Franka became involved in Ten Days for World Development, an ecumenical project designed to educate Canadians about global development issues and social justice.[20] Her partner at the time, Matthew, was funded by the World Council of Churches to travel to developing countries in southeastern Africa and talk to people about the political and economic pressures they were facing, especially due to the Rhodesian War. She went with him and interviewed people in refugee camps in Tanzania, Zambia, Botswana, and Mozambique.[21] The people they met through this project encouraged them to document experiences in South Africa, which was not part of the original plan. This work involved sneaking into South Africa on tourist visas and mailing tapes of the interviews out of the country. They took this precaution so that they would not have to take the tapes through customs and risk having the interviews destroyed, having their contacts exposed, or being jailed themselves.

During this project Franka learned about human rights abuses perpetuated by trade inequities in these countries:

> What I was learning was that our affluence in Canada and the United States and Europe is really dependent on the poverty in the Third World, that there's a very close connection, and you could really see it and name it. One of the grounds of the dependence and its unfairness was bringing over wealth to us from them, which was unfair trade. The fact was that at that time many Third World countries had just become independent from Britain and the countries, then, say the ones that produced coffee and tea, were nationalizing their coffee and tea trades in the hopes that would bring money into Tanzania and Sri Lanka. They wanted to nationalize the trade. It happened in Nigeria, Ghana. I think of the names of people who were instrumental in bringing about independence, men who spent many years in prison, in and out, and then became the head of the country and nationalized these things. And then the bottom of the market fell out so that nobody would buy the coffee or tea. They lost profits because, for Sri Lanka, they were totally dependent on two big companies to buy their tea and process it and so forth. With coffee I know it was Nestlé and General Foods. Tanzania had built not a coffee factory but an instant coffee factory to really do the process, but they couldn't sell it. They couldn't sell it![22]

Franka began to think about what assistance the organizations to which she belonged might offer countries facing these kinds of trade problems. "We knew that Tanzania wasn't able to sell any coffee," she said, "so we thought, 'We could sell it here.' Sri Lanka could only sell loose tea in a large quantity for a low price, and we thought, 'We should somehow buy coffee made into tea bags there.' We thought we would try to get the churches that were involved in Ten Days to do this." Unfortunately, none of the organizations she approached were ready to undertake the venture. Franka related: "So we talked to Ten Days and then to the United Church and to Oxfam,[23] and none of them said, 'We can do that.' You know, Ten Days said, 'We can't do that. We're an educational organization. We can't do this; it's just too . . . We're not a business. We can't do that.'"

Franka and Matthew refused to drop the project: "We decided *we* would do it." With the help of a two activist friends, in 1981 Franka and her partner started Bridgehead Trading. "We were able to use this small amount of money really to help us," she explained, "and we lived very, very simply. And we did it." They would buy instant coffee from Tanzania's factory at a fair price and then sell it around Toronto, particularly in churches. They also developed relationships with coffee producers in Nicaragua and began to import, roast, and distribute their coffee.

In this process Franka found herself challenged to do new things. She recalled: "Our books had to be done and audited. I did something that I had never done before. I had never even taken math—higher math—in high school or any math in university. But I had no trouble doing the books for Bridgehead, and I really enjoyed it." She laughed as she talked about having fun going over the numbers. It was also during the time she created Bridgehead that Clearwater United Church asked her to become its pastor and she accepted, a position she held until she retired in 2000, though she continues to volunteer in the church.

Bridgehead's fair trading model became a success. After Franka and her group had proven it could work, other organizations were willing to take it over and to make it into a bigger project. In 1984 Franka and her business partners were happy to turn Bridgehead over to Oxfam Canada, which then incorporated the business into an official nonprofit organization.[24]

Franka has remained very active on issues of global poverty and development. She also continues to attend public demonstrations, particularly those against the wars in the Middle East, with her current partner, Sophie, and the rest of the Clearwater congregation. Her participation in the founding of Bridgehead and her early work in the fair trade movement in North America continue to be among the highlights of her life.[25] Franka said, "That was the most exciting, risky, wonderful social activism that I've done!"

Bridgehead is a concrete political articulation of the cosmology of relationship that my participants espouse. Franka met individual people who were facing economic difficulties and understood herself to be in relationship with them. She wanted to help. Her help, then, came not as charity but in a balanced exchange of money for goods, an exchange between equals in a globalized community. She engineered this exchange by building on her existing networks, namely United Church congregations and ecumenical relief organizations.

Franka's understanding of herself in relationship with coffee producers in Tanzania, and later Nicaragua, motivated her action, which took the form of insisting to people who were in relationship to her—that is, friends, fellow United Church members, and colleagues—that they, too, were already in relationship to these people who needed help. She defines sin as "breaking connections," something she attributes to "hierarchy and patriarchy." She conceived the inequality between Canadian people and people in newly postcolonial countries to be something that could be rectified by righting relationships between individuals through economic justice, that is, through a fair exchange of money and goods. This system was something that was not possible on the level of nations, but it became possible when envisioned on the scale of relationships between individuals and between communities.

Franka's experience and leadership in developing a viable fair trade organization have inspired participation in new movements around economic justice among Clearwater congregants. During my fieldwork Christine became involved in a project to sell fair trade olive oil through the Toronto-based organization Zatoun to raise money for Palestinian farmers and used the announcement time provided in the worship service to encourage members to purchase it through her.[26] When someone remarked that the olive oil seemed expensive, Marjorie retorted, "That is the price of justice!" "That's right," said Christine, and many people nodded emphatically. Later Yarrow Collective members began offering this oil for sale as well and discussed the project over their Listserv. The worldview of relationship, on which Franka centered her Bridgehead project, continues to influence the ways members of her congregation, and members of Toronto's spiritual activist communities more broadly, conceive of economic fairness and global justice.

Care Ethics and Social Justice

As Franka's story demonstrates, envisioning connection between self, community, and world places the individual in an important position, both in coming to political self-consciousness and in affecting those around her. Franka said: "I think you can't be unpolitical. I think it's impossible to be. If you're not active, then you're actively for whatever the majority is for. I mean, if you don't make a stand, then you're just letting whatever is be. In other words, you're for the status quo. So, if you aren't active, then you *are* being active—you're being active for the status quo, of course [*laughs*]. . . . I don't think you can *not* be political. Feminists say the personal is political. So all of life is political." This perspective not only challenges the division of the world into separate spheres, as discussed in the previous chapter, but it also makes individual awareness, along with mental and emotional health, important components of work for social change.

The concern for self-care embedded in this cosmology of relationship is shared with feminist care ethics. Feminist care ethics burgeoned in the 1980s as a response to justice reasoning, especially as articulated by John Rawls.[27] Nel Noddings and Carol Gilligan are credited as founders of the field. While they come to ethical concerns from different disciplines, Noddings from philosophy and Gilligan from psychology, both attempt to elaborate uniquely female ethical systems that can stand in opposition to the inequities they understand to be inherent in justice reasoning.

Noddings argues that women are predisposed to have concern for immediate and concrete others, actual people one knows. She articulates an ethical system based on the mother-child relationship, which for her is the primary relationship that all people experience. She argues that women both do and should approach moral quandaries from the position of "one-caring," that is, as a caregiver. Because of her emphasis on only immediate, personal relationships, she argues that moral agents are only obligated to help those closest to them.[28] Solving global problems is untenable within her system.[29]

Gilligan, in response to Lawrence Kohlberg's theory of moral development, which privileged boys over girls and men over women, offers a theory in which justice reasoning and care reasoning are two incompatible moral orientations.[30] While individuals may alternate between these orientations when assessing moral quandaries, she claims that men are much more strongly disposed toward justice reasoning, whereas about half of women are disposed toward justice reasoning and half toward care reasoning. The distinction for her is that justice reasoning is concerned with sets of universal rules or laws for given situations, whereas care reasoning is concerned with the maintenance of personal relationships and meeting the needs of concrete individuals in specific situations.[31] She argues that women are more likely than men to want more information about the individual people involved in a moral conflict and that the social circumstances and emotional responses of these people are important to women in reasoning moral solutions to problems.[32]

Within these systems of care ethics, care of the moral agent's self is a requisite factor in solving ethical dilemmas. Noddings argues that the self must be taken into consideration when one is assessing the needs of individuals in a particular situation. Writing of her one-caring, Noddings says: "She needs no special justification to care for herself for, if she is not supported and cared for, she may be entirely lost as one-caring. If caring is to be maintained, clearly, the one-caring must be maintained. She must be strong, courageous, and capable of joy."[33]

Gilligan also emphasizes the importance of self-care within a care ethics system. Of the development of moral reasoning she writes, "Concern for the self re-emerges to guide a new understanding of relationship as a dynamic process of interaction rather than a bond of mutual dependence. This reassessment centers on a new and more active understanding of care that includes both self and other in the realization of their interdependence."[34] The prioritizing of self-care stands in contrast to ethical systems of justice, such as the Rawlsian "veil of ignorance," in which it is necessary for the moral agent to ignore her own attributes and interests.[35]

I am persuaded by much of the engaged criticism of care ethics in this original form from within feminist communities that an ethics of care alone is untenable for a variety of reasons.[36] Just as traditional justice reasoning brackets off specific areas of moral inquiry, such a care ethics restricts moral reasoning to one's immediate circles.[37] As feminist philosopher Amy Mullin explains the quandary, a viable ethical system based on caregiving must "challenge assumptions that self-sacrifice should be the norm without going to the opposite extreme of concluding that acts of unreciprocated care are unhealthy."[38] Moreover, the assessment of needs on which this kind of care ethics is based suffers from the limited perspective of the moral agent, in this case the caregiver.[39] This limitation reinforces the chauvinism of a dominating, white-normative feminism—one that has been profoundly critiqued by those it excludes.[40] As Mullin argues, it is equally unsafe to assume either that the interests of caregivers and care receivers (in her formulation mothers and children) will be continually at odds with one another or that they will always line up conveniently.[41]

Care ethics in these original forms replaces the blind objectivity of justice ethics with a crowded subjectivity. If with justice reasoning we cannot see the individual trees, with care reasoning alone we cannot see the forest. Either of these positions leaves us stranded, with very limited and specific perspectives. Moreover, an ethics of care relies on an ability to assess the validity and urgency of the needs of those involved in the moral quandary. Without an idea of fairness or equity, how is one to make a correct assessment? As Virginia Held writes, "We can agree that caring relationships need a floor of justice."[42]

I am also concerned that care ethics has the potential to replicate traditional practices of gendering moral responsibility, not unlike the first-wave Victorian activists who were out to mother the world in order to make up for the problems caused by the male-dominated state. The fair trade movement can serve as an example. Reading morals back into the market may create especially urgent problems for women, as they are traditionally tasked both with responsibility for household purchasing, understood as a form of care, and with the moral purity of those in the home, also conceived as care.[43] If these responsibilities are seen as conflicting—that is, if maintaining the home and its ideal abundance through consumer purchases is seen to be in conflict with maintaining moral purity through ethical consumption choices—it creates a moral bind. This hazard combines with political concerns that focusing too much on household success and comfort distracts from care about others outside the home and breeds complacency, concerns that Omri

Elisha has articulated as "the spiritual injuries of class."[44] These moral failings, not only their own but those of their intimates, are laid at women's feet.

If one takes the critiques of both justice ethics and traditional care ethics seriously, it becomes clear that neither alone is sufficient. Some care ethicists insist that the two perspectives are mutually exclusive, as two entirely different ways of assessing the same situation, and that while individuals may shift from one perspective to another when prompted, they cannot hold both simultaneously.[45] However, there are ethical systems that do attempt to meld the fairness and equity of justice theory with traditional care ethics' attention to differences in personal situation and sensitivity to social context.

Later work in care ethics disrupts the assumption that genuine concern can only be expressed for concrete others.[46] Ethicists theorize ways that care may be pushed beyond immediate interactions, extended to political and social programs, and considered as a global responsibility.[47] Feminist intersectionality theory, developed by Kimberlé Crenshaw, Patricia Hill Collins, and others, builds on the idea of basing justice on individual circumstances and social positionality, including factors such as gender, race, sexual orientation, and class, but presents the resulting ethical demands in less gender-essentializing ways.[48] Further, my participants articulate an ethical worldview that reflects these more recent shifts to incorporate values of both care and justice. Following their usage, I am calling this ethical system "social justice."[49]

In her study of anti-colonial movements in Victorian Britain, Leela Gandhi describes the power of "affective communities," that is, groups of people who make conscious decisions to care about each other, to be friends. Drawing on Jacques Derrida's "politics of friendship,"[50] Gandhi highlights ways in which identification with cultural "others" resisted the colonial constructions of identity predicated upon insurmountable differences between people. Gandhi roots social change in "that critical conjuncture when some of the selves who make up a culture loosen themselves from the security and comfort of old affiliations and identifications to make an unexpected 'gesture' of friendship to those on the other side of the fence."[51] My participants' social justice ethics have much in common with the utopian socialism of Gandhi's late Victorians.

In social justice ethics my participants take the ethics of care and apply it beyond gender and home to other global concerns such as economic development and exploitation, class, race and ethnicity, religion, the status of Indigenous people, and environmental preservation. They express an attitude that it is important to ask others what they need first, not assume the privileged position of condescending caretaker. This approach is a conscious effort to mitigate the dynamics of power inherent in their "positions of privilege" via others who are "suffering oppression,"[52] an attitude that manifests in projects such as fair trade, global education, and grassroots organizing. My participants operate an ethics of care from a cared-for perspective, reminiscent of Peruvian liberation theologian Gustavo Gutiérrez and his articulation of a "preferential option for the poor."[53] This approach becomes especially significant in the context of historical North American reform movements in general, but particularly those of Canada, such as residential schools and the moral reform movements of "Toronto the Good" in the Victorian era.[54]

How successful is a social justice strategy in mitigating privilege and connecting with those whom my participants would wish to help? The least successful project along this line was Yarrow's desire to find an immigrant community within Toronto with whom they could be in active solidarity, that is, ally themselves politically and provide support through resource sharing. The project was modeled on the relationship of Starhawk's Reclaiming Witchcraft collective with the Salvadoran community in San Francisco. Betty brought the idea to the Yarrow Collective in a group "visioning" meeting, and people seemed excited about it, particularly as a way to negotiate and mitigate the predominantly white character of the group.[55]

In the Reclaiming tradition of which many Yarrow members are a part, there is a distinction between different kinds of power. This idea comes from Starhawk's formulation in her book *Truth or Dare*, in which she distinguishes between "power over," "power with," and "power from within"—or put another way, coercive authority, community strength, and inner strength rooted in the living world.[56] The Yarrow solidarity project was envisioned as engaging a power-with model.

However, the solidarity project did not go past the stage of initial excitement. Conflicts arose between members over perceived racism and cultural appropriation within the group related to Heidi's channeling of African spirits, as described in chapter 1. Even before the conflict, Betty had expressed concern that the Yarrow Collective was too white and therefore potentially less sensitive about issues of racism than it should be. The solidarity project was proposed by her as part of a plan to change that. The new conflict around cultural appropriation led Yarrow members to decide that they should clean their own house before they invited others into it—that they should engage in antioppression training together to address these issues before they sought out coalition with an immigrant community.

Clearwater chose a different path in dealing with issues of privilege and oppression. At the time I began fieldwork with the congregation, its members were at the end of a two-year sponsorship of an Iranian immigrant family to Canada. The family did not attend services, but members of the church who were on the support committee reported on their needs and progress and what they needed from the congregation as well as what Immigration Canada required from the church to complete the sponsorship process. This option allowed the family members themselves to determine the levels of interaction they desired with the church, within the structure of required interaction set out by Canadian immigration law. Clearwater used the unique privilege it receives both as a Canadian institution and a Christian church to redirect resources to those who do not have such privilege, in this case a Muslim family desiring to immigrate to Canada. This is well in keeping with an explicit project on the part of the Clearwater congregation to use social privilege in favor of oppressed and disadvantaged people, the metonym for which was the sale of its church building in the 1980s and donation of the proceeds to charity.

The social privilege Clearwater draws on is also the result of a long history of government lobbying by the larger United Church body and other Christian churches. Clearwater is able to spend social capital afforded to Christian institutions in Canada, even though it, as a congregation, does not endorse such privileging. In contrast, Yarrow and the

Toronto Catholic Worker, as religious communities without stable positions in officially recognized Christian churches, do not have this kind of clout.

The Catholic Worker community combines approaches, working in active coalition with Aboriginal Canadian groups, welcoming international students and visitors, and supporting refugees and helping them file claims with the Canadian government. Through both formal and informal networks, Catholic Worker members try to provide support and assistance to diverse groups and individuals who ask for it. Built into the quotidian activities of the Worker community is redirection of resources gained through social privilege into the mitigation of oppressions caused by the same system, that is, North American society.

Agency and Privilege

Social justice ethics must account not only for relationships between ethical subjects but also for relationships between agents and systems of power. Feminist ethnographers Marla Frederick, R. Marie Griffith, and Saba Mahmood trouble the easy binary of accommodation-resistance to which scholars and activists commonly turn in describing such relationships.[57] They each argue that, in the cases of the women with whom they worked,[58] labeling particular actions as exclusively subversive or supportive of structural power reduces complex social interactions beyond recognition, forcing them into an imposed dichotomy. Mahmood, for example, uses Michel Foucault's model of "subjectivation," in which "the very processes and conditions that secure a subject's subordination are also the means through which she becomes a self-conscious entity and agent."[59] Mahmood combines this analysis of power, in which it constructs the very subjects who resist and accommodate it, with Aristotelian ethics to explore alternatives to Western, liberal, feminist understandings of agency and freedom. In particular, she wants to disrupt models that find ethical subjects exclusively in moments of resistance to cultural norms and open the investigation to include ways in which women embrace and strive to embody such norms.

Public protests provide an opportunity to think through activists' multilayered interactions with authority. The public demonstrations in which religiously motivated activists take part presuppose the inevitability of state power. What is more, in order for religious terms, symbols, and rituals to be persuasive forms of protest, the state and other citizens must desire to be in line with them. Others must share religious values and prioritize them as important. My participants do not endorse a government built on Christianity, explicitly or otherwise. Indeed, one of the greatest challenges for them is how to draw on religious privilege in such a way that it does not perpetuate the hierarchies upon which that privilege is based.

As Frederick has written in the context of African American women's activism, "To protest, to get involved, to speak out, to run for public office, each involves a certain level of risk."[60] Social hierarchies of privilege and oppression mediate these risks. This is well demonstrated by Ruth Frankenberg when she argues that race defines possibilities and boundaries in white women's lives as well as the lives of women of color but that those limits take different forms and carry different costs.[61]

For example, Jenna, a Catholic activist, was forced to confront her own assumptions about her right to safety through interactions with an activist colleague from Colombia, Kimy Pernía Domicó. Leader of the Indigenous Embera Katío people, Domicó came to Canada in 1999 to speak before Parliament against a dam project that threatened his people's homes, farmland, and burial grounds. A few months after attending the Quebec City protests to speak on behalf of his people at the Summit of the Americas, he was forcibly disappeared on June 2, 2001. His murder was confirmed by a right-wing paramilitary leader in late 2006.[62] Jenna recounted her experience with him at the protests:

There was a fellow named Kimy Pernía Domicó, who is from Colombia, and you may know that soon after he was there he was kidnapped in Columbia. So shortly before that he was here, and . . . soon after, in June, he was disappeared. And I remember he was with us for part of the day, and we had dinner with him, and he had gone up to the fence and was taking footage or someone had taken footage of what was happening up at the fence, and he looked at it and said, "My God, my people will never believe this is happening to white people!" So it was just such an interesting comment that made me go, "Wow." You know? And yet to feel that as a white person you should be safe when there's just so much violence and oppression in the system, why would you think that you would be able to be safe from that?[63]

Jenna's experience of sharing surprise with an Indigenous Colombian man at the violence with which white Canadian protesters were met threw into relief her assumptions that some people—white North American people—should be safe from violence and that violence was something that happened to poor people of color. Having these assumptions made explicit, she realized the injustice inherent in them.

Of course, the terrorist attacks of September 11 followed and ushered in new sets of assumptions about safety and vulnerability, what Judith Butler has called "the dislocation from First World privilege."[64] This has involved both concern about real and potential violence caused by Others, foreign Muslims, and real violence perpetuated by Canadian, American, and European law enforcement agencies against their own citizens. Such state violence is justified as a rational, measured, and necessary response to, or even a means of preventing, the terrifyingly irrational violence of others.[65] In this way a deeply violent secular state erases its own violence and ascribes it to Others.

As political activists, many of my participants are forced to confront advantages as well as disadvantages that come with different facets of their identities, be it white privilege or other preferential treatment based on presumed socioeconomic class, gender, or religion. Because they may afford their bearers social privilege, some of these identities provide opportunities for intervention in structures of oppression. This may take the form of morally embarrassing perpetrators of injustices, as in the popular crowd chant "Shame! Shame!" in direct response to aggressive police actions. It may also take the form of providing public witness to violations, informing police that activists see what they are doing, with the implication that authorities and the media will care what they think, regardless of the same institutions' potential dismissal of others.

Laura spoke about her feelings marching with Clearwater members under the church banner. At times she feels sheepish about being publicly active with her church, and it is something she joked about having to "come out of the closet" about to fellow activists in other contexts. Despite her misgivings about being publicly associated with the church, as her story illustrates, she feels that the public perception afforded by the church can help others:

> We went to one of the earliest Peace Day marches, when they were still talking about possible war with Iraq, and then afterward we joined up with an OCAP march that was a very small group of people who were taking over some housing, some abandoned housing, and we joined them.[66] And that was interesting because it was a very small group, and the police were just brutal! There were so many of them and horses, and they were just brutal and dragging some of the people off. And it was interesting there to be under the banner because a lot of onlookers came up and said, "What's the church doing here?!" So I like to think, I'm not sure if it's true though, but I like to think it had some influence on the police because they were really, I mean, you couldn't even stand on the sidewalk, for heaven's sake! It was really ridiculous. And a number of us spoke out, and they backed off a bit. And there was one incident where a kid, or a man actually, crossed the street and kind of got dragged off, and we were quite vociferous, and that was the last dragging off, and so in that case it probably is good [to be there representing the church]. Yeah, as a witness and a voice.[67]

For Laura the church presence influenced police to behave less violently toward other activists. Further, she believes that marching under the banner forced onlookers to reassess the protest and consider its messages more carefully.

Angel understands identity-based intervention in a different way. For her it would be wrong to use her privilege precisely because she would be exercising power to which other people do not have access. She explained:

> I try to limit myself in terms of the kinds of compromises I'm willing to make because I look at the state and I don't believe that the federal government can actually fix what's there. I think that the whole construction is just problematic, and so I think it would be a compromise to, you know, run for office in the federal government. So I do place a lot of limits on the compromises I'm willing to make. Like I'm not willing to negotiate with the police. *Ever.* And that's mostly where

I place my limitations, listening to the radical voices and determining, "Okay, if I do this, it's just playing my privilege card." Because there are a lot of people who don't necessarily have the same choices I have. If I go and chitchat with the police and sort of flirt with them, like I can do that because I'm a cute white girl whose parents are both employed and any [government] record will pull that up. So that makes a big difference because I know a lot of people who can't make those choices.[68]

Taking advantage of the preferential treatment she may receive based on her identity is unacceptable to Angel, even if she uses it for the benefit of others, such as negotiating with the police in protest situations. She is deeply suspicious of any benefits she may gain through her position as a young, white, (apparently) middle-class woman because they are based in a corrupt and unfair system.

The same identities that may positively influence police may lead to the dismissal of activists' messages. Lavender complained, for example, that police did not take the Quebec City Women's Protest seriously because it was a women-only demonstration.[69] Women may also face targeting and harassment *as women*, such as sexual harassment of topless women in anti-war marches. Furthermore, even though some of these racial, classed, and gendered identities may translate into more comfortable, or at least respectful, treatment by police in protest situations, it cannot be depended upon with any certainty. The massive teargassing of Quebec City, indiscriminant in terms not only of protesters' identities and affiliations but also of involvement with the protests at all (entire residential neighborhoods suffered from the gas), testifies to the arbitrary nature of identity-based social privileges in protest environments.

Some activists, like Laura, try to share the social privilege they gain through their identities and church affiliations with other activists who have a less protected status. Others, like Angel, try to distance themselves from such advantages in order to minimize their complicity in systems of power. Both strategies involve complex negotiations with state authority and social privilege and take into account hierarchies of race, class, gender, and religion within an implicitly Christian culture.

The Yarrow Collective offers a different instance of negotiating systems of power. Despite similar understandings of magical energies at work in occult and ceremonial magic traditions, such as the Rosicrucians, the Freemasons, the Order of the Golden Dawn, Aleister Crowley's Ordo Templi Orientalis, and esoteric Satanism,[70] my contemporary Pagan participants distance themselves from Crowley and Satanism, for obvious reasons. At a Yarrow reading group meeting near Halloween that took place at the home of Heidi, the woman who channeled spirits, the presence of her cats prompted the group to rehash the urban legend that Satanists kill cats at Halloween.[71] Heidi and River took the main roles in the conversation, but the group seemed to agree that this story was something everyone knew to be true. They pointed out that it was too bad that the Humane Society would not adopt out cats near the end of October because of this threat but that it was a good precaution to take.

The "fact" that Satanists kill cats on Halloween as part of their rituals is a myth, a story also told about Wiccans and other contemporary Pagans by conservative Christians.[72] By perpetuating this story, the contemporary Pagan reading group members participate in the "othering" discourse at its heart:[73] "We are good people, but there really are bad people who do despicable things on Halloween, and we must protect children and animals from them—it's just not us who do these things." This story serves to center these women within the local community and to distance them and their magic from "Satanists" and *their* magic, magic that is portrayed as harmful and sadistic.[74] To overextend Gayatri Spivak,[75] "White witches are saving black cats from black witches." Reworking and re-centering these rumors does not challenge the systems of power underlying them but does place these women in a different relationship to them.

The fair trade movement, endorsed by participants from all three groups, affords further insight into ways that activists' resistance is shaped by the very forces it seeks to counter. Fair trade contrasts itself with free market capitalism. Based on the idea that free trade privileges Western corporations and exploits workers in developing countries, fair trade resists this exploitation by paying producers mutually agreed amounts for goods, amounts that exceed "market price," the lowest price desperate producers can be forced to accept. Consumers who buy fair trade products withhold money from nonparticipating companies and redirect it to companies that trade fairly. Yet this resistance takes place within the framework of global capitalism. Voting with dollars accommodates a worldview in which dollars matter. Rather than opting out of the whole system, fair trade suppliers, distributors, and consumers work within it to limit its negative effects.

The philosophy behind fair trade further reveals aspects of self-discipline inherent in activist worlds. Consumers deliberately pay more than they must for goods. This practice was highlighted by the exchange between Marjorie and the Clearwater member who complained that Christine's fair trade olive oil seemed expensive. Marjorie's reply, "That is the price of justice!" communicates that acting ethically costs the agent something. This is similar to attitudes toward tithing that Frederick found among her participants: it is sometimes painful to give money to the church when one has little, but reciprocity with God requires the return of his financial blessings.[76] Both of these acts, tithing and buying fairly traded goods, call into question values underlying broader consumer culture.

Mahmood takes up disciplines of the self, arguing that within the conservative mosque movement, women train themselves to desire pious behavior, such as praying regularly or behaving modestly. Her respondents do not "assume that the desire to pray is natural, but that it *must be created* through a set of disciplinary acts"; following the Aristotelian tradition of moral agency, "desire in this model is not the *antecedent* to, or cause of, moral action, but its *product*."[77] In this approach one does the right thing not because one desires it but because it is right. While desire and rightness may diverge in the beginning, over time the repetition of the act becomes habit, and the habituation produces a desire for the act that was not in one's heart before.

While my participants for the most part do not articulate such a worldview, there are certain aspects of their activism that they describe in similar terms. Training oneself into proper action is an aspect of Clearwater's Amnesty International letter writing events. Annie and Marjorie found it difficult to make themselves write their letters. Trying to write alone, they felt overwhelmed by the awfulness, by their lack of power to prevent the human rights abuses the letters denounced. Yet they felt that writing the letters was important. To solve their problem, they created a monthly drop-in so that everyone in Clearwater and their neighboring congregations could receive social support while writing.[78] In doing so, however, they also created an environment in which they receive social *pressure* to write their letters. They now have social obligations to others for which they are held accountable. As far as Annie is concerned, the good that comes of writing Amnesty International letters is more important than her aversion to it.[79] She created a situation in which she forces herself to act ethically.

Cross-Cultural Energies

Because an ethical agent's relationships with others are the basis of the system, within a social justice cosmology, as in feminist care ethics, self-care becomes an important element of activist work. This valuing of personal well-being as contributing to global well-being places the Toronto Catholic Worker, the Yarrow Collective, and Clearwater in historical line with spiritual and therapeutic trends in North America. Such movements incorporate personal energies as powerful tools for change within individuals and in the external world, and as renewable resources, with proper care. Self-help or recovery movements are just the latest manifestations of these self-healing trends in North American culture and religiosity, what historian Jackson Lears calls the "therapeutic worldview."[80] This concern with the self contrasts with understandings of human agency and energy within many secular activist communities, which incorporate cultural trends that disparage self-care as self-indulgence.

These various therapeutic understandings of power, influence, and energies add up to a long tradition in North American religiosity of belief in the power of spiritual energy.[81] Lears pinpoints a shift at the turn of the twentieth century from therapies based on ideas of "psychic scarcity," that is, depleted mental energies, to therapies based on ideas of "psychic abundance," a shift that he argues is linked to changes in economics and class interests. Contemporary self-help movements draw on ideas of hidden stores of strength and power inside each individual that, when properly accessed, can heal emotional wounds and bring happiness and contentment.[82] Andrew Reiser writes of movements based on theories of mind over matter that "some of these movements coexisted peaceably with traditional religious practices; others, pushing beyond the limits of orthodoxy, found new homes in Theosophy, mind cure, Spiritualism, and Christian Science; still others made a religion out of consumerism, seeking transcendence in the new world of material abundance."[83] Beryl Satter emphasizes that new strategies for physical and emotional health through spiritual means were taken up by large numbers of women. In fact, "they were first understood as the components of a new 'woman's religion."[84] The therapeutic worldviews at the heart of these movements are based on the idea that there is a relationship between the internal world of the individual and the external world.

Belief in spiritual and mental powers can be found across religious boundaries. Lears discusses the Victorian notion of "influence," which he calls "a primitive theory of psychological manipulation."[85] One articulation of the belief in influence is "mesmerism," also known as "electro-biology" or "animal magnetism."[86] Contemporary language of spiritual "energy" can be traced in large part to mesmerism. Alex Owen writes of healing within British mesmerism, "A belief in the ability to transfer either thoughts or physical sensation was relevant for a healing practice which relied upon the concept of a transfer of energy." Such healing involved the exchange of "positive energy for another's depleted vitality."[87]

Promoted in North America in the form of mesmerism, "influence" found its way into more specifically religious expressions, such as New Thought, Christian Science, Spiritualism, and evangelical Christianity.[88] Ann Braude explores how closely tied popular understandings of electricity and spiritual power were in mid-nineteenth-century North America, the time when many of these religions, which embrace notions of spiritual energies, developed.[89] Pamela Klassen discusses the popularization of similar technological concepts, such as "radio-mind," among liberal Protestants.[90] And Lears writes, "Under the aegis of the Protestant cure of souls, influence was enlisted as part of a program of holistic regeneration, melding body and mind, transforming mesmerism into a force for good."[91] Spiritual influence in these religions took on a positive role.[92] Notions of spiritual energies as healing have cycled back into the wider culture through New Thought into psychology and self-help.[93] When critics complain that they sense religious influence in Twelve-Step programs, it is likely these histories of ongoing and diverse religious engagement underlying the explicit injunction of submission to a higher power that concern them.[94]

Beyond historical trajectories of European influence, my participants also interact with understandings of spiritual power drawn from other cultures. Supernatural and religious understandings based in transplanted African traditions are one such example. Yvonne Chireau argues persuasively for the shared nature of supernatural beliefs among both African Americans and Anglo Americans during settlement through the present.[95] Jacqui Alexander describes the transfer of African ideas of the sacred to the Caribbean and on to North and South America.[96] Especially in Toronto, where there are significant Caribbean spiritual communities, such as Ifa and Spiritual Baptist churches,[97] the influence of traditional African, Caribbean, and African Canadian spiritualities is important in understandings of the sacred and the supernatural.

Beyond indirect cultural influence of African spiritual traditions on my participants, there are also direct links within their groups to such traditions. Members of Clearwater's host church have ties to the Caribbean, and in addition to Franka's work there, Marjorie also spent time in South Africa. Catholic Worker hosts immigrants and students directly from Africa. And in Yarrow the connection is split between the two women at the center of the conflict about spirit possession. Betty has a close friend who is a priestess in Ifa, and Betty's partner is also Caribbean Canadian. Heidi received her calling to spiritual healing and mediumship in South Africa.

Native American and Aboriginal / First Nations Canadian spiritualities also impact spiritual self-understandings,[98] especially among the Clearwater congregation, in which they are explicitly invoked. When Franka was pastor, for example, her interest in both process theology and community engagement encouraged her to learn about other religious traditions and theologies of immanence. This was motivated in part because the congregation's commitment to feminism and nonhierarchical structures forced them to discard many hymns and rewrite traditional liturgy.[99] She said: "We were very thin liturgically for awhile, until we built up the hymns we found. And then when *Voices United* came out, a lot of the hymns that we had been using were included and so forth. I wrote some, just a little bit, of the things that were used for liturgical responses."[100]

In this search for alternatives to traditional theology and liturgy, the congregation began to experiment with elements from other traditions. Some members became very interested in Buddhist meditation, while others interacted with Aboriginal Canadian communities. Franka recounted a talk by an elder in the early 1980s about his struggles with alcoholism: "He said that when he really wanted to drink, he would hold onto a tree root, and the tree would help him, or he'd put his hands in a stream, and the stream would strengthen him. While he was in the city, he would hold onto a rock instead, and the rock would strengthen him. That became a time really powerful to me, realizing the presence of the Spirit in all of creation."[101] The elder's articulation of connection to the earth, the immanence of deity in creation, moved Franka deeply and helped her verbalize her personal theology in a new way.

Franka heard this Native elder's story at a time when the long and painfully mixed history of relationships between the United Church and Aboriginal communities in Canada was becoming increasingly prominent. Like the Catholic and Anglican Churches, the United Church and its Methodist and Presbyterian precursors participated in the federal residential schools program, under the auspices of which children were removed from Aboriginal communities and placed in church-run boarding schools.[102] Along with creating environments in which vulnerable children were abused and even killed, the residential school system in Canada actively worked to disrupt traditional forms of life by refusing to teach children about their heritage, forcing them to abandon their languages, and actively working toward the assimilation of Aboriginal children into Anglo Canadian society.[103]

The United Church formally apologized to Aboriginal Canadians for its role in the catastrophe, while class action lawsuits continued to be slowly resolved through Canadian courts.[104] The United Church has also embarked on programs of "repentance and reconciliation," including a "Healing Fund" to give grants to projects within First Nations communities.[105] During my fieldwork at Clearwater, one of the activities printed up in the bulletin and announced during the service every week was a program of study, hosted by one of the neighboring United Churches, in understanding the relationship of the United Church to Canadian Aboriginal communities and ways to work toward reconciliation.[106] This was an issue that the congregation took seriously and openly discussed.

From the perspective of Canadian First Nations people and their allies, apologies and investigations can only mean so much in the context of ongoing colonialism. Canada remains a settler nation.[107] The Idle No More movement for Aboriginal sovereignty and care for the earth, which in practical terms often means resisting corporate mining, logging, and pipeline projects, was launched in December 2012.[108] This is an ongoing protest movement that continues to negotiate issues of solidarity across lines of race and citizenship and in the face of colonial history.[109]

Conscious of colonial context, Clearwater does not arbitrarily reference ideas about spiritual energy drawn from Aboriginal Canadian and Native American cosmologies. Rather, members draw upon these ideas while attempting to acknowledge the troubled historical relationship between the church and Aboriginal communities. This is usually reflected in the ways First Nations stories contrast with contemporary Anglo Canadian values. For example, Laura read a story during service one Sunday that specifically compared Aboriginal ideas of justice, rooted in healing and community, with historical interpretations of biblical justice, which Laura understands as emphasizing systemized and equal punishment for affronts to individuals, "an eye for an eye."[110]

In the First Nations story a man who is caught stealing food from his neighbors is told by a community matriarch that he must work for the family from whom he stole; however, the family must also make amends for not noticing how hungry and desperate he and his family had become. They must continue to employ him and help him support his family after he has paid back his debt. Moreover, the elder tells the whole community that they, too, are responsible for the family's hunger, so everyone in the community, including the elder, must make up for this neglect and aid the family with blankets, clothes, and food. Laura talked about how different this story was from contemporary Anglo Canadian notions of punitive justice and how similar it was to her notion of Christianity and right relationship. A few weeks later Annie brought up this story as one in which notions of justice and right relationship are clear, as opposed to biblical Scripture, in which notions of social justice are often obscured.[111]

In their use of Native materials, Clearwater members may leave themselves open to charges of cultural misappropriation. On the one hand, such labeling does not take into account their sincere concern to be in right relationship not only with the earth but with living Aboriginal Canadians. On the other hand, the problem that many predominantly white people regard Native spirituality as a commodity to be consumed, disregard the cultural context of the ideas they take up, and do nothing to aid material conditions or rectify political oppressions of the Native groups from whom they "borrow" is not lightly dismissed. As Laura Donaldson writes in her criticism of "New Age Native Americanism," "A more responsible attitude acknowledges that spiritual growth requires life-long discipline and commitment as well as a mutual relationship with one's resource traditions."[112]

Clearwater members are very serious about doing the work necessary to become good allies to Aboriginal Canadian individuals and communities. This work both influences and is supported by their interactions with Native American spiritualities. As Pamela Klassen cautions, "The embrace of difference found in ritual proximity is not an innocent encounter, nor is it entirely hegemonic."[113] Clearwater's use of Aboriginal Canadian spiritual resources is not a clear-cut case of misuse, but it can also never be free of histories of exploitation and systemic inequality. Instead, Clearwater's religious borrowing reflects complicated relationships between contemporary communities.

Discussions of value, or lack thereof, in religious participation must include an exploration of the notion of metaphysical forces or, in the language of many of my participants, energy. Through their understandings of spiritual energy as active in physical and psychological worlds, they place themselves in context with a long history of Western religious and folk traditions. My participants supplement these understandings with material drawn from other cultures, such as Canadian Aboriginal and Native American traditions.

Taking Care of Yourself Is Radical

Belief in connection between the interiority of individuals and their exterior environments pairs with an understanding of personal well-being as crucial to effective action in the world, political as well as metaphysical. As agents of change, which requires personal energy, my participants understand their health and well-being, both physical and psychological, to be crucial to their political work. Lavender, a contemporary Pagan, said: "You know, the personal is political is spiritual is economic. You can't separate anything. It's all one."[114] This belief is also reflected in ritual.

Religiously motivated activists refuse to accept a split between individual and community as obvious, natural, or necessary. In their views the interconnection between the individual, community, and world drives political engagement but not self-sacrifice, as the health of the individual is a crucial component of large-scale change. River explained: "To me the personal and political are interchangeable, and this is partly feminism and partly Reclaiming. They talk about three legs of the cauldron, which are political work, inner healing, and personal practice. And to me it all goes together."[115] Like River and fellow Yarrow members, United Church and Catholic participants expressed the feminist axiom "the personal is political" but did so within the context of their religious motivation for activism.[116]

My participants articulate religious worldviews in which they may not see change in their lifetimes but are compelled to work toward it as best they can nonetheless. In the words of Clearwater member Annie, "You are part of a community that is doing the work."[117] Within this view world problems are not going to be solved right away. Deborah spoke to this aching uncertainty instead of the triumphalism of revolutionary eschatology:

You know, I'm not always sure that I'm ever going to change things. And I guess this is the big connection between political activism and religion or spirituality, that it's the hope, it's the feeling that no matter what you might think on any one day, despair is out. . . . So depending on what you look at, you can be very hopeful or say, you know, really, we're not making much difference, but you have to hope. And that's where spirituality nourishes my activism. That above all, being reminded on at least a weekly basis of what things are important after all. And that message of hope.[118]

Rather than an ideal of political purity and martyrdom, the religiously motivated social justice activists with whom I spoke understand humans as fallible and damaged, simply doing what they are able. Within this view all anyone can ask of you is to do the best you can; taking care of yourself is part of the job.

If activists don't stay healthy, then it just means more people burn out and leave activist work. From this perspective it can be argued that *not* taking care of yourself, not working on personal problems, is selfish. River talked about the importance not only of food or rest but of ritual for sustaining activist work: "It's what you bring to your spiritual practice and that you can send energy out and that energy has an effect. And at another level people can participate in it, and the community can support what people are doing. And to me, if you're going to be in this for the long haul, and not just as a college, university, whatever, thing, you've got to have something that gives you an anchor, and spirituality gives me an anchor."[119] This ethic of self-care also manifests in other ways, such as activists declaring some time off from political work. At the time of our interview, River was in the middle of a self-declared "activist sabbatical."

It is here we can examine some of the sliding between self-care and world change that critics of such cosmologies repudiate. Wendy Kaminer has criticized the focus on individual improvement perpetuated by therapeutic self-help as disempowering and as a distraction from systemic oppressions in North American culture. Of "co-dependency," depression, lack of self-esteem, and abusive relationships, she writes, "Problems like these are political as well as personal; they require collective as well as individual action and objectivity as well as introspection." Kaminer is concerned that self-help movements, the Twelve-Step movement in particular, channel women's justified dissatisfaction with their personal situations into self-pity, rather than political action. Comparing them to consciousness-raising groups of second-wave feminism, Kaminer sees Twelve-Step support groups as lacking any political dimension, thus encouraging people to work on the self *instead* of the world.[120]

Sociologist Verta Taylor disagrees with Kaminer's assessment of self-help as purely self-indulgent and disempowering.[121] She urges suspicion of popular critiques of self-help, arguing that self-help is often the object of discomfort and disrespect precisely because it is a "female enterprise" that calls into question dominant discourses on gender. She writes, "Not only do self-help participants empower themselves, but they also challenge the gender code embedded in medical, legal, and mental health institutions." She also makes the point that in the very act of seeking and joining a support group, women prove that they do not view their problems as purely personal. Women's self-help engages in the fundamentally feminist project of disrupting traditional ideas of public and private.[122]

Including self-care in the realm of activism may indeed lend political significance to minor personal actions, as critics warn. One of my participants who could be understood to fit this description is Nora, a contemporary Pagan. When we spoke, Nora had not been to a political demonstration in a long time because she feels that street protests do not effectively communicate with those on the other side of issues and that they perpetuate bad energy. At the end of our interview, she talked a bit about this:

There's something about the energy of protests that doesn't fit right with me. Not all protests, some protests. I think that when we move, there is a place for sacred outrage, a sense of sacred indignation about the mistreatment of other human beings. There is a very fine line between that and just falling, I think, which I see a lot in people, falling into their own personal rage without even consciousness around it. And it's really toxic energy. It does not make a point. In fact, on an energetic level, it really undermines the political agenda of an organization or of a protest or of an activity.[123]

Despite her avoidance of overtly political engagement, Nora nevertheless considers herself to be an activist. She makes her own line of natural cosmetics, and, more significant for her, she actively works to network and bring other entrepreneurial women together as well as serve as a role model for other people through her self-confidence in everyday interactions. She described her approach:

Walk into a subway like you have a real, absolute right to be there, and it's amazing how much it twists people's energy. I know that because I used to not take up space, not feel entitled to be there, and

I was invisible. And now I'm not wearing anything particularly flashy sometimes, and people see my energy. . . . I think the best explanation would be if you met somebody who was Christian and they talked a really good talk but they didn't live it and if you met somebody who didn't necessarily say that they were anything but they were really, really, amazingly deep and lived by sort of basic spiritual precepts and they had no rhetoric, who would be more empowering to you? And who would be ultimately more political in terms of being able to change the world?[124]

She considers her current projects to be just as political as her previous participation in demonstrations. For Nora empowering herself and other women, serving as an example for others, is inherently political.

However, this perceived relationship between self and world need not mean disengagement from the world in favor of individual improvement, as Kaminer and others are concerned it must. The assumption that religious participation is the result or cause of self-centeredness and withdrawal from political engagement does not hold with my participants. Compare, for example, Nora's networking and role modeling to Franka's involvement in fair trade movement or with participants from all three groups in the Quebec City protests for global justice (as discussed in chapter 2).

Self-Care and Marxist Praxis

My participants do not unthinkingly accept the significance of spiritual energies and personal balance that are fundamental to cosmologies of relationship. There are many trends within contemporary North American culture that ridicule such worldviews as naive, even dangerously self-delusional. Such perspectives can be found in many of the activist communities with which my participants identify as well as in scholarship on activism. Addressing other academics, labor historian Lynne Marks writes, "For those on the left, the reluctance to deal with religion may simply be explained by a more materialist focus and by a personal secularism, often based in deep-seated hostility to religion (linked in come cases to troubling childhood memories of religious patriarchy, misogyny, and oppression)."[125]

There are also gendered issues at work here. Tracy Fessenden demonstrates that during the Victorian era religion itself became closely associated with the white, middle-class private sphere and, as a result, continues to be perceived in gendered terms.[126] This relegation leaves religiosity subject to androcentric suspicions of all things associated with femininity and provides a rationale within social movements to, if not openly spurn religion, then generally ignore it as irrelevant.

North American activist communities are influenced by particular strands of Marxism that dismiss religion. This process occurs directly, through reading, and indirectly, through models of political engagement and activism inherited from the New Left in the 1960s.[127] As activist Becky Thompson writes, "For activists who came of age in Communist or New Left politics, grappling with spirituality can feel like coming out of a spiritual closet."[128]

The International Socialists (is) are a Marxist group that for many of my participants exemplified stereotypes of unsustainable organizing on the Left. At the time I conducted my fieldwork, the Toronto is had a reputation among other activists as a predatory organization. Its members regularly visited other groups to try to redirect them to work on is projects. Given an email address, even for ostensibly social or specific purposes, organizers had been known to hound nonmembers with group emails. Additionally, it was not uncommon at the time for International Socialist members to express an interest in a particular issue—for example, the accessibility of abortion, the anniversary of the bombing of Hiroshima and Nagasaki, or sexual diversity education— only to bring the solution to the issue back around to their version of the struggle of the proletariat for class revolution and to highjack other groups' meetings with endless discussion of this topic. Members of the is drove themselves hard and expected equally frantic energy levels from others.

In informal discussions Catholic Worker members joked about the problems they have experienced with the International Socialists. During a Yarrow meeting I also overheard a particular Pagan group in town disparagingly referred to as "the is of Paganism" in reference to its aggressiveness in "correcting" other Pagans' ritual practices and theologies. River even said, in the context of discussing the importance of building community: "You just have to worry if the IS is it [*laughs*]. Some day someone is going to do a workshop on 'Okay, how did the IS screw up *your* movement?'"[129] Toronto activist groups such as the IS interpret Marxist theory in such a way that self-care has no place in political work, particularly not spiritual care.

Marxist theories of political action, such as those embraced by the IS, share the public and private split articulated and fostered by the Enlightenment and the industrial revolution. Such theories require and reinforce an assumed dichotomy. Like other formulations of this split, these interpretations of Marxism leave the private sphere as morally inferior to the public, in that personal needs come after those of class. Within this model human energy is not renewable in the way it is within cosmologies of psychic abundance. Moreover, such a worldview assumes that we are always and already in crisis. Not only is the problem urgent, but revolution is imminent. The self-care so necessary to my participants in their understandings of how change comes about is glossed as self-indulgent and harmfully distracting within these particular Marxist frameworks.[130] Many activists end up arguing for a conservative personal asceticism, advocating what feminist ethicist Lisa Tessman names "burdened virtues," that is, traits that may be beneficial in the larger context of political struggle but do not contribute to, or may even impede, the flourishing of those who bear them.[131]

In their involvement with transcendence, religions compete with the transcendence that such strands of Marxism promote, the proletarian revolution.[132] For example, whereas historically in Protestant Christianity the salvation of the individual soul is important, within these Marxist political theories the individual is not the focus of change, but rather the collective is.[133] We are all at the mercy of the blind trajectory of history. It is through the collective that the individual may find salvation. While such Marxist praxis presents itself as uniquely pragmatic, as opposed to the misguided naïveté of religion,[134] it nonetheless posits transcendent forces at work in the world, forces that literally rival those of religions. These types of Marxism provide their own teleological eschatology.

Distrust of individual needs and desires and concern over competing notions of transcendence gives these versions of Marxism much in common with various formulations of Christianity, particularly notions of predestination. Susan McClary writes, for example, "The political folk song is the Left's version of the Calvinist hymn: words are foregrounded to control 'the meaning,' music effaced to the status of vehicle, all untoward appeals to the body eliminated."[135] The distractions of bodily needs, personal desires, or, in McClary's case, the groove are all subordinated to political message. In making economic class the unit of historical change and agency, as opposed to the individual or the family,[136] these interpretations of Marxism can accommodate care of the self, in any form other than participation in class struggle, only in negative terms. Such self-care detracts from work for the underclass more generally but also forestalls the imminent class revolution.

The denigration of self-care within some secularly oriented activist communities does not go unnoticed by spiritually motivated activists. Most important, the emphasis on Manichaean divisions between good and bad people, predicated on divisions between proletariat and bourgeoisie, or those enlightened about the true nature of the world and those suffering from false consciousness, alienates many of my participants. Said River, a contemporary Pagan, speaking of coalition work in political projects: "Sometimes I can get along better with people who are of different faiths than I can with people who are a-spiritual. Because there doesn't necessarily seem to be a belief in that difference between the opponent and the enemy, realizing that we're all human beings at the fundamental end."[137]

Despite the contrast with certain strands of Marxist praxis at work in Toronto activist communities, it would be misleading to cast the projects of my participants as entirely at odds with Marxist cosmologies more generally. Religiously motivated social justice activists are clearly influenced by Marxist analyses, particularly those relating to the material dimensions of global justice. Nonetheless, I suggest that it is the refraction of Marxist concerns through the lenses of liberation theology and feminism that allows for the place of individual health and self-care within their worldviews, rather than the self-negating theories of political revolution espoused by groups like the International Socialists.

It is also important to note that there are circumstances in which religiously motivated activists do place themselves in harm's way, particularly within the context of public demonstrations. In Quebec City protesters against the FTAA confronted physical danger, challenging state and economic power in the name of global community. While my participants strive for balance between self-care and work for others, particular practices may fall on either side of the divide.

Ritual of Relationship

I would like to close this exploration of social justice with a final example of work born of a cosmology of connection. Three members of the Yarrow Collective spontaneously performed a ritual the day before the Summer Solstice gathering (discussed in chapter 1). Ward's Island, where the group's Solstice ritual was to take place, was where a young girl's murdered remains had been found earlier that spring. Holly Jones, ten years old, was abducted on her way home from a friend's house on May 12, 2003. Her remains were found the day after her disappearance in two weighted bags off Ward's Island, the easternmost island in the Toronto Island chain in Lake Ontario. The tragedy of her death rocked Toronto in the summer of 2003, and a pall of concern and fear, especially fear for the safety of children, shrouded the city while the police searched for her killer. On the morning of the Yarrow Collective's Solstice ritual, newspapers announced that the police had arrested a suspect in her murder.

After the Solstice ritual, during the social time, River, Heidi, and Antonia mentioned that they had come down the day before to clear the space and "to do what we needed to make the space feel safe."[138] They had done magical work in the space we used for ritual and also on the other side of the island, where police had found Holly's remains (fig. 8). The women felt that there was a connection between their work and the apprehension of Holly's murderer. They did not claim that they had made it happen, but they felt that there was a connection between their work and the work that others had been doing around Holly, her killer, and then the arrest.

Heidi talked about noticing feelings of different energies that were connected to the people who had hurt Holly Jones. One was heavy and scary—she took this to be the man later arrested—and one was light and manic. She wasn't sure who that person was "or whether he'll be dangerous on his own." Heidi, Antonia, and River felt it was very important to do something with that energy flying around the city, especially if the collective was going to be doing energy work at Ward's Island later, so they plunked themselves down on the grass by the ferry dock and the boardwalk and interacted with the energies, trying to understand what the energies meant and what they, as Witches, could do to help the imbalance that the energies caused. Heidi reported that they worked for a long time, wrapping up after a couple hours of trance and energy work. She giggled that they were right out where anyone could see them and guessed that some people must have thought that they were pretty weird, but she didn't care. She felt that the three of them were providing a very important service for the people of the city, for Holly, and for her family.

After the report several of the collective members thanked Antonia, Heidi, and River for the work that they had done, both in terms of helping the people of Toronto and in terms of clearing the space that we had just used for the Solstice ritual. Yarrow members felt that the murder had damaged everyone in the city. Ward's Island was well loved by many in the collective as a peaceful and beautiful place. The murder and desecration caused a breech.[139] Especially while the murderer remained unapprehended, the city itself was tainted. For them it felt like no one, especially no child, was safe.

By getting involved with the energies they felt that day, the three women put efforts into rectifying the imbalance that the murder had created. While no one believed that their work had "caused" Holly's murderer to be caught, other members did feel that by adding their directed energies to the hopes and anxieties of everyone in the city, the three members had helped in righting the balance of things. In however small a way, they helped make things right, both in terms of helping cleanse the aura of tragedy and pain that Holly's remains brought to Ward's Island and in terms of adding energy to the efforts to bring Holly's killer to justice. This is an example of a ritual in which the focus was not on self-improvement but one in which ideas of interconnection were nonetheless extremely important.

Religiously motivated feminists such as Nora and Franka would probably both be hard pressed to argue that their actions are political in the same kinds of ways. Compared to Nora's role modeling and feminist networking, Franka's fair trade activism clearly has a greater demonstrable impact on other people, on political and economic relationships between Canada and nations in the developing world, and between Canadian consumers and workers who produce their goods. Nonetheless, the worldview of relationship, which both women articulate, allows for a diversity of actions to be considered politically relevant.

Some of the activists with whom my participants work dismiss self-inclusive cosmologies because they allow actions such as Nora's role modeling or the cleansing of the city performed by Yarrow's River, Heidi, and Antonia into political consideration. What these critics neglect, however, is that the same worldview at work in such inclusion also inspires and supports major projects and actions such as Franka's, which have a clearly visible political impact. My participants refuse to accept the premise upon which such criticism is based, that personal well-being can be extricated from assessments of global justice. As Marla Frederick writes: "Women's refashioning of their world may not always coincide with traditional interpretations of radical politics. Nevertheless, the communities they create and the life changes they inspire speak to the agentive possibilities of their faith."[140]

Religiously motivated feminist activists understand the place and role of the individual in the world as one developed through relationship to others, in contrast to secular economic models that promote isolated autonomy. This reflects concerns of traditional feminist care ethics, but the inclusion of people in different cultures and parts of the world in the category of those to whom one is connected broadens its original focus. Moreover, through emphasizing fairness and equity as necessary components of relationship, social justice provides a further option to choosing either traditional feminist care ethics or justice reasoning alone. None of these formulations can entirely escape larger structures of power, however, as we saw in the exploration of ways activist projects of resistance necessarily reinscribe existing state and economic systems.

Elizabeth Pritchard has argued that agency is "eminently social," that it is through conscious connection to others that one enacts agency and not through individual resistance to transcendent power and its systems.[141] Despite the value they place upon resistance as part of activist identity, the cosmology of relationship articulated by my participants offers an alternative to formulations of agency as exclusively found in individual resistance. Locating change neither exclusively within the individual nor exclusively within the public sphere, formulations of social justice disrupt the binary assumptions of certain Marxist political theories latent in my participants' secular activist communities. At the same time, religiously motivated feminists also cultivate left-wing economic and political activism as religiously virtuous endeavors within theologies that focus far more on saving lives for this world than saving souls for the next.

Conclusion

In thinking through relationships between religion and politics in the contemporary world, it is often easier to see their coordination in conservative projects than in other configurations. This is in part because conservative Christianity is vocal in insisting on its right to represent "real" religion but also because, due to their commitment to making space for other religious and nonreligious voices, progressive activists tend to downplay personal religious motivations, opting instead to emphasize shared ethical discourses. For practical reasons both scholarship and popular attitudes have also generally taken this divide for granted. The religious motivations of protesters blocking access to birth control clinics, for example, are deduced from their signs, chants, and rhetoric. Because those escorting women across the picket lines are not publicly presenting their work as "religious," they are usually glossed as "secular," the opposite of the kind of religious work being performed by protesters. To know any better, you would have to start talking to people, and they would likewise have to be willing to provide complicated answers.

My initial interest in this research grew out of particular silences and constructed invisibilities that I began to perceive in communities with which I was engaged. As I moved across activist spaces in Toronto, there were many people of faith, often the same individuals working on different causes, who were open about their religious motivations. Yet there also seemed to be tacit agreement among broader progressive communities, of which these same committed people were members, that religion was something that only people on the other side of the issues did. In venerable anthropological tradition I conducted fieldwork because I wanted to talk about what a community was not talking about.

Some of the challenges of articulating a project like this one are in distinguishing between political philosophy, advocacy scholarship, and ethnographic work. While I certainly have my own feelings about the futility of trying to legislate religion out of the public sphere, or out of popular discourse more generally, my argument here is not prescriptive in that sense. Rather, my purpose has been to explore, explain, and critically analyze ways in which religion already plays an important role for feminist activists in Toronto and, more broadly, in progressive communities across North America.

Tracing the Arguments

As political activists who also identify with religious institutions, my participants believe that religion and political action are interconnected. In doing so, they draw on a history of interaction between feminism and religion in North America. This approach has implications both for religious ritualizing and for public demonstrations. As I discussed in chapter 1, ritual is a main focus of these politically oriented religious groups. I considered some of the issues on which their rites focus, including self-worth, mutual support, and social change. Within the understanding of these activists, ritual provides means through which to explore alternatives to the social alienation, exploitation, and disconnection they perceive in the world.

Ritual is profoundly world altering for my participants and they understand it as efficacious in several ways. Ritual can serve to heal the self and one's social relationships, thus improving communities. This improvement is not solely personal, however. It is understood as effecting cultural change through subverting systemic oppressions and social privilege. The personal healing and growth sought through ritual necessarily include increased political consciousness.

Ritual also serves to renew personal energy and interpersonal connections necessary for sustained activist work. This aspect of ritual includes both assertions of the personal worth of the individual in the world and the strengthening of connections with other activists. Ritual increases solidarity and focuses collective energies. It creates the community requisite to make social change possible. Moreover, within this worldview ritual is more than simply a symbolic expression of personal worth and community connection. Ritual is considered instrumental; it can bring about concrete change. All three of the groups with whom I did fieldwork perform specific rituals that are meant to improve the world: ease suffering, increase justice and equality, and bring comfort globally.

Religiously motivated feminist activists communicate some of these world-changing possibilities through the use of religious ritual in their political actions. My participants attend public demonstrations with their religious groups and integrate ritual into protest, bringing religion and politics together in innovative ways. Ritualizing is part of their participation in the alternative communities created by major anti-globalization protests, temporary communities that offer brief instantiations of other possible social structures. Such public religiosity can be fruitfully compared to other public displays of religion and shares characteristics with rituals of pilgrimage found within many different and disparate religious traditions.

When religion is so explicitly brought into public dialogue, it can cause religiously motivated activists concern about endorsing social hierarchies that favor one religion, in the North American case, Christianity, over all others. It may also trigger mixed reactions from fellow activists. My participants strategically engage a distinction between "religion" and "spirituality" to position themselves in specific relationships to their faith traditions and their political communities, a choice that is also linked to gendered experience.

The logic behind the popular dichotomy of religion versus spirituality is that personal encounter with the transcendent is inherently an individual experience, one that is made less genuine, less pure, less true, through interaction with community and institutional authority. This attitude, while deeply indebted to Reformation critiques of Catholicism, also draws upon uniquely North American religious traditions. Historically, belief in spirit energies and metaphysical connections locate religious experience in the individual and her interactions with the world. Different elements of these beliefs can be traced through North American religious history. Today these trends manifest in the popular denigration of institutionalized religion and the lauding of personalized spiritualties.

This semantic shift does not actually mean that these are brand-new postmodern ideas. Instead, in its popular usage and among my participants, the language of spirituality, while based on a rejection of religion in the public sphere, in fact facilitates discussion of religious experience, albeit with a change in focus. In the popular distinction between religion and spirituality, religion represents institutional authority, rote ritual, and hierarchical power, whereas spirituality represents meaningful personal experience, rejection of institution, and do-it-yourself initiative. Nonetheless, in assuming religion to be a domineering public institution and spirituality to be an admirable personal recognition of connection to the world, the rhetoric of spirituality versus religion turns religion into a specific manifestation of a universal spirituality. This usage flips the assumed dichotomy, confining religion to a slightly embarrassing, private preference and expanding spirituality to a wholesome, universally accessible experience that is nonthreatening to the integrity of the public sphere. Advocating spirituality as a phenomenon that transcends particular identities and religious institutions also contributes to the creation of a third space, outside the male-dominated hierarchies of Christianity and the secular state, from which traditionally marginalized people can launch critiques of both.

Even as they accommodate it through strategic use of language, religiously motivated feminist activists do not unequivocally embrace a sharp divide between public and private. In the introduction I argued that women's reform work in the Progressive Era focused on extending the private sphere of women's influence into the public sphere in order to solve social problems such as poverty, prostitution, juvenile delinquency, rape, and alcoholism. Projecting the Christian home into public space, Progressive Era women reformers offered a private model for the solution of public problems. Contemporary religiously motivated feminists distance themselves from the cultural chauvinism and gendered essentialism of such an approach but also offer an intimate model for the solution of global problems. Replacing the idea of the Christian home with a new principle, contemporary social justice feminists articulate the idea of relationship, or personal connection, as a way to ameliorate the harms of global exploitation and social injustice. This action does not so much extend the private sphere into the public as offer a worldview in which the private and public intermingle in complex ways.

Taking seriously the feminist axiom that "the personal is political," my participants understand the public and private spheres as being connected. They articulate a cosmology of relationship, an ethical worldview they call "social justice" that denotes interconnection and mutual responsibility for the well-being of others. Social justice melds the importance of self-care and interpersonal relationships of traditional feminist care ethics with the emphasis on fairness and equality of justice ethics. It also requires confronting the personal advantages, as well as disadvantages, of social privilege accorded by race, class, gender, and religion. Within such a cosmology of interconnection, religious participation is not extraneous to political work for social change, and religious discourse is not incompatible with healthy democracies.

Personal Reflections

This project really began for me in the tear gas clouds of the Quebec City anti-FTAA protest in April 2001. Between then and now are the demoralizingly entangled tragedies of September 11, the rise of even more blatant police repression in the service of international corporate interests, the latest wars in the Middle East, the Great Recession, and the 2016 U.S. presidential election. Nonetheless, there are also the Occupy, Idle No More, Standing Rock, Black Lives Matter, and Women's March movements. The trajectories of all these and related phenomena can be traced across the sinews of this book.

When I was conducting my fieldwork among the amazing and dedicated activists I feature here, I was often confused at what I took to be their condescension to me as an American in Canada, a place where I ended up living for nearly fifteen years. The messages I received were that I must be so grateful to be here, away from the brutal racism, buffoonish politics, and general mess of the United States. And yet I would often be receiving these messages as we walked together at protests against the policies of the province of Ontario or the Canadian federal government, policies that we all agreed were racist, exploitative, and undemocratic, part of a larger globalized problem that transcended national borders. In fact, returning home to Toronto from visits to the States, my car was almost always searched by Canadian customs agents, sometimes while painfully young soldiers holding machine guns kept watch. For someone who arrived in Ontario under Mike Harris and left Canada under the premiership of Stephen Harper—to return to Obama's America no less—I remained perplexed by my friends' confidence that things were better north of the border.

The election of Justin Trudeau has helped me make more sense of that confidence. Suddenly the "socialist utopia" that Canada never was during my time there clicks into clearer view. The concerns of Trudeau and his government for gender equality, meaningful First Nations reconciliation, poverty amelioration, and anti-racism reflect fairly well the issues that have always been in the hearts of my participants, even as we all suffered under Harper and the global repression he seemed so perplexingly pleased to perpetuate. Former participants from all three of my fieldwork communities lit up—didn't the world?—over Trudeau's literal open-armed embrace of Syrian refugees in December 2015 as they arrived at the Toronto Pearson airport, "Welcome to your new home."

My point, of course, is not that Trudeau has solved everything. The federal government will always be an unwieldy and conservative mechanism, tangled with corporate interests. Threats to First Nations land, resources, and sovereignty continue. The planet is melting, burning, and storming, all at the same time. Sexual violence remains virulent. Racism, religious distrust, and hopelessness poison discourse across the globe, and that includes Canadian communities.

But I can say to my friends: I get it now. I understand why you were so confident that things could be different. Even now, as the whole world faces an uncertain future in the wake of the U.S. presidential election, culmination of recent populist movements in the West, Canada is indeed positioned to demonstrate some alternatives. While I am committed to staying and fighting the good fight south of the border, it is hard not to gaze wistfully across it these days. Nonetheless, choosing to stand with those who cannot run has always been the heart of social justice work. This is the work that my participants consciously commit to again and again. In their communities, even in their disagreements, they provide models for being fully human *together*, rather than in spite of each other.

As religiously motivated feminist activists prove, we miss out on a larger perspective if we approach the relationship of religion to politics as one of antagonism, incompatible in all but their most conservative manifestations. Limiting ourselves to a recognition of religion in only harmful and restrictive forms does not actually keep us safe from its dangers, real or imagined. Instead, by accepting the conservative line that only the most restrictive and hierarchal forms of, for example, Christianity, are true religion, we relinquish religion's power as a force for progressive social change.

The contemporary Pagan, United Church Protestant, and Catholic women with whom I worked find in their religions support for their deep commitment to social change. Their religious communities help sustain concerted patience in the face of hopelessness and frustration inherent in work for long-term goals, such as global justice, peace, health, sexual freedom, and gender equality. Religion also helps them maintain compassion for others' suffering and empathy for people on opposite sides of their political issues. They perform rituals that are meant to improve the world and that increase their senses of self-worth and their connections to each other.

They participate in their religious communities despite familiarity with criticisms of ritual as self-indulgent and unproductive. These groups reject the seeming dichotomy of using ritual for self-improvement or therapeutic purposes and using ritual for effecting political or social change. In the work of the Yarrow Collective, the Toronto Catholic Worker, and the Clearwater United Church congregation, approaches to self-healing and political and social change are understood as dialectical, rather than contradictory. Within their cosmologies of relationship, it is impossible to make any real changes in one realm without making real changes in the other. While there may be conflict within the groups about the perfect balance of ritual to direct action, on the whole each group rejects the forced choice of improving themselves or improving the world and instead insists on the deeply radical possibility of doing both.

Source Acknowledgments

Portions of the introduction are adapted from "Feminism and Religion: Intersections between Western Activism, Theology and Theory," *Religion Compass* 6, no. 7 (July 2012): 354–68.

Portions of chapter 1 are adapted from "Second Nature: Contemporary Pagan Ritual Borrowing in Progressive Christian Communities," in "Feminism, Activism and Spirituality," special issue, *Canadian Women's Studies / cahier de la femme* 29, nos. 1–2 (2011): 16–23.

Portions of chapter 2 are adapted from "Ritual Actions: Feminist Spirituality in Anti-Globalization Protests," in *Feminist Spirituality: The Next Generation*, ed. Chris Klassen (Lanham MD: Lexington Books, 2009), 159–77.

Portions of chapter 3 are adapted from "Spiritual, but Religious: 'Spirituality' among Religiously Motivated Activists in North America," *Culture and Religion* 8, no. 1 (2007): 51–69, http://www.tandfonline.com/10.1080/14755610601157120.

Notes

Introduction

1. Mahmood, *Religious Difference*; Najmabadi, "(Un)Veiling Feminism"; Shukrallah, "Impact of the Islamic Movement."

2. Sered, *Priestess*, 185.

3. J. Z. Smith, *Imagining Religion*; Orsi, "Snakes Alive"; C. Smith, "Introduction"; P. Berger, "Desecularization"; C. Taylor, *Modern Social Imaginaries*; Asad, *Formations of the Secular*.

4. J. Z. Smith, *Imagining Religion*; Moore, *Religious Outsiders*; Fessenden, "Disappearances"; Orsi, *History and Presence*.

5. For works critical of religion in the public sphere, and in general, see Hitchens, *God Is Not Great* and *Morality*; Dawkins, *God Delusion*, *Magic of Reality*, and *Brief Candle*; Harris, *End of Faith*, *Letter to a Christian Nation*, and *Waking Up*; Dennett, *Breaking the Spell*. For a response to Dawkins that applies well to the other authors, see Eagleton, "Lunging, Flailing, Mispunching."

    For analysis of such assumptions, see Jakobsen and Pellegrini, "World Secularisms," and "Introduction"; P. Berger, "Desecularization"; Asad, *Formations of the Secular*; C. Smith, "Introduction"; Taylor, *Modern Social Imaginaries* and *Secular Age*; Bruce, *God Is Dead*; and C. Smith, "Correcting a Curious Neglect."

6. Dawkins, *God Delusion*; Hitchens, *God Is Not Great*; and Harris, *End of Faith* and *Letter*.

7. Lilla, *Stillborn God*. For refutation of this position on evolutionary grounds, see de Waal, *Bonobo and the Atheist*. For criticism of these arguments by someone on the Left who is also critical of conservative Christianity, see Hedges, *I Don't Believe*. See also Wilder, "I Don't Believe."

8. Charles, *Religulous*. See also Maher, interview with Conan O'Brien.

9. For a discussion of these arguments and the theologies underlying them, see Stout, *Democracy and Tradition*. For an overview of the movement, see Hankins, *American Evangelicals*. For examples of evangelical Christian

communities that challenge these bifurcations, see Gasaway, *Progressive Evangelicals*; and Elisha, *Moral Ambition*.

10. Falwell, interview with Pat Robertson. My purpose in using this quote is not to suggest that it is cutting-edge currency in the movement (in fact both Falwell and Robertson later tried to distance themselves from the statement) but instead to demonstrate explicitly the worldview that repudiates a distinction between public legislation and biblical law.

11. On Dominionist theology, see Phillips, *American Theocracy*; Sharlet, "Jesus Plus Nothing," "Soldiers for Christ," "Sex as a Weapon," and *Family*. There are also websites that anthologize news pieces on conservative Christianity and politics; see, for example, Wilson and Clarkson, *Talk to Action*; and Handleman, *Revealer*.

12. Connolly, "Belief, Spirituality, and Time." For an insightful analysis of the construction of such dialectical relationships, using Western liberal feminism and Islamic fundamentalisms as case studies, see Moallem, "Transnationalism, Feminism, and Fundamentalism." See also Mahmood, *Religious Difference*.

13. For a tracing of the historical trajectory of these conflicts in North American culture, see Wuthnow, *Christianity*.

14. Jakobsen and Pellegrini, "World Secularisms," 23.

15. Frederick, *Between Sundays*, 82–91; Griffith, *God's Daughters*, 205; Elisha, *Moral Ambition*.

16. Harris, *Letter*; Hitchens, *God Is Not Great*; Lilla, *Stillborn God*. For analysis, see Yip and Nynäs, "Reframing the Intersection"; Fedele and Knibbe, "Introduction."

17. Gerber, *Seeking the Straight*; Erzen, *Straight to Jesus*; DeRogatis, *Saving Sex*; Burack, *Tough Love*; Wilson, "Erupting Clash"; Moslener, *Virgin Nation*. See also Casanova, "Nativism"; Mahmood, *Politics of Piety* and *Religious Difference*.

18. Merry, *Gender Violence*; Naples, *Women's Activism*; Grewal and Kaplan, *Introduction*.

19. Tong, *Feminist Thought*.

20. Roof, *Generation of Seekers*; Heelas, "Spiritual Revolution"; Fedele and Knibbe, "Introduction"; Bender, *New Metaphysicals*.

21. Geertz, "Religion as a Cultural System"; J. Z. Smith, *Imagining Religion*; Asad, *Genealogies of Religion* and *Formations of the Secular*; Masuzawa, *Invention of World Religions*.

22. Tong, *Feminist Thought*.

23. Foucault, *Discipline and Punish*; Asad, *Genealogies of Religion* and *Formations of the Secular*; Taylor, *Modern Social Imaginaries*; Mahmood, *Politics of Piety* and *Religious Difference*.

24. For one of the earliest explications of this distinction, see Jaggar, *Feminist Politics*. For a slightly later explication, see Pateman, *Disorder of Women*.

25. Riley, *"Am I That Name"*; Butler, *Gender Trouble*.

26. Jaggar, *Feminist Politics*; Kent, "Confluence of Race"; Tong, *Feminist Thought*; Eller, *Myth of Matriarchal Prehistory*.

27. Hewitt, *No Permanent Waves*; Laughlin and Castledine, *Breaking the Wave*; Moynaugh and Forestell, General Introduction; Cobble, Gordon, and Henry, *Feminism Unfinished*.

28. Tong, *Feminist Thought*.

29. Klassen, Goldberg, and Lefabvre, *Women and Religion*; Castelli and Rodman, *Women, Gender, Religion*.

30. Tong *Feminist Thought*; Braude, "Women's History"; Sered, *Priestess*; Gilligan, *In a Different Voice*.

31. Pascoe, *Relations of Rescue*; Higginbotham, *Righteous Discontent*; Pellauer, *Toward a Tradition*; Moslener *Virgin Nation*; Van Osselaer, "Religion, Family and Domesticity."

32. Pascoe, *Relations*, 9.

33. Pascoe, *Relations*, 17, 21, 13.

34. Strange, *Toronto's Girl Problem* and "From Modern Babylon"; Valverde, *Age of Light*; Jenson, "Was It for 'Want of Courage,'" 32.

35. Weisenfeld, *African American Women*, 88, 90.

36. Collier-Thomas, *Jesus, Jobs and Justice*. A related space-making process occurred with the blending of missionizing and music for female gospel singers, legitimizing public performance as respectable. Jackson, *Singing in My Soul*, esp. 39–40. On an earlier community of African American women who leveraged a different kind of feminine role modeling into social activism, see Morrow, *Persons of Color*.

37. Higginbotham, *Righteous Discontent*; Wollcott, *Remaking*; Franklin and Collier-Thomas, "For the Race in General"; Butler, *Women in the Church*. In *Your Spirits Walk beside Us*, however, Savage emphasizes that African American churches were forced to take on all problems within the community because racism made it impossible to create other socially viable, independent institutions within areas such as business, philanthropy, and politics.

For discussion of the impact of the history of the "politics of respectability" on contemporary black women, see Frederick, *Between Sundays*,

12–13 and 185–90. In *Black Mega-Church* Tucker-Worgs argues that the "dual gendered spheres" ideology continues to limit women within contemporary African American churches at the same time that it has historically provided them with opportunities for public action.

On respectability's role for a Chinese Canadian professional, see Llewellyn, "Teaching June Cleaver." While especially significant for women of color as they negotiated intersecting oppressions, the politics of respectability were also mobilized by women marginalized by other identity markers, such as age. See Robinson and Ruff, *Out of the Mouths of Babes*.

38. Braude, *Radical Spirits*; Foster, *Women, Family, Utopia*; Owen, *Darkened Room*; Satter, *Each Mind a Kingdom*.

39. Pascoe, *Relations*; Gordon, "Black and White Visions."

40. Braude, *Radical Spirits*.

41. Satter, *Each Mind*; Pascoe, *Relations*; Higginbotham, *Righteous Discontent*; Wollcott, *Remaking Respectability*; Yung, *Unbound*. See also Pascoe, *What Comes Naturally*; Griffith, *Born Again Bodies*. In "Social Motherhood," however, Jones suggests that caregivers were often more conscious of the risks of condescension than later historians give them credit for.

42. Echols, *Daring*; Jaggar, *Feminist Politics*; Levy, *Women and Violence*; Merry, *Gender Violence*.

43. Jaggar, *Feminist Politics*.

44. Gimbutas, *Goddesses and Gods* and *Civilization of the Goddess*; Christ, *Laughter of Aphrodite* and *Rebirth of the Goddess*; Eisler, *Chalice and the Blade*. For critiques, see Eller, *Living* and *Gentlemen*; and Ruether, *Goddesses*.

45. Jaggar, *Feminist Politics*; Echols, *Daring*.

46. For example, Christ, *Laughter* and *Rebirth*.

47. Fessenden, "Disappearances"; Sands, "Feminisms and Secularisms."

48. Evans, *Personal Politics* and *Journeys*; Ruether, "Rosemary Radford Ruether"; Williams, "Delores Williams"; Braude, "Faith, Feminism and History."

49. Evans, *Personal Politics*; Echols, *Daring to Be Bad*, 182–84. For complicating perspectives, see Braude, "Faith, Feminism and History"; and Savage, *Your Spirits*.

50. Cited in Echols, *Daring to Be Bad*, 184.

51. Echols, *Daring to Be Bad*, 184, 251–57, 283–84.

52. On Paganism, see Starhawk, *Spiral Dance*; Eller, *Living*; M. Adler, *Drawing Down the Moon*; Christ, *Laughter*; Griffin, "Goddess Spirituality and Wicca";

Pike, *New Age and Neopagan Religions.* On Afrocentric traditions, see Teish, *Jambalaya*; Badejo, *Osun Seegesi*; Chireau, *Black Magic.* See also Duncan, *This Spot of Ground.* On Mestiza identity, see Anzaldúa, *Borderlands.*

53. Evans, *Personal Politics*; C. Klassen, "Confronting the Gap."
54. For example, Mohanty, "Under Western Eyes"; Lorde, "Open Letter to Mary Daly."
55. Crenshaw, "Mapping the Margins"; Kent, "Confluence"; Gluck et al., "Whose Feminism"; hooks, *Ain't I a Woman*; Levy, *Violence*; Williams, "Delores Williams."
56. Lorde, "Open Letter"; Mohanty, "Under Western Eyes"; Donaldson, "On Medicine Women."
57. Orleck, *Common Sense.*
58. Echols, *Daring*; B. Smith, "'Feisty Characters.'"
59. Walker, *In Search of Our Mothers' Gardens*; Williams, *Sisters in the Wilderness*; Gilkes, "If It Wasn't for the Women"; Razak, "Her Blue Body."
60. Isasi-Díaz, *Mujerista Theology* and *En la Lucha.*
61. Heller, *Cross-Purposes.*
62. Zack, *Inclusive Feminism*; Gillis, Howie, and Munford, *Third Wave Feminism*; Llewellyn, "Across Generations"; Vincett, "Generational Change in Goddess Feminism."
63. For example, in spaces such as the "Feminist Theory and Religious Reflection" at the American Academy of Religion.
64. Anderson and Young, *Women and Religious Traditions*; Castelli and Rosamond, *Women, Gender, Religion*; Sharma and Young, *Her Voice.*
65. Ruether, *Goddesses*; Ford, "Hierarchical Inversions"; Hassan, "Feminist Theology"; Bynum, *Holy Feast.*
66. Hiltebeitl and Erndl, *Is the Goddess a Feminist*; Ruether, *Goddesses.*
67. Ruether, *Goddesses*; Christ, *Laughter.*
68. Daly, *Beyond God the Father,* 19.
69. Christ, *Laughter*; Goldenberg, *Changing of the Gods.*
70. Plaskow, *Standing Again at Sinai,* 161–65; Kuikman, "Women in Judaism"; R. Adler, *Engendering Judaism*; Kedar, "Metaphors of God"; Young, "Women in Christianity," 163–92, 171.
71. Kiukman, "Women in Judaism," 57; Reuther, *Goddesses,* 90–97, 112–22, 127–37.
72. Plaskow, *Coming of Lilith*; Diamant, *Red Tent*; Walton, "Lilith's Daughters"; Ruether, *Goddesses*; Schüssler Fiorenza, *In Memory of Her.*
73. Clarke, "Women in Islam"; Ford, "Hierarchical Inversions."
74. Hassan, "Feminist Theology," 92.
75. Spretnak, *Politics of Women's Spirituality*; Christ, *Laughter* and *Rebirth.*

76. Teish, *Jambalaya*; Badejo, *Osun Seegesi*; Chireau, *Black Magic*; Anzaldúa, *Borderlands*; Eller, *Living*; Salmonsen, *Enchanted Feminism*; Starhawk, *Spiral Dance*.

77. Gallant, "Imagination, Empowerment and Imaginary Figures"; M. Adler, *Drawing Down the Moon*; Pike, *Earthly Bodies*; Ruether, *Goddesses*; Razak, "Her Blue Body."

78. Christ, *Laughter* and *Rebirth*; Daly, *Outercourse*.

79. Christ, "Musings on the Goddess"; Ruether, "Rosemary Radford Ruether," "Response to Naomi Goldenberg," and *Goddesses*.

80. Razak, "Her Blue Body."

81. Eller, *Myth*; Peskowitz, "Unweaving."

82. Hiltebeitl and Erndl, *Is the Goddess a Feminist*; Rountree, "Goddess Pilgrims as Tourists"; Donaldson, "On Medicine Women."

83. Ruether, "Response," 6 and *Goddesses*.

84. Braude, *Transforming the Faiths*.

85. Sered, *Priestess*; J. Z. Smith, *Imagining Religion*; C. Smith, "Introduction"; Orsi "Snakes Alive."

86. On theology, see Weisenfeld, "Invisible Women"; Chireau, *Black Magic*. On ritual, see Bell, *Ritual*, 237–42; Sered, *Women as Ritual Experts*; Duncan, *This Spot*, 97–123. On mysticism, see Bynum, *Holy Feast*; Brown, *Mama Lola*. On sacrifice, see Jay, *Throughout Your Generations*; Dubisch, *In a Different Place*; Mizruchi, "Place of Ritual in Our Time."

87. Sered, *Priestess*.

88. Sered, *Women as Ritual* and *Priestess*; Boddy, *Wombs and Alien*; Asad, *Genealogies of Religion* and *Formations of the Secular*; J. Z. Smith, *Imagining Religion*; Orsi, "Snakes Alive."

89. Such as those explored by Braude, *Radical Spirits*; K. M. Brown, *Mama Lola*; Boddy, *Wombs*.

90. Sered, *Priestess*, 182–93.

91. Sered, *Priestess*, 281.

92. Braude, "Women's History," 93.

93. Braude, "Women's History," 90.

94. Bell, *Ritual*, 257; Mahmood, *Politics of Piety*; Griffith, *God's Daughters*; P. Berger, "Secularization and Desecularization."

95. Littman, *In Her Own Time*; Frederick, *Between Sundays*; P. Klassen, *Blessed Events*; Griffith, *God's Daughters*; Orsi, *Thank You*; Stacey, *Brave New Families*; Stacey and Gerrard, "We Are Not Doormats"; Ginsberg, *Contested Lives*; Mahmood, *Politics*.

96. Abu-Lughod, "Romance of Resistance."

97. Mahmood, *Politics of Piety*.

98. Griffith, *God's Daughters*.

99. Pritchard, "Agency without Transcendence."

100. Merry, *Gender Violence*; see also Jung, Hunt, and Balakrishnan, *Good Sex*.

101. Hassan, "Riffat Hassan"; Moallem, "Transnationalism"; Mahmood, *Politics* and *Religious Difference*; Merry, *Gender Violence*.

102. On colonial projects globally, see Loomba, *Colonialism/Postcolonialism*; Stevenson, "Colonialism and First Nations Women"; Ahmed, *Women and Gender*; Mahmood, *Religious Difference*; Stoler, *Carnal Knowledge*. In the West: J. Roy, *Rhetorical Campaigns*; Corrigan and Neal, *Religious Intolerance in America*, 49–72; Frink, "Women, the Family, and the Fate"; Mattingly, "Uncovering Forgotten Habits"; Foster, *Women, Family, Utopia*; Pascoe, *Relations of Rescue*; Corrigan and Neal, *Religious Intolerance*, 73–98; Bennett, "'Until This Curse of Polygamy.'" Note that Mormonism and Catholicism colluded in this process by also denouncing each other through patterns established by Protestantism. See Grow, "Whore of Babylon."

103. Levy, *Violence*; Merry, *Gender Violence*; O'Toole et al., "Roots."

104. Mollenkott, "Virginia Ramey Mollenkott," 60–61.

105. Wadud, *Qur'an and Woman* and *Inside the Gender Jihad*; Hassan, "Feminist Theology" and "Riffat Hassan"; al-Hibri, "Azizah al-Hibri."

106. Hassan, "Feminist Theology," 86. For pragmatic examples of this strategy, see Hammer, *American Muslim Women*; and Basrudin, *Humanizing the Sacred*. For a Muslim, feminist critique of this approach, see Hidayatullah, *Feminist Edges of the Qur'an*.

107. Hassan, "Feminist Theology" and "Riffat Hassan"; Ahmed, *Women and Gender*, 41–63; Imam, "Muslim Religious Right"; Ali, *Sexual Ethics and Islam*.

108. Hassan, "Riffat Hassan"; al-Hibri, "Azizah al-Hibri."

109. Cavanaugh, "Colonialism and Religious Violence"; Goodchild, *Theology*; Butler, *Precarious Life*.

110. For example, Braude, *Radical Spirits*; Foster, *Women, Family, Utopia*; Higginbotham, *Righteous Discontent*; Loades, *Feminist Theology*; Muir and Whiteley, "Introduction"; Pellauer, *Toward a Tradition*; Warne, *Literature as Pulpit* and "Nellie McClung's Social Gospel"; Yellin, *Women and Sisters*.

111. Two notable exceptions to this trend include volumes of memoirs: Braude, *Faiths of Our Fathers*, based on the Harvard "Religion and the Feminist Movement" conference mentioned earlier; and Evans, *Journeys*, based on interviews with women active in the feminist movement following involvement in the Civil Rights movement.

112. Evans, *Personal Politics*; Braude, "Faith, Feminism and History"; Llewellyn and Trzebiatowska, "Secular and Religious Feminism"; C. Klassen, "Confronting the Gap."

113. Exceptions include Ward, *La Leche League*; and Grayson, "Necessity Was the Midwife." See also Koehlinger, "'Are You the White Sisters or the Black Sisters.'"

114. B. Smith, "Fiesty Characters." For example, see Harris, "From the Kennedy Commission."

115. Gluck et al., "Whose Feminism." See also Cobble et al., *Feminism Unfinished*.

116. Thompson, *Promise*.

117. For example, Bendroth, *Fundamentalism*; Ginsburg, *Contested Lives*; Griffith, *God's Daughters*; Stacey and Gerrard, "We Are Not Doormats."

118. Exceptions include Braude, *Faiths*; Alpert, *Voices of the Religious Left*; Nepstad, *Convictions of the Soul* and *Religion and War Resistance*; Bouma, "Jesus Was a Feminist"; Herzog and Braude, *Gendering Religion and Politics*; Pauli, *Radical Religion*; and Gasaway, *Progressive*.

119. Alpert, *Voices*; C. Smith, *Emergence of Liberation* and "Correcting"; Cannon, *Just Spirituality*.

120. Brock, *Journeys by Heart*; Isasi-Díaz, *Mujerista Theology* and *En la Lucha*; Johnson, *She Who Is*; McFague, *Super, Natural Christians*; Moody, *Women Encounter God*; Williams, *Sisters in the Wilderness*. An exception to this trend is Ruether, *America, Amerikkka*.

121. For classic texts of thealogy that are still recommended by practitioners of goddess spirituality to newcomers, see Budapest, *Holy Book*; Christ, *Rebirth*; Spretnak *Politics of Women's Spirituality*. Starhawk's books stand as exceptions to this trend and do focus explicitly on activism. See Starhawk, *Truth or Dare* and *Webs of Power*.

122. Davie, *Women in the Presence*; Ginsburg, *Contested Lives*; H. Berger, *Community of Witches*; Jacobs, "Women-Centered Healing Rites"; Luhrmann, *Persuasions*; Neitz, "In Goddess We Trust"; Pike, *Earthly Bodies*; Bednarowski, *Religious Imagination*; Sered, *Priestess*.

123. Winter, Lummis, and Stokes, *Defecting in Place*.

124. Finley, "Political Activism and Feminist Spirituality."

125. Eller, *Living*; M. Adler, *Drawing Down the Moon*; Wilcox, *Queer Women and Religious Individualism*.

126. For more information on each of these traditions, see later descriptions.

127. *Participant-observation* is a methodological term within anthropology and ethnography. I attended events and, with the explicit permission of each group, participated in their activities for the purpose of better under-

standing and explaining the experience in my research. This structured fieldwork took place over a year, from April 2003 to April 2004.

128. See Starhawk, *Spiral Dance, Dreaming,* and *Webs of Power.* For an ethnography of the San Francisco Reclaiming Collective, see Salmonsen, *Enchanted Feminism.* NightMare, *Witchcraft and the Web* and *Pagan*; and Starhawk and NightMare, *Pagan Book.* NightMare publicly left the Reclaiming tradition in 2012.

129. I discuss this in more detail in chapter 1.

130. Braude, "Women's History."

131. I stress here that there are many politically active Muslim, Jewish, Hindu, and other religious groups in Toronto as well. My choices of field study should in no way imply that these are the only feminist religious groups at work on social justice issues.

132. Christ, *Laughter.*

133. Hutton, *Triumph of the Moon.*

134. Starhawk, *Spiral Dance.*

135. All nineteen Pagan women with whom I spoke are white; there are two women of color in the United Church sample and four in the Catholic. That puts the study at just 10 percent of the women with whom I spoke being women of color.

136. For discussion of this aspect of the feminist movement and the responses of women of color, see Thompson, *Promise.*

137. This is the alternative term I heard most often among my participants.

138. Long, *Significations,* 9.

139. Frederick, *Between Sundays.*

140. My approach here is influenced by work addressing "lived religion." See Hall, *Lived Religion in America.*

141. Griffth, *God's Daughters,* 12.

142. See Riegle, *Dorothy Day*; C. Byrne, *Catholic Worker.* For a history of earlier publications, see Klejment and Klejment, *Dorothy Day.* A classic memoir with an ethnographic bent is Ellis, *Year at the Catholic Worker.*

143. Moloney, *American Catholic Lay Groups*; Thorn, Runkel, and Mountin, *Dorothy Day*; McKanan, *Catholic Worker after Dorothy*; Zwick and Zwick, *Catholic Worker Movement*; Parrish and Taylor, "Seeking Authenticity."

144. Chernus, "Dorothy Day and the Catholic Worker Movement"; Coy, "Experiment in Personalist Politics"; Klejment and Roberts, *American Catholic Pacifism*; Kosek, *Acts of Conscience*; Baker, *Go to the Worker.*

145. Klejment and Klejment, *Dorothy Day,* xxv.

146. The *Catholic Worker* continues to be published and still sells for one cent a copy, with yearlong subscriptions available for twenty-five cents. Write to:

Catholic Worker, 36 East First Street, New York, NY 10003, United States. For a scholarly analysis, see Bordon, "Communitarian Journalism." McKanan, *Touching the World*; Nepstad, *Religion and War Resistance*.

147. See the Catholic Worker website for information about international community connections: http://www.catholicworker.org (accessed May 20, 2016). For studies on other Catholic Worker communities, see Allahyari, *Visions of Charity*; Spickard, "Ritual, Symbol, and Experience"; and Yukich, "Boundary Work."

148. The choices of these members can be productively compared to various types of Catholics who have broken with Vatican authority. See J. Byrne, *Other Catholics*.

149. For an overview, see Schweitzer, *United Church of Canada*.

150. On the relationship between the denomination and progressive social causes, see P. Klassen, *Spirits of Protestantism*.

151. United Church of Canada, "Social Action."

152. An essential belief in the autonomy of the individual and the validity of personal spiritual experience lies at the heart of contemporary Paganism. This heterodoxy allows for mutual acceptance, even when one person's experience contradicts another's. Therefore, no definition of contemporary Paganism, or Wicca, should be considered absolute or exclusive. For general information about contemporary Paganism and Wicca in North America, see M. Adler, *Drawing Down the Moon*; H. Berger, Leach, and Shafer, *Voices from the Pagan Census*; Pike, *New Age and Contemporary Pagan* and *Earthly Bodies*; Clifton, *Her Hidden Children*; Eller, *Living*; York, *Pagan Theology*; Luhrmann, *Persuasions*; Lewis, *Magical Religion*; Magliocco, *Witching Culture*; and Hutton, *Triumph of the Moon*. Starhawk, *Spiral Dance*; Clifton, *Her Hidden Children*; Zwissler, "In Memorium Maleficarum" and "Witches Tears."

153. Clifton, *Her Hidden Children*; Bado-Fralick, *Coming to the Edge*; Starhawk, *Spiral Dance* and *Webs of Power*; M. Adler, *Drawing Down the Moon*; Berger, *Community of Witches*; Griffin, "Goddess Spirituality"; and Ruether, *Goddesses*, 274–98.

154. On the relationship between feminism and contemporary Paganism, see Griffin, "Webs of Women"; Eller, *Myth* and *Living*; C. Klassen, "Colonial Mythology"; Ruether, *Goddesses*; and Zwissler, "In Memorium Maleficarum."

155. See Starhawk, *Webs of Power*; Ruether, *Goddesses*.

156. Wiccans and other contemporary Pagans in general use computer technology to organize their groups, educate themselves, and share their knowledge with others. See Cowan, *Cyberhenge*.

157. Albanese, *Republic of Mind and Spirit*.

158. On the New Left, see O'Neill, *New Left*. On feminism's relationship to the New Left, see Echols, *Daring to Be Bad*; Evans, *Personal Politics*; Tong, *Feminist Thought*.

159. On Canadian self-identity in deliberate contrast to the United States, especially around issues of race and multiculturalism, see Stevenson, *Building Nations from Diversity*; De B'Béri, "Politics of Knowledge," 25; Reid-Maroney, "History, Historiography"; Duncan, *This Spot*.

160. For more information, see chapter 2.

161. "Cosmology. A theory of, or set of beliefs concerning, the nature of the universe and the cosmos. These beliefs may include postulates of the structure, organization and functioning of the supernatural, natural and social worlds." Seymour-Smith, "Cosmology," 55. Claude Lévi-Strauss's structuralism was an inspiration for this usage, but it is one engaged by diverse scholars, including Mary Douglas and Talal Asad. For example, Asad uses it to discuss the perceived structure of the universe within medieval Christianity. Asad, *Genealogies*. See also Abramson and Holbraad, *Framing Cosmologies*.

1. Changing Rituals, Changing Worlds

1. There is usually no nonparticipatory audience anticipated in the case of regular or holiday rites. Everyone present is expected to be there to participate, even if they are not regular members of the community.

2. For an overview of the discussion, see Grimes, *Craft*, 186–97.

3. Grimes, *Craft*, 187.

4. J. Z. Smith, *To Take Place*, 103.

5. J. Z. Smith, "Bare Facts," 63.

6. Goodchild, *Capitalism and Religion*, 103–4.

7. Goodchild, *Theology of Money*.

8. Bell, *Ritual Theory*, 32.

9. Grimes, *Craft*, 166; Mitchell, *Colonising Egypt*.

10. Bado-Fralick, *Coming to the Edge*, 8.

11. Lavender, contemporary Pagan, July 18, 2003.

12. Regina, Catholic, August 1, 2003.

13. Bell writes: "In the newer model, ritual is primarily a medium of expression, a special type of language suited to what it is there to express, namely internal spiritual-emotional resources tied to our true identities but frequently unknown and underdeveloped. Ritual expression of these internal dimensions will unleash their healing power for the self and others." *Ritual*, 241.

14. For an ethnographic account of another group negotiating criticisms of shared rituals, see Fedele, "Créativité et incertitude."
15. On women, spirit possession, and power dynamics related to gender and colonial histories, see Brown, *Mama Lola*; Keller, *Hammer and the Flute*; Boddy, *Wombs and Alien Spirits*; Johnson and Keller, "Work of Possession(s)"; Kenyon, *Spirits and Slaves*.
16. M. Adler, *Drawing Down the Moon*. On distinguishing this practice from ancient Greek theurgy, see Hutton, "Paganism and Polemic."
17. Coleman, *Re-riting Woman*.
18. On racialized discourses surrounding and constructing Atlantic spirit possession traditions, see K. M. Brown, *Mama Lola*; and Johnson, "Toward an Atlantic Genealogy."
19. Wendy, United Church, March 28, 2004.
20. Saturday, June 21, 2003.
21. Holly Jones was a ten-year-old girl who was found murdered earlier in the spring. I discuss the impact her death had on the city in chapter 4.
22. October 31, 2003.
23. Star, contemporary Pagan, July 28, 2003.
24. April 11, 2004.
25. Jim later published an account of his abduction. Loney, *Captivity*.
26. April 11, 2004.
27. On the importance of circles in women's ritualizing, see Northup, *Ritualizing Women*. On specifically Pagan understanding of circles, see Bado-Fralick, *Coming to the Edge*.
28. The notion that there is something in religious symbols and ritual patterns that transcends specific cultural contexts and represents a human universal is one deconstructed by anthropologists of religion, yet it remains a popular discourse. Matthew Engelke even found investment in ceremonial practices, especially rites of passage, among British secular humanists, who identified them as something from which specific religious overlays could be removed, leaving them merely meaningful human practices. Engelke, "Christianity." On shared ritualization among U.S. atheists, see Cimino and Smith, *Atheist Awakening*.
29. See chapter 3 for discussion of "spirituality" and "religion."
30. Dufferin Grove News, "Home." As of 2012, the park has been turned over to City of Toronto Parks, Forestry and Recreation Division, but there is still very active community engagement in planning its space and events, as well as continued resistance to city efforts to "standardize" its management to make it more like other parks. See Dufferin Grove News, "About Us."

31. Night of Dread is put on by Toronto artist David Anderson and his Clay and Paper Theatre collective. See Clay and Paper Theatre, http://www.clayandpapertheatre.org/.

32. On Christian use of Pagan elements as "ritual washing," see Zwissler, "Second Nature."

33. For a discussion of this trend in North American religion more generally, see Albanese, *Nature Religion* and *Reconsidering Nature Religion*. On deliberate "fusing" of Christian and Goddess elements within Christian communities in the West, see Vincett, "Fusers." See also Beavis, "Christian Goddess Spirituality."

34. While the trangressive boundary crossings themselves were clearly part of the fun, Paganism's self-conscious embrace of ritualized play may have been experienced by these Christian practitioners as giving permission to be silly. As Bado-Fralick and Sachs-Norris have noted, in Western traditions "the connections between play and religion are often overlooked if not hidden outright or even shunned." Bado-Fralick and Sachs Norris, *Toying with God*, 170.

35. On contemporary Pagan ritual experimentation, see Magliocco, "Ritual" and *Witching Culture*. "Affinities" quote from Maxine, contemporary Pagan, July 29, 2003. Other Pagans such as Lavender, contemporary Pagan, July 18, 2003, and Bea, contemporary Pagan, January 22, 2004, also discussed positive personal connections to Christianity.

36. Hutton, *Triumph of the Moon*; Clifton, *Her Hidden Children*.

37. Grimes, *Ritual Criticism*, 125.

38. Laura, United Church, July 30, 2003.

39. Grimes argues that such attitudes reflect larger cultural discourses about the self, writing, "Experimenting with ritual is an expression of a specifically North American ethos, one that posits experience as a primary value." *Ritual Criticism*, 111.

40. Bell, *Ritual*, 241.

41. Grimes, *Ritual Criticism*, 111.

42. Thomson, *Promise*, 359.

43. Goodchild *Capitalism and Religion*, 179.

44. Kaminer, *I'm Dysfunctional*.

45. Wuthnow, *Sharing the Journey*, 3.

46. For an examination of the construction of "religion" over and against "magic" in the fields of religious studies and anthropology, see Styers, *Making Magic*.

47. Long, *Significations*, 4.

48. Alexander, *Pedagogies of Crossing*, 296.

49. Frederick, *Between Sundays*, 88, 103–4.

50. Lincoln and Mamiya, *Black Church*, 12, qtd. in Frederick, *Between Sundays*, 233n17.

51. See chapter 3; and Albanese, *America*, 103; Cogliano, *No King*, 17; Massa, *Anti-Catholicism*, 56; Orsi, *History and Presence*.

52. Angel, Catholic, April 2, 2003.

53. Deborah, United Church, July 22, 2003.

54. Conversation, March 21, 2004. I discuss this further in chapter 3.

55. See Zatoun, "Zatoun Is Palestine in a Bottle." Franka's fair trade coffee project is discussed in depth in chapter 4.

56. Donna, United Church, July 28, 2003.

57. April 2, 2004.

58. KAIROS, "Home."

59. My participants and their groups do not universally welcome the International Socialists. This conflicted with Donna's desire that Clearwater engage in more networking with them. See chapter 4 for more detailed discussion.

60. Annie, United Church, March 14, 2004.

61. See chapter 4 for a discussion of local Marxist groups and their responses to religious affiliation.

62. Northup, *Ritualizing Women*, 87.

63. Deborah, United Church, July 22, 2003.

64. Camille, contemporary Pagan, February 5, 2004.

65. Sue, contemporary Pagan, July 16, 2003.

66. On the notion of personal agency in contemporary feminist scholarship and a parochialization of this understanding of agency, see Mahmood *Politics of Piety*. Mahmood writes, "Agentival capacity is entailed not only in those acts that resist norms but also in the multiple ways in which one *inhabits* norms" (15). She also writes, "The concept of agency should be delinked from the goals of progressive politics, a tethering that has often led to the incarceration of the notion of agency within the trope of resistance against oppressive and domineering notions of power" (34). I discuss the significance of Mahmood's theory for the forms of action my participants engage in chapter 4.

67. River, contemporary Pagan, June 26, 2003.

68. For an ethnographic example of this approach in another feminist community, see Fedele, *Looking for Mary Magdalene*.

69. As Lesley Northup articulates this understanding: "All efficacious ritual performance leads inexorably to transformation. Because ritual is

constitutive of reality, it is reality itself that is radically altered." Northup, *Ritualizing Women*, 105.

70. Griffith, *God's Daughters*, 212.
71. Northup, *Ritualizing Women*, 86.
72. J. Z. Smith, "Bare Facts," 63.
73. Grimes, *Craft*, 315.
74. Anna Reading, a Greenham activist, argues that the collective activity of composing and singing songs together creates institutional memory of core values for activist communities. Reading, "Singing for My Life."
75. Regina, Catholic, August 1, 2003.
76. Donna, United Church, July 28, 2003.
77. With a nod to Durkheim, *Elementary Forms*. Obviously rituals can do many things and include multiple power dynamics. They do not always contribute to group cohesion and identity, especially when they reinforce preexisting social hierarchies. Grimes, *Craft*, 304–6.
78. Emily, Catholic, July 24, 2003.
79. River, contemporary Pagan, June 26, 2003.
80. River, contemporary Pagan, June 26, 2003.
81. Grimes, *Craft*, 312, 325.

2. "The Shrine Was Human Rights"

1. On religion in the public sphere, see Habermas, *Between Facts and Norms* and *Structural Transformation*. See also Promey, "Public Display of Religion."
2. On the anti-globalization movement, see Graeber, *Direct Action*; Flusty, *De-Coca-Colonization*; Leite, *World Social Forum*; Santos, *Rise of the Global*; Starhawk, *Webs of Power*; Starr, *Global Revolt*. On frustrations within the Occupy movement, see Juris, "Reflections on #Occupy Everywhere"; Mitchell, Harcourt, and Taussig, *Occupy*.
3. Leclair, "Carnivals against Capital." For a broader discussion of the relationship of carnival to modernization, secularization, and capitalism, see also Taylor, *Modern Social Imaginaries*.
4. Term invented by Bey, *T.A.Z.* For further discussion, see Flusty, *De-Coca-Colonization*, 190–92.
5. Bakhtin, *Rabelais and His World*, 10.
6. Bell, *Ritual*, 257.
7. On the importance of the period of preparation to pilgrimage experiences, see Kaell, *Walking Where Jesus Walked*.
8. See Starhawk, *Webs of Power*; Leite, *World Social Forum*; Flusty, *De-Coca-Colonization*; Graeber, *Direct Action*.

9. "Cleanup Crews Erase Memory of Summit Protests."

10. The People's Summit began on April 16, 2001. See Common Frontiers Canada, "Building a Hemispheric Social Alliance in the Americas"; Mutume, "Quebec Braces for Anti-Globalisation Protests."

11. For example, Chossudovsky, "Quebec Wall"; "Thousands Converge on Quebec."

12. The route of the official march was the focus of controversy, as discussed later.

13. Panetta, "Quebec Judge Rules."

14. Petrunic, "Activist Groups."

15. On the black bloc, see Starr, "Violence"; Danaher and Mark, *Insurrection*; Starhawk, *Webs of Power*; Flusty, *De-Coca-Colonization*, 189–90; Conway, "Civil Resistance"; Panetta, "Violence Blamed"; Graeber, *Direct Action*, 149–58; Juris, "Violence Performed and Imagined."

16. For example, Lavender, contemporary Pagan, July 18, 2003; Jenna, Catholic, July 10, 2003; Judy, United Church, March 16, 2004; Angel, Catholic, April 2, 2003.

17. On the color coding, see Flusty, *De-Coca-Colonization*, 194; Starhawk, *Webs of Power*, 85–86.

18. Despite protester efforts, it was tear gas entering the building that finally ended up disrupting summit meetings. Daro, "Edge Effects."

19. Petrunic, "Activist Groups."

20. Panetta, "Violence Blamed."

21. See Starhawk, *Spiral Dance, Truth or Dare*, and *Webs of Power*. For an ethnography of the San Francisco Reclaiming Collective, see Salmonsen, *Enchanted Feminism*.

22. See Acker and Brightwell, *Off Our Rockers*; Toronto Raging Grannies, http://torontoraginggrannies.nonprofitnet.ca/ (accessed January 19, 2007; site discontinued); and Roy, *Raging Grannies*.

23. See Organizing Autonomous Telecoms, "Home."

24. See Food Not Bombs, "Home."

25. Angel, Catholic, April 4, 2003.

26. Starhawk, "Weaving a Web of Solidarity." Also qtd. in Starhawk, *Webs of Power*, 81.

27. Judy, United Church, January 16, 2004.

28. Conway, "Civil Resistance," 510.

29. Lavender, contemporary Pagan, July 17, 2003.

30. Starhawk, "Weaving a Web."

31. Starhawk, "Weaving a Web."

32. Lavender, contemporary Pagan, July 18, 2003.

33. Roberts, "Dancing into the Revolution."

34. Craig, "Debating Desire."

35. Jenna, Catholic, July 10, 2003.

36. Lavender, contemporary Pagan, July 18, 2003.

37. Abby, Catholic, February 16, 2004; Roberts, "Dancing into the Revolution," 11.

38. Abby, Catholic, February 16, 2004.

39. This document is available on many activist websites and has become a focus for water rights activism. Citizens of Bolivia, Canada, United States, India, and Brazil, "Cochabamba Declaration"; also available in Starhawk, *Webs of Power*, 83. Lavender, contemporary Pagan, July 18, 2003; River, contemporary Pagan, June 26, 2003. Starhawk, *Webs of Power*, 90–91.

40. Judy, United Church, March 16, 2004; Regina, Catholic, August 1, 2003; Abby, Catholic, February 16, 2004.

41. Jenna, Catholic, July 10, 2003.

42. Jesse, Catholic, March 17, 2004; River, contemporary Pagan, June 26, 2003; Sue, contemporary Pagan, July 17, 2003; Antonia, contemporary Pagan, July 21, 2003. See also Starhawk, *Webs of Power*, 87–88, 90–91.

43. Angel, Catholic April 2, 2003.

44. Sue, contemporary Pagan, July 16, 2003.

45. Camille, contemporary Pagan, February 5, 2004.

46. On determining the efficacy of such ritualization, see later discussion.

47. Literature on definitions of pilgrimage includes Badone and Roseman, "Approaches"; Bhardwaj and Rinschede, "Pilgrimage"; Coleman John Eade, "Introduction"; Eade and Sallnow, "Introduction"; Morinis, "Introduction"; Nolan and Nolan, *Christian Pilgrimage*; Reader, "Introduction"; Stoddard, "Defining and Classifying"; Turner and Turner, *Image and Pilgrimage*; Winkleman and Dubisch, "Introduction."

48. Frey, *Pilgrim Stories*, 219–22, 228–29.

49. Lavender, contemporary Pagan, July 18, 2003.

50. Angel, Catholic, April 2, 2003.

51. River, contemporary Pagan, June 26, 2003.

52. On "summit-hoping" as an opportunity available only to the privileged, see Daro, "Edge Effects."

53. Betty, contemporary Pagan, July 14, 2003.

54. Jenna, Catholic, July 10, 2003.

55. Morinis suggests a typology of sacred journeys including devotional, instrumental, normative, obligatory, wandering, and initiatory. Morinis, "Introduction," 10–11.

56. Reader, "Introduction," 5; Morinis, "Introduction," 4; Preston, "Spiritual Magnetism," 33.

57. Reader, "Introduction," 5–10; Preston, "Spiritual Magnetism," 44.
58. Angel, Catholic, April 2, 2003; River, contemporary Pagan, June 26, 2003; Jenna, Catholic, July 10, 2003; Sue, contemporary Pagan, July 17, 2003; Antonia, contemporary Pagan, July 21, 2003.
59. Albanese, *America*, 495.
60. Morinis, "Introduction," 4.
61. Porter, "Pilgrimage and the IDIC Ethic," 172.
62. Pike, *Earthly Bodies*. Gilmore, "Embers, Dust and Ashes" and "Fires of the Heart." For an overview of pilgrimage theory in light of contemporary Pagan pilgrimage practices more specifically, see Zwissler, "Pagan Pilgrimage"; Ivakhiv, "Green Pilgrimage."
63. Turner, *Dramas, Fields, and Metaphors*.
64. Cohen, "Pilgrimage and Tourism," 50.
65. Jenna, Catholic, July 10, 2003.
66. Lavender, contemporary Pagan, July 18, 2003.
67. Turtlekneader, Pagan Listserv email received by author, September 15, 2003.
68. Maddrell et al., *Christian Pilgrimage*.
69. Bielo, "Materializing the Bible."
70. Daro, "Edge Effects," 182.
71. Conway, "Ethnographic Approaches."
72. Fife, "Extending the Metaphor," 140.
73. Lavender, contemporary Pagan, July 18, 2003.
74. For other descriptions of this space, see Starhawk, *Webs of Power*, 84; Flusty, *De-Coca-Colonization*, 194–95.
75. Thanks to David Ferris for his account of this action (personal communication, April 21, 2001).
76. For an overview of the Turners' *communitas* and Eade and Sallnow's conflict theory, see Zwissler, "Pagan Pilgrimage."
77. Turner, *Ritual Process*, 96.
78. Turner and Turner, *Christian Pilgrimage*.
79. Grimes, *Symbol and Conquest*, 68, 73, 69. Grimes notes another difference, that is, the necessity of each form of ritualized movement to have nonparticipating spectators. He argues that parades have the most need of spectators, followed by processions and then pilgrimages (74). This raises issues about the role of marches and protest actions in anti-globalization protests. On one hand, the whole point of going to protest is to register publicly one's opposition to the policies of the conference (e.g., FTAA or WTO). That implies that one's actions will have impact beyond the march itself. On the

other hand, there is also an element of personal experience of the event, going to feel what it is like to participate (see, e.g., Camille's quote about the goal of ritualizing around violence, below) and to support other protesters.

80. Bakhtin, *Rabelais*.

81. Angel, Catholic, April 2, 2003; River, contemporary Pagan, June 26, 2003; Jenna, Catholic, July 10, 2003; Camille, Catholic, July 15, 2003; Lavender, contemporary Pagan, July 18, 2003; Antonia, contemporary Pagan, July 21, 2003.

82. Lavender, contemporary Pagan, July 18, 2003.

83. Jenna, Catholic, July 10, 2003.

84. Lavender, contemporary Pagan, July 18, 2003.

85. Anderson, *Imagined Communities*, 6.

86. Flusty, *De-Coca-Colonization*, 182.

87. Flusty, *De-Coca-Colonization*, 183.

88. Anderson, *Imagined Communities*, 6.

89. For a summary and discussion of these forces, see Flusty, *De-Coca-Colonization*, 1–21, 169–73.

90. Asad, "What Do Human Rights Do." See also Goodchild, *Theology*.

91. Clarke, *Fictions of Justice*.

92. Mahmood, *Religious Difference*. Mahmood draws on Lindkvist, "Politics of Article 18."

93. Loenen, "Safeguarding Religious Freedom"; Gürsel, "Regulating Women's Bodies"; Stuart, "Right to Freedom."

94. On religions as offering models of and models for reality, see Geertz's use of Kluckholn's terms in Geertz, "Religion as a Cultural System."

95. Eade and Sallnow, "Introduction," 15.

96. For example, Kane, "Stigmatic Cults and Pilgrimage."

97. Starhawk, *Webs of Power*, 93.

98. See, for example, Walkom, "Demonstrators' Dilemma."

99. Walkom, "Quebec City's Carnival"; Bustos, "Outside the Fence"; "Quebec City."

100. For an articulation of such views, see Conway, "Civil Resistance." For a discussion of corporate property destruction and fighting with police as "performative violence," a specific and planned type of both protest and radical identity formation, see Juris, "Violence Performed."

101. River, contemporary Pagan, June 26, 2003.

102. Angel, Catholic, April 2, 2003. For a description of activists turning others in to the police, see Conway, "Civil Resistance," 514–15.

103. River, contemporary Pagan, June 26, 2003; Lavender, contemporary

Pagan, July 18, 2003. Starhawk, *Webs of Power*, 91. See also "Turning Point for Activists."

104. Lavender, contemporary Pagan, July 18, 2003. See also Acker and Brightwell, *Off Our Rockers*, 207–8.

105. River, contemporary Pagan, June 26, 2003; Bea, contemporary Pagan, January 22, 2004.

106. River, contemporary Pagan, June 26, 2003.

107. Lavender, contemporary Pagan, July 18, 2003.

108. Daro, "Edge Effects," discusses ways that men from local, or "hosting," communities may utilize international protests as opportunity to street-fight with police or loot, yet their actions are collapsed into the protest and ascribed to visiting activists in media reports. To complicate matters further, law enforcement plants "provocateurs" among crowds to incite violence, which in turn provides excuse for mass arrests of all protesters in the area. See Juris, "Violence Performed."

109. Angel, Catholic, April 2, 2003.

110. Lavender, contemporary Pagan, July 18, 2003.

111. Starhawk, *Webs of Power*, 93.

112. Coleman, "Do You Believe in Pilgrimage," 363.

113. York, "Contemporary Pagan Pilgrimages," 139.

114. For scholarly distinctions between pilgrimage and tourism, see Badone and Roseman, "Approaches"; Zwissler, "Pagan Pilgrimage"; Swatos, *On the Road*; Kaell, "Notes on Pilgrimage"; Bielo, "Materializing the Bible"; Bremer, "Touristic Angle of Vision"; Stausberg, *Religion and Tourism*; Badone, "Conventional and Unconventional." On pilgrimage as a reflection of authenticity, see Dunn, "Historical and Modern Signs."

115. Frey, *On and Off*, 107.

116. Angel, Catholic, April 2, 2003; Lavender, contemporary Pagan, July 18, 2003; Jenna, Catholic, July 10, 2003; Judy, United Church, March 16, 2004; Carrie, contemporary Pagan, February 8, 2004; Ashley, contemporary Pagan, March 9, 2004.

117. Linda, Catholic, June 27, 2003.

118. Laidlaw, "Battle of St. Jean."

119. Olajos and Salem, "Riot Control Agents"; Ahronheim, "Medics Report." This publication is from On the Ground, a collective of street medics, people with medical training who attend demonstrations to help activists and anyone else in the protest space who may need medical attention.

120. Starhawk writes, "I would once not have considered bringing a gas mask to an action; after Quebec City it was tops on my wish list for a fiftieth birthday present." *Webs*, 226.

121. On dangers of secondhand exposure to tear gas, see Hankin and Ramsay, "Investigation of Accidental Secondary Exposure."

122. Di Matteo, "Foggy over Tear Gas Safety."

123. Cantarow, "Not Tears Alone," 16–17; Hu et al., "Tear Gas"; Heinrich, "Possible Lethal Effects."

124. Di Matteo, "Foggy"; Goldberg, "Tear Gas."

125. On the Ground Collective, *Health and Safety*; Laidlaw, "Battle"; Clarot et al., "Lethal Head Injury."

126. Lavender, contemporary Pagan, July 18, 2003.

127. Churchill, *Pacifism as Pathology*. For a critique of Churchill, see Starhawk, *Webs of Power*, 211–12.

128. Starhawk, "'Many Roads to Morning': Rethinking Nonviolence," *Webs of Power*.

129. Mahmood, *Politics of Piety*, 15, 34.

130. Butler, *Precarious Life*, xxvii.

131. Antonia, contemporary Pagan, July 21, 2003.

132. Judy, United Church, March 16, 2004.

133. Several scholars address the issue of pilgrimage as metaphor for inner experience. See, for example, Reader, "Introduction," 9; Frey, *On and Off*, 228; Morinis, "Introduction," 4; York, "Contemporary Pagan," 138; Robinson, "Pilgrimage and Mission," 172.

134. Angel, Catholic, April 2, 2003.

135. Sue, contemporary Pagan, July 16, 2003.

136. River, contemporary Pagan, July 26, 2003. On feelings of homecoming, see Reader, "Conclusions." There is also literature on a genre of "homecoming" pilgrimage. See, for example, Bon, "Secular Journeys"; Hyndman-Rizk, "Return to Hadchit"; Sax, *Mountain Goddess*.

137. Lavender, contemporary Pagan, July 18, 2003.

138. Tomlin, "Protestants and Pilgrimage," 110.

139. Bunyan, *Pilgrim's Progress*.

140. Nolan and Nolan, *Christian Pilgrimage*, 44.

141. Coleman, "Pilgrim Voices," 7; Lock, "Bowing Down to Wood"; Coleman and Elsner, "Tradition as Play."

142. On contemporary Pagan pilgrimage practices, see Dubish, "Encountering Gods and Goddesses" and "Epilogue"; Fedele, *Looking for Mary Magdalene*; Rountree, "Goddess Pilgrims as Tourists"; and Zwissler, "Pagan Pilgrimage."

143. Magliocco, "Ritual," 104, 114.

144. Robinson, "Pilgrimage," 171; York, "Contemporary Pagan," 140.

145. Zwissler, "Pagan Pilgrimage."

146. Grimes, "Infelicitous Performances."

147. Jenna, Catholic, July 10, 2003; Camille, contemporary Pagan, February 5, 2004; Camille, Catholic, July 15, 2003.

148. Judy, United Church, March 16, 2004; Abby, Catholic, February 16, 2004; Camille, contemporary Pagan, February 5, 2004.

149. Sociologist Stephen Hart argues that activists often self-censor because they believe that the more generic the description of their aims and the less surprising their actions, the broader the appeal of their calls for change will be. Hart contrasts this "constrained discourse" with "expansive discourse" grounded in personal experience and passion about the cause. Hart, *Cultural Dilemmas*.

150. Lavender, contemporary Pagan, July 18, 2003; Jesse, Catholic, March 17, 2004.

151. Lavender, contemporary Pagan, July 18, 2003; Abby, Catholic, February 16, 2004; Judy, United Church, March 16, 2004.

152. Lavender, contemporary Pagan, July 18, 2003; Jenna, Catholic, July 10, 2003.

153. Jenna, Catholic, July 10, 2003.

154. Judy, United Church, March 16, 2004; Angel, Catholic, April 2, 2003.

155. Camille, contemporary Pagan, February 5, 2004.

156. Abby, Catholic, February 16, 2004.

157. Angel, Catholic, April 2, 2003; Abby, Catholic, February 16, 2004; Antonia, contemporary Pagan, July 21, 2003. Starhawk, *Webs of Power*, 90–91.

158. Roberts, "Dancing," 1. On Women in Black, see Women in Black, "Who Are Women in Black?"

159. Judy, United Church, March 16, 2004; Jenna, Catholic, July 10, 2003; Abby, Catholic, February 16, 2004.

160. Jenna, Catholic, July 10, 2003; Abby, Catholic, February 16, 2004; Lavender, contemporary Pagan, July 18, 2003; River, contemporary Pagan, June 26, 2003; Camille, contemporary Pagan, February 5, 2004.

161. Lavender, contemporary Pagan, July 18, 2003; River, contemporary Pagan, July 26, 2003.

162. Angel, Catholic, April 2, 2003.

163. Judy, United Church, March 16, 2004.

3. *"Spirituality" as Third Choice*

1. Fedele and Knibbe, "Introduction"; Bender, *New Metaphysicals*; Frederick, *Between Sundays*; Fuller, *Spiritual, but Not Religious*; P. Klassen, *Blessed Events*; Roof, *Generation of Seekers*; Winter, Lummis, and Stokes, *Defecting in Place*; Wuthnow, *After Heaven*.

2. Latour, *We Have Never Been Modern*, 38.

3. On the "protean" nature of the term *spirituality*, see P. Klassen, "Procreating Women," 79. On the use of a discourse of authenticity, see C. Taylor, *Ethics of Authenticity*.

4. Sarah, contemporary Pagan, June 24, 2003. Note her use of New Testament terms.

5. Laura, United Church, June 30, 2003.

6. Angel, Catholic, April 2, 2003.

7. Grace, United Church, July 23, 2003.

8. For example, Asad, *Formations of the Secular*; Goodchild, *Theology of Money*; Jakobsen and Pellegrini, "Introduction"; Keane, *Christian Moderns*.

9. Wolffe, "Exploring the History," 7.

10. Orsi, *History and Presence*. For Catholic responses, see Pasulka, "Eagle."

11. Albanese, *America*, 103.

12. Wolffe, "Exploring," 7. See also Fatovic, "Anti-Catholic Roots."

13. See, for example, Marotti, *Religious Ideology*; Fenton, "Birth"; Carter, "'Traitorous Religion.'" In North America this animosity had both specific racial dimensions and violent impact on individual lives and communities. See Roediger, *Wages of Whiteness*; Ignatiev, *How the Irish Became White*; and Gordon, *Great Arizona Orphan Abduction*.

14. "While scholars disagree as to how real the threat of an Anglican Episcopal establishment in the American colonies was, the spirited debate over the prospect of such an establishment was genuine. New Englanders feared that the establishment of an Anglican hierarchy in America would be the first step toward the establishment of popery in New England." Cogliano, *No King*, 42, 8. See also Fenton, "Birth."

15. Cogliano, *No King*, 17.

16. Kenny, "Prejudice That Rarely Utters Its Name, 639; Wolffe, "Exploring," 9. On the history of British negotiation with Catholicism in the integration of Quebec, see Stevenson, *Building Nations from Diversity*, esp. 21–26 and 42–69 on concerns about Irish immigration and their relationship to anti-Catholicism in both Canada and the United States.

17. Tumbleson, *Catholicism*, 12. Note that it was not only Protestants who used Catholicism as a foil against which to prove their own modernity, though Protestantism set the terms. Joskowicz, *Modernity of Others*.

18. Tumbleson, *Catholicism*, 13, 15.

19. Fatovic, "Anti-Catholic Roots."

20. Roy, *Rhetorical Campaigns*, 192, 38.

21. Massa, *Anti-Catholicism in America*. One might rightly wonder at the subtitle, "The Last Acceptable Prejudice," but note it is also shared by Jenkins, *New Anti-Catholicism*.

22. Orsi, "U.S. Catholics," 41. See also Pasulka, "Eagle."

23. Massa, *Anti-Catholicism*, 56.

24. Fatovic, "Anti-Catholic Roots."

25. Fenton, "Birth of a Protestant Nation," 33.

26. J. Z. Smith, *Imagining Religion*, 42.

27. Orsi, "Snakes Alive," 104. See also Moore, *Religious Outsiders*.

28. Asad, "Construction of Religion."

29. Wasserstrom, *Religion after Religion*, 239.

30. Albanese, *America*, 103, 419.

31. Schmidt, *Restless Souls*.

32. C. Smith, "Introduction," 44.

33. R. Marie Griffith makes the further point that unconscious suspicion of Catholicism affects the work of contemporary scholars of gender and religion. Griffith, "Crossing the Catholic Divide." However, Jody Roy emphasizes a distinction between contemporary concerns with injustices within the church and the historical anti-Catholicism of nativist groups. Roy, "Playing the Anti-Catholic Card."

34. C. Smith, "Introduction," 19, 70.

35. On this process, see Keane, *Christian Moderns*.

36. Latour, *We Have Never Been Modern*.

37. For a classic example of this objectification of Muslim women, see Daly, *Gyn/Ecology*. For critiques, see, for example, Mahmood, *Politics of Piety*; al-Hibri, "Azizah al-Hibri"; Ahmed, *Women and Gender*; Abu-Lughod, *Do Muslim Women Need Saving*; Mohanty, "Under Western Eyes"; Hammer, "To Work for Change."

38. For discussion, see Taves and Bender, "Introduction." See also Fitzgerald, "Encompassing Religion."

39. Najmabadi, "(Un)Veiling Feminism," 41.

40. Jakobsen and Pellegrini, "World Secularisms"; Alcoff and Caputo, "Introduction;" Wilcox, "When Sheila's a Lesbian."

41. Goodchild, *Capitalism and Religion* and *Theology of Money*; Graeber, *Debt*.

42. For example, Carrette and King, *Selling Spirituality*.

43. Bender, *New Metaphysicals*; Eller, *Living*; see also Zwissler, "Second Nature"; Knibbe, "Obscuring the Role."

44. Sointu and Woodhead, "Spirituality, Gender."

45. Reilly, "Introduction," 9.

46. The literature on this is vast. See, for example, Scott, "Sexularism"; S. Ahmed, *Queer Phenomenology*; Mahmood, *Religious Difference*; Braude, "Women's History."

47. For summary, see McEwan, "Point"; Watson, "Privilege Delusion" and "It Stands to Reason."

48. Echols, *Daring to Be Bad*; Gluck et al., "Whose Feminism"; Evans, *Personal Politics*.

49. Dawkins later apologized, vaguely, for his initial reaction that (presumably non-Muslim?) American women should not complain about sexual harassment because Muslim women are much more oppressed. Dawkins, "Who Is 'Belittling' What."

50. Examples abound. A particularly well-argued analysis can be found in Hoodfar, "Veil in Their Minds." See also Scott, *Politics of the Veil*.

51. On using secularism to unmark dominant religious values, see Fessenden, *Culture and Redemption*; Mahmood, "Can Secularism Be Other-Wise." On the early history of constructing Protestantism as generic and inclusive, see Fenton, "Birth." On making religious values hard to subject to systems of laws and justice, see Asad, *Formations of the Secular*; C. Smith, "Introduction"; Mahmood, *Religious Difference*.

52. Puar, *Terrorist Assemblages*.

53. Hala, "Impact of the Islamic Movement"; Najmabadi, "(Un)Veiling Feminism"; Mahmood, *Religious Difference*.

54. Scott, "Sexularism."

55. Jakobsen and Pellegrini, "Introduction," 22.

56. Said, *Orientalism*. See also Brauner, "Cannibals, Witches, Shrews." Connolly, "Belief, Spirituality, and Time," 141. Jakobsen and Pellegrini, "Introduction," 10–11; Cavanaugh, "Colonialism and Religious Violence."

57. Jakobsen and Pellegrini, "Introduction"; Levitt, "Other Moderns"; Mahmood, *Religious Difference*.

58. Bruce, *God Is Dead*, xiii.

59. P. Berger, "Desecularization," 3. See also Orsi, "Snakes Alive."

60. C. Smith, "Introduction," 16; C. Taylor, *Modern Social Imaginaries*, 196; Chakrabarty, *Provincializing Europe*; Jakobsen and Pelegrini, "Introduction."

61. Jakobsen and Pellegrini, "World Secularisms," 23.

62. Marx, *Marx on Religion*.

63. Regina, Catholic, August 1, 2003.

64. Judy, United Church, March 16, 2004.

65. Judy, United Church, March 16, 2004.

66. Fessenden, *Culture and Redemption.*
67. Weintraub, "Theory and Politics," 7.
68. Goodchild, *Theology of Money,* 11.
69. Weintraub, "Theory and Politics," 11.
70. Casanova, *Public Religion,* 42.
71. Habermas, *Between Facts and Norm* and *Structural Transformation*; Fraser, "Rethinking the Public Sphere" and *Scales of Justice*; Reilly, "Introduction."
72. Heelas, "Spiritual Revolution," 357.
73. Bruce, *God Is Dead,* 3.
74. Heelas, "Spiritual Revolution," 104.
75. Bruce, *God Is Dead,* 22–25; Elisha, *Moral Ambition.*
76. Northup, *Ritualizing Women,* 94.
77. Many contemporary Pagans understand the term *New Age* to have connotations of frivolousness and cultural appropriation, as Fedele and Knibbe discuss in "Introduction." The group with which I did participant-observation reflects this disdain; River even occasionally punned the term to rhyme with *sewage.* That said, many of the members engaged in activities that Heelas would include within the category of New Age, such as spiritual healing, herbalism, soundings, communicating with spirit guides, and divination.
78. This seems to bear out among others' work as well. For example, Fedele, *Looking for Mary Magdalene*; Trullson, "Cultivating the Sacred."
79. P. Berger, "Secularization and Desecularization," 296; Cassanova, *Public Religions,* 57–58; Wald, *Religion and Politics,* 34.
80. Craig, "Debating Desire."
81. For similar challenges experienced among social justice–oriented Evangelicals, see Elisha, *Moral Ambition*; Bielo, *Emerging Evangelicals*; and Gasaway, *Progressive Evangelicals.*
82. Deborah, United Church, July 22, 2003.
83. Wacker, "Holy Spirit," 54; Fox, "Culture of Liberal Progressivism," 643.
84. Wacker "Holy Spirit," 42.
85. Heelas, "Spiritual Revolution," 370.
86. Albanese, "Religion and the American Experience," 349.
87. Moore, *Religious Outsiders,* 170; Williams, *God's Own Party.*
88. Stacy and Gerard, "We Are Not Doormats"; Moslener, *Virgin Nation.*
89. Griffith, *God's Daughters.*
90. P. Klassen, "Procreating Women," 84.
91. Ginsburg, *Contested Lives.*
92. Lavender, contemporary Pagan, July 18, 2003.
93. Winter, Lummis, and Stokes, *Defecting in Place.*

94. Agatha, Catholic, April 8, 2004.

95. Emily, Catholic, July 24, 2003.

96. Regina, Catholic, August 1, 2003.

97. Donna, United Church, July 28, 2003.

98. Expressed during the introductions to collective meetings (July 2 and September 29, 2003) and during interviews with founding members, some of whom include River (June 26, 2003), Betty (July14, 2003), Bea (January 22, 2004), Carrie (February 8, 2004), and Ashley (March 9, 2003).

99. C. Taylor, *Ethics of Authenticity*.

100. Moore, *Religious Outsiders*, xi.

101. Judy, United Church, March 16, 2004.

102. Bea, contemporary Pagan, January 22, 2004.

103. Angel, Catholic, April 2, 2003.

104. Judy, United Church, March 16, 2004.

105. Bender, *Heaven's Kitchen*, 70; Bruce *God Is Dead*, 199; P. Klassen, "Procreating Women," 79; Fedele and Knibbe, "Introduction."

106. P. Klassen, *Blessed Events*, 68; Mitchell, *Spirituality and the State*.

107. Angel, Catholic, April 2, 2003.

108. Deborah, United Church, July 22, 2003.

109. Maxine, contemporary Pagan, July 29, 2003.

110. Angel, Catholic, April 2, 2003; Maxine, contemporary Pagan, July 29, 2003.

111. Orientation toward Goddess worship in combination with their primary identities as Christian places Annie and Christine within a contemporary movement that Beavis has called "Christian Goddess Spirituality" in an article by the same name. See also Vincett, "Fusers"; and Fedele, *Looking for Mary Magdelene*.

112. Braude, *Radical Spirits*; Lears, *Fables of Abundance*.

113. Hutton, *Triumph of the Moon*; Aloi, "Rooted in the Occult Revival"; Clifton, *Her Hidden Children*; Zwissler, "Witches' Tears."

114. Knibbe, "Obscuring the Role"; Wilcox, "Spirituality, Activism."

115. Angel, Catholic, April 2, 2003.

116. Judy, United Church, March 16, 2004; Bea, contemporary Pagan, January 22, 2004.

117. For ethnographies of communities that similarly treat spirituality as a trans-tradition technique, see Fedele, *Looking for Mary Magdelene*; Eller, *Living*; Bender, *New Metaphysicals*; and Wilcox, "Spirituality, Activism." See also Zwissler, "Second Nature."

118. Pearson, *Wicca and the Christian Heritage*. On the significance of Christian apostolic succession to modern occult figures, such as Aleister Crowley, see J. Byrne, *Other Catholics*, 87–124.

119. Hutton, *Triumph of the Moon*, 80–81.

4. Self, Community

1. See, for example, Abu-Lughod, "Romance of Resistance"; Stacy and Gerrard, "We Are Not Doormats"; Griffith, *God's Daughters*; P. Klassen, *Blessed Events*; Mahmood, *Politics of Piety*; Rouse, *Engaged Surrender*; Najmabadi, "(Un)Veiling Feminism."
2. She writes, "I want to move away from an antagonistic and dualistic framework-one in which norms are conceptualized on the model of doing and undoing, consolidation and subversion—and instead think about the variety of ways in which norms are lived and inhabited, aspired to, reached for, and consummated." Mahmood, *Politics of Piety*, 23.
3. Pritchard, "Agency without Transcendence," 270.
4. Fineman, "Vulnerable Subject"; Mackenzie, "Importance of Relational Autonomy."
5. Goodchild, *Theology of Money*, 256.
6. Goodchild, *Theology of Money*, xxii.
7. Regina, Catholic, August 1, 2003.
8. Tiffany, Catholic, June 27, 2003.
9. Franka, United Church, July 2, 2003.
10. Grace, United Church, July 23, 2003.
11. Lavender, contemporary Pagan, July 18, 2003.
12. For internal critiques of short-term charity projects of this sort, see Elisha, *Moral Ambition*.
13. Tiffany, June 27, 2003.
14. River, contemporary Pagan, July 24, 2003.
15. Regina, August 1, 2003.
16. J. Z. Smith, "Influence of Symbols," 143.
17. Goodchild, *Capitalism and Religion* and *Theology of Money*.
18. Goodchild, *Capitalism and Religion*, 200.
19. Goodchild, *Theology of Money*, 59.
20. Ten Days for World Development became Ten Days for Global Justice and is now incorporated into KAIROS: Canadian Ecumenical Justice Initiatives. See KAIROS, "Be Not Afraid."
21. The groups that were supporting Franka's project and funding refugee camps were also giving money to revolutionary struggles in these places. Franka said: "The World Council of Churches had given grants of money to the liberation groups, say, ANC, in southern Africa, South Africa and Rhodesia, or Zimbabwe now, but Rhodesia then. And they were being accused—well,

cuso and the World Council of Churches—were all being accused of supporting terrorism. So, I mean that was the big thing" (July 2, 2003).

cuso, Canadian University Service Overseas, has been mainly funded through the Canadian International Development Agency since 1968. For its beginnings and its role in these struggles, see Canadian University Service Overseas, "Our History."

The World Council of Churches is an ecumenical organization involving most of the world's Christian denominations, including Orthodox traditions but excluding the Roman Catholic Church, with which it has, nonetheless, worked closely. The organization was founded in 1948. See World Council of Churches, "History."

22. Franka, United Church, July 2, 2003. The following comments are all from this interview.

23. Oxfam Canada, "Introduction to Oxfam."

24. See Bridgehead, "History."

25. The fair trade movement in North America is largely traced to Edna Ruth Byler, an American Mennonite whose efforts on behalf of women in Puerto Rico grew into the organization known today as Ten Thousand Villages. See DeCarlo, *Fair Trade*; Lyon and Moberg, *Fair Trade*; K. Brown, *Buying into Fair Trade*.

26. See Zatoun, "Zatoun Is Palestine in a Bottle."

27. Rawls, *Theory of Justice*.

28. Noddings, *Caring*, 47, 79, 86.

29. In contrast, Patricia Hill Collins articulates ways in which an ethic of caring, rather than facilitating withdrawal from the world, as Noddings proposes, actually provides a foundation for political activism. Collins shows how the tradition of "other-mothering," that is, caring for children who are not one's direct blood relations, serves as a model and motivation for activism to serve African American communities and other oppressed groups. Collins, "Black Women and Motherhood."

30. Gilligan, *In a Different Voice*.

31. Gilligan, "Moral Orientation," 34.

32. Gilligan, *In a Different Voice* and "Moral Orientation."

33. Noddings, *Caring*, 100.

34. Gilligan, "Do the Social Sciences Have an Adequate Theory."

35. Rawls, *Theory of Justice*.

36. See Bell, *Rethinking Ethics*.

37. Benhabib, "Generalized and the Concrete Other." Marilyn Friedman contends that care ethics, especially as articulated as gendered, *do* stand up to empirical inquiry. Arguing that they are outside the realm of

rational evaluation merely serves to further marginalize feminist ethics and subvert care as a valid ethical tool. Moreover, the gendering of ethical orientations—that is, linking men with cold justice reasoning and women with warm caring reasoning—is both born of and reinforces traditional gender roles within Western culture. She maintains that by lauding care ethics as superior to justice ethics and by arguing that concern with care ethics is the result of women's current condition, care ethicists end up celebrating women's current oppression under patriarchy, a problem with feminist essentializing in general. Friedman, "Beyond Caring." Joan Tronto also argues that just like traditional justice ethics, care ethics limit women's moral purview to only the "private sphere" of domesticity and personal relationships, "the feminine approach to caring bears the burden of accepting traditional gender divisions in a society that devalues what women do." Tronto, "Women and Caring," 112. On the way care ethics restricts moral reasoning, see, for example, Noddings, *Caring*, 86; Bell, *Rethinking Ethics*, 36–48.

38. Mullin, *Reconceiving Pregnancy*, 188.

39. Tronto, "Women and Caring."

40. DuPlessis and Snitow, *Feminist Memoir Project*; Mohanty, "Under Western Eyes"; al-Hibri, "Azizah al-Hibri"; Williams, "Delores Williams"; Peskowitz, "Unweaving."

41. Mullin, *Reconceiving Pregnancy*, 188. See also Dodds, "Dependence, Care, and Vulnerability."

42. Held, "Feminist Moral Inquiry," 173.

43. Van Osselaer, "Religion, Family and Domesticity"; Elisha, *Moral Ambition*.

44. Elisha, *Moral Ambition*.

45. Gilligan, "Moral Orientation."

46. For an overview of this newer work, see Held, "Taking Care."

47. Held, *Ethics of Care*; Ruddick, *Maternal Thinking* and "Making Connections." Bubeck, *Care, Gender, and Justice*; Mackenzie, Rogers, and Dodds, "Introduction." Held, "Care and Justice."

48. Crenshaw, "Demarginalizing the Intersection" and "From Private Violence"; Collins, *Black Feminist Thought* and "Intersectionality's Definitional Dilemmas"; Cho, Crenshaw, and McCall, "Toward a Field"; MacKinnon, "Intersectionality as Method."

49. The term *social justice* has many meanings in popular and theological discourse. In this project I am not offering an exclusive definition of *social justice* but, rather, an exploration of ways the term is used in practice by particular communities.

50. Derrida, *Politics of Friendship*.

51. Gandhi, *Affective Communities*, 189.

52. These terms were used ubiquitously with all three groups and are part of current discourse within Toronto activist groups more broadly, a discourse they share with social justice activists in North America and abroad.

53. Gutiérrez, *Theology of Liberation*.

54. On Victorian reform in general, see Pascoe, *Relations of Rescue*; Yung, *Unbound Feet*; Wollcott, *Remaking Respectability*. On residential schools, see Milloy, *National Crime*; Chrisjohn, Young, and Maraun, *Circle Game*; Schissel and Wotherspoon, "Legacy of Residential Schools." On Toronto the Good, see Valverde, *Age of Light*.

55. Yarrow Collective meeting, September 29, 2003.

56. Starhawk, *Truth or Dare*, 8–10.

57. Frederick, *Between Sundays*; Griffith, *God's Daughters*; Mahmood, *Politics of Piety*. Considering agency from beyond the binary of accommodating or resisting structures of power is central in their work, but see esp. Frederick, *Between Sundays*, 5–6 and 212–20; Griffith, *God's Daughters*, 199–213; and Mahmood, *Politics of Piety*, 5–32.

58. Participants in the Black Church in North Carolina, in the conservative Christian Women Aglow movement in North America, and in the conservative Muslim mosque movement in Egypt, respectively.

59. Mahmood, *Politics of Piety*, 17.

60. Frederick, *Between Sundays*, 94.

61. Frankenberg, *White Women, Race Matters*.

62. Woods, "Plea over Harper's Columbia Visit"; "Where People Disappear"; International Centre for Human Rights and Democratic Development, "John Humphrey Freedom Award Past Winners"; Council of Canadians / Conseil des Canadiens, "Remembering Water Justice Activist."

63. Jenna, Catholic, July 10, 2003.

64. Butler, *Precarious Life*, xii; see also Brunner, "Occidentalism."

65. Cavanaugh, "Colonialism and Religious Violence"; Goodchild, *Theology*; Butler, *Precarious Life*.

66. The Ontario Coalition against Poverty (OCAP) advocates for housing for the homeless and includes homeless people in its actions. See Ontario Coalition against Poverty, "About." Many supporters believe it is the visible presence of poor people, along with confrontational rhetoric, that causes police to target the group and the media to cover it negatively.

67. Laura, United Church, July 30, 2003.

68. Angel, Catholic, April 1, 2003.

69. Lavender, contemporary Pagan, July 18, 2003.

70. For an overview of the history of ceremonial magic groups in Britain, see Hutton, *Triumph of the Moon*, esp. chapter 5, "Finding a High Magic," 66–83; and Albanese, *Republic of Mind*, 21–65. Aleister Crowley's formulations of "magick" have found particular influence in various forms of contemporary Paganism through Gerald Gardiner, arguably the founder of contemporary Witchcraft. See M. Adler, *Drawing Down the Moon*, 60–66; and Hutton, *Triumph of the Moon*, 205–41. Crowley's ideas about magic and spiritual energies can be found throughout contemporary Pagan communities and, more generally, in popular understandings of spiritual power. For example, a famous quote from one of his treatises on magic shows up in different forms, often detached from him entirely: "Magick is the Science and Art of causing Change to occur in conformity with Will. Every intentional act is a Magickal Act." Crowley, *Magick*, 126–27. For a discussion of magic in contemporary Pagan communities more generally, see M. Adler, *Drawing Down the Moon*, 1–40. In addition to its circulation within contemporary Pagan and New Age circles, Crowley's formulation of magic is picked up by Anton LaVey in his version of Satanism, in which magic is understood as an extension of will, or manifesting one's will in the world. LaVey, *Satanic Bible*.

71. There actually was a contemporary case of animal cruelty in Toronto that garnered national media attention. An art school student and two accomplices tortured to death a feral cat, capturing the horror on film. They were turned into the police by a roommate, tried, and convicted. See "Cruelty to Cat" and "Animal Activists"; DiManno, "Unspeakable Horror"; Wente, "How Katie Got Her Man." A documentary film was made about the case and its aftermath, critically investigating the claims of the defendants that their actions constituted "art" and therefore should be protected as free expression. Asher, *Casuistry*. The documentary was screened at the Toronto International Film Festival in 2004 to much controversy. "Head of Animal Group."

72. On Satanic rumors generally, see Victor, *Satanic Panic*; Frankfurter, "Beyond Magic" and *Evil Incarnate*; Richardson, Best, and Bromley, *Satanism*; Cohn, *Europe's Inner Demons*. For the specific issue of the rumor of Satanists killing cats, see Victor, "Dynamics of Rumor Panics," 227. For links to rumors surrounding other animal deaths, such as cattle mutilations, see Balch and Gilliam, "Devil Worship," 258–59. On conservative Christians' perpetuation of this myth, see Balch and Gilliam, "Devil Worship," 254–55; Victor, *Satanic Panic*, 234. For how rumors operated historically in specific contexts, see Ostling, *Between the Devil*. On their stubborn survival within academe in new forms, see Ostling, "Babyfat and Belladonna"; Zwissler, "In Memorium

Maleficarum." For a parody of Christian justification for killing cats, see "Dave," "Are Cats for True Christians." While the parody was created to satirize the Jehovah's Witness publication *Watch Tower Magazine*, it has, nonetheless, engaged many comment thread contributors, some of whom approach the text earnestly. See, for example, the discussion spurred by a reposting by "J.R., U.S.A." to the discussion thread "Are Cats for True Christians," Paradise Cafe Discussions.

73. Victor, "Dynamics" and *Satanic Panic*; Frankfurter, "Beyond Magic" and *Evil Incarnate*.
74. For a religious Satanist's critique of contemporary Paganism's disowning of Satanism, see Baddeley, *Lucifer Rising*, 64.
75. Spivak, "Can the Subaltern Speak." Spivak's focus is powerful deconstruction of colonial *sati* rumors.
76. Frederick, *Between Sundays*, 171.
77. Mahmood, *Politics of Piety*, 122–26, 156–61, 126.
78. This drop-in is now facilitated by the Justice, Peace and Environment group.
79. Annie, United Church, March 14, 2004.
80. Lears, *No Place of Grace*, 47; see also P. Klassen, *Spirits of Protestantism*.
81. For a thorough investigation of metaphysical traditions, see Albanese, *Republic of Mind*; on contemporary groups that inherit such traditions, see Bender, *New Metaphysicals*.
82. Lears, *No Place of Grace*, 53, 54.
83. Reiser, *Chautauqua Moment*, 238.
84. Satter, *Each Mind a Kingdom*, 240.
85. Lears, *Fables of Abundance*, 60.
86. Lears, *Fables of Abundance*, 61; Owen, *Darkened Room*, 109.
87. Owen, *Darkened Room*, 109.
88. Lears, *Fables of Abundance*, 62.
89. Braude, *Radical Spirits*, 4–5, 23.
90. P. Klassen, *Spirits of Protestantism*.
91. Lears, *Fables of Abundance*, 62.
92. Braude, *Radical Spirits*, 146; P. Klassen, *Spirits of Protestantism*.
93. Satter, *Each Mind a Kingdom*, 239–43, 4–5.
94. Kaminer, *I'm Dysfunctional*, 49–53; Bender, *New Metaphysicals*.
95. Yvnne Chireau, *Black Magic*. See also Albanese, *Republic of Mind*, esp. chapter 2, "Atlantic Journeys, Native Grounds," 66–120.
96. Alexander, "Pedagogies of the Sacred."
97. Duncan, *This Spot of Ground*.

98. On ways that North American Protestantism has been deeply influenced by outside traditions of healing, see P. Klassen, *Spirits of Protestantism*.

99. For similar experiences of cultural borrowing, in this case Asian traditions, by Anglicans, see P. Klassen, "Ritual Appropriation."

100. Franka, United Church, July 2, 2003.

101. Franka, United Church, July 2, 2003.

102. For a United Church perspective on its role in the residential schools project, see United Church of Canada, "Truth and Reconciliation Commission."

103. Chrisjohn, Young, and Maraun, *Circle Game*; Milloy, *National Crime*; Schissel and Wotherspoon, "Legacy."

104. United Church of Canada, "Apology to Former Students." For the church this apology is seen as an extension of the 1986 *Apology to First Nations*, which did not deal explicitly with complicity in the residential school project. United Church of Canada, *Toward Justice and Right Relationship*. The Truth and Reconciliation Commission of Canada posts the outcomes of related court cases. See the Truth and Reconciliation Commission of Canada, "Resources."

105. See United Church of Canada, *Healing Fund*.

106. "Toward Justice and Right Relationship: A Beginning." Described in the bulletin as follows: "How we as church can live in right relation with Aboriginal Canadians after the Residential Schools, a five-week video study." Qtd. from Clearwater bulletin, March 21, 2004. See United Church of Canada, *Toward Justice and Right Relationship*.

107. King, *Fishing in Contested Waters*.

108. Idle No More, http://www.idlenomore.ca/. See also Graveline, "IDLE NO MORE"; Scott, "Forces That Conspire." Idle No More participants also contributed to the Standing Rock Dakota Access Pipeline protest in the western United States.

109. Wotherspoon and Hansen, "'Idle No More' Movement"; Friedel, "Understanding the Nature." Obviously, Idle No More began well after my fieldwork ended. However, many participants from all three communities have since been involved in Idle No More protests and projects, in addition to support for Standing Rock.

110. March 7, 2004. I was not able to get the citation of Laura's reading.

111. Personal communication, March 21, 2004.

112. Donaldson, "On Medicine Women," 250.

113. P. Klassen, "Ritual Appropriation," 367.

114. Lavender, contemporary Pagan, July 18, 2003.

115. River, contemporary Pagan, July 26, 2003.

116. Franka, United Church, July 2, 2003; Grace, United Church, July 23, 2003; Emily, Catholic, July 24, 2003.

117. Personal communication, March 21, 2004.

118. Deborah, United Church, July 22, 2003.

119. River, contemporary Pagan, July 26, 2003.

120. Kaminer, *I'm Dysfunctional*, 15, 79, 95. Sarita Srivastava levels a similar critique against institutional anti-racism and anti-oppression trainings because they locate social change exclusively within the individual, blocking systemic change by emphasizing personal therapy and an unattainable political purity. Srivastava, "You're Calling Me a Racist." The Yarrow Collective was in the process of scheduling a weekend anti-oppression training when my fieldwork ended.

121. V. Taylor, *Rock-a-Bye-Baby*. First, she emphasizes that critiques of twelve-step programs should not be automatically extrapolated to the self-help movement as a whole (7). Second, she roots the self-help movement historically as intertwined with moral reform movements in 1920s North America, movements closely interrelated with feminist concerns. Third, she argues that though self-help may focus on the individual, it is always in the context of social connection. She writes, "Even if women's self-help takes the individual to be the locus of change, it encourages the collective pursuit of personal problems that can be seen as a direct result of men's domination and women's subordination" (9). She disagrees with Kaminer here and, instead of seeing declawed feminism, sees proto-feminist organizing (150).

122. Taylor, *Rock-a-Bye-Baby*, 165, 126, 179. Taylor's assessment coincides with Robert Wuthnow's appraisal of the role of small groups in social change. In *Sharing the Journey* Wuthnow writes: "We need to acknowledge that small, informal groups may divert attention from larger social issues. But we also must be practical enough to know that a utopian redirection of energy will never happen. What can happen is a small investment of time and effort. And that will happen only through existing social networks" (359).

123. Nora, contemporary Pagan, June 24, 2003.

124. Nora, contemporary Pagan, June 24, 2003.

125. Marks, "Challenging Binaries," 118.

126. Fessenden, "Gendering Religion."

127. On the New Left, see O'Neill, *New Left*; Gosse, *Rethinking the New Left*. On feminism's relationship to the New Left, see Evans, *Personal Politics*; Echols, *Daring to Be Bad*; and Tong, *Feminist Thought*.

128. Thompson, *Promise and a Way of Life*, 359.

129. River, contemporary Pagan, June 26, 2003.

130. I am not suggesting that this is the only possible reading of Marx but that this is a particular strand of Marxism present in secularly oriented activist communities, with which my participants interact.

131. Tessman, *Burdened Virtues*.

132. For a Canadian Socialist perspective on competition between religious cosmologies and Marxism, see Löwy, "Marxism and Religion."

133. Mouffe, *Return of the Political*, 13, qtd. in Gandhi, *Affective Communities*, 196n34.

134. Even in writing to persuade fellow activists not to dismiss Muslims as potential allies in socialist struggles, for example, Dave Crouch offers an explanation for his interest in religion: "As a boy I was attracted to the ritual of the Anglican church, which I attended regularly. All the same, I don't recall having any genuine religious conviction until my early 20s, when I had a powerful sense that my fate was in the hands of a higher being. In retrospect this was probably a reflection of the personal upheaval, poverty and hopelessness I experienced at the time. I was bitterly angry about society and could conceivably have been attracted to a religious sect, to violence, or religious violence. Instead I found Marxism offered a more effective understanding of the world and a guide to changing it." Crouch, "Bolsheviks and Islam."

135. McClary, "Same as It Ever Was."

136. Marx and Engels, *Communist Manifesto*, 80–95.

137. River, contemporary Pagan, June 26, 2003.

138. Heidi and Antonia mentioned this work again at the collective meeting on July 2, 2003.

139. Grimes discusses a rite by a ritual performance group to purify a mountain retreat after a murder in the area. Grimes, *Ritual Criticism*, 114.

140. Frederick, *Between Sundays*, 12.

141. Pritchard, "Agency," 280.

Bibliography

Abramson, Allen, and Martin Holbraad, eds. *Framing Cosmologies: The Anthropology of Worlds*. Manchester: Manchester University Press, 2014.

Abu-Lughod, Lila. *Do Muslim Women Need Saving?* Cambridge: Harvard University Press, 2013.

———. "The Romance of Resistance: Tracing Transformations of Power through Bedouin Women." *American Ethnologist* 17, no. 1 (1990): 41–55.

Acker, Allison, and Betty Brightwell. *Off Our Rockers and into Trouble: The Raging Grannies*. Victoria BC: TouchWood Editions, 2004.

Adler, Margot. *Drawing Down the Moon: Witches, Druids, Goddess-Worshippers, and Other Pagans in America Today*. Boston: Beacon Press, 1986.

Adler, Rachel. *Engendering Judaism: An Inclusive Theology and Ethics*. Philadelphia: Jewish Publication Society, 1998.

Ahmed, Leila. *Women and Gender in Islam: Historical Roots of a Modern Debate*. New Haven: Yale University Press, 1992.

Ahmed, Sara. *Queer Phenomenology: Orientations, Objects, Others*. Durham NC: Duke University Press, 2006.

Ahronheim, Sarah. "Medics Report from the Front." *Canadian Dimensions* 13, no. 3 (May–June 2001): 6.

Albanese, Catherine. *America: Religion and Religions*. 3rd ed. Belmont CA: Wadsworth Publishing Co., 1999.

———. *Nature Religion in America: From Algonkian Indians to the New Age*. Chicago: University of Chicago Press, 1990.

———. *Reconsidering Nature Religion*. Harrisburg PA: Trinity Press International, 2002.

———. "Religion and the American Experience: A Century Later." *Church History* 57, no. 3 (1988): 337–51.

———. *A Republic of Mind and Spirit: A Cultural History of American Metaphysical Religion*. New Haven CT: Yale University Press, 2007.

Alcoff, Linda Martin, and John. D. Caputo. "Introduction: Feminism, Sexuality, and the Return of Religion." In *Feminism, Sexuality and the Return of*

Religion, edited by Linda Martin Alcoff and John D. Caputo, 1–16. Bloomington: Indiana University Press, 2011.

Alexander, M. Jacqui. *Pedagogies of Crossing: Meditations on Feminism, Sexual Politics, Memory, and the Sacred.* Durham NC: Duke University Press, 2005.

al-Hibri, Azizah. "Azizah al-Hibri." In *Transforming the Faiths of Our Fathers: Women Who Changed American Religion*, edited by Ann Braude, 47–54. Boston: Beacon Press, 2004.

Ali, Kecia. *Sexual Ethics and Islam: Feminist Reflections on Qur'an, Hadith, and Jurisprudence.* 2006. Reprint, Braintree MA: Oneworld Publications, 2016.

Allahyari, Rebecca Anne. *Visions of Charity: Volunteer Workers and Moral Community.* Berkeley: University of California Press, 2000.

Aloi, Peg. "Rooted in the Occult Revival: Neo-Paganism's Evolving Relationship with Popular Media." In *Handbook of Contemporary Paganism*, edited by Murphy Pizza and James R. Lewis, 539–76. Boston: Brill, 2009.

Alpert, Rebecca T., ed. *Voices of the Religious Left: A Contemporary Sourcebook.* Philadelphia: Temple University Press, 2000.

Anderson, Benedict. *Imagined Communities: Reflections on the Origins and Spread of Nationalism.* Rev. ed. 1983. Reprint, London: Verso, 1991.

Anderson, Leona M., and Pamela Dickey Young. *Women and Religious Traditions.* New York: Oxford University Press, 2010.

"Animal Activists Want Tougher Sentences for Cruelty." CBC News, March 29, 2002. http://www.cbc.ca/canada/toronto/story/2002/03/29/mar2902 _cats.html (accessed November 12, 2006; page discontinued).

Anzaldúa, Gloria. *Borderlands / La Frontera: The New Mestiza.* 3rd ed. Minneapolis: Aunt Lute, 2007.

Asad, Talal. *Formations of the Secular: Christianity, Islam, Modernity.* Stanford: Stanford University Press, 2003.

———. *Genealogies of Religion: Discipline and Reasons of Power in Christianity and Islam.* Baltimore: Johns Hopkins University Press, 1993.

———. "What Do Human Rights Do? An Anthropological Enquiry." *Theory and Event* 4, no. 4 (October 2000). https://muse.jhu.edu/article/32601 (accessed May 2, 2017).

Asher, Zev, dir. *Casuistry: The Art of Killing a Cat.* Toronto: Rough Age Projectiles, 2004. Film, 91 mins.

Baddeley, Gavin. *Lucifer Rising: A Book of Sin, Devil Worship, and Rock 'n' Roll.* New York: Plexus, 1999.

Badejo, Diedre. *Osun Seegesi: The Elegant Deity of Wealth, Power, and Femininity.* Trenton NJ: Africa World Press, 1996.

Bado-Fralick, Nikki. *Coming to the Edge of the Circle: A Wiccan Initiation Ritual.* Oxford: Oxford University Press, 2005.

Bado-Fralick, Nikki, and Rebecca Sachs Norris. *Toying with God: The World of Religious Games and Dolls*. Waco TX: Baylor University Press, 2010.

Badone, Ellen. "Conventional and Unconventional Pilgrimages: Conceptualizing Sacred Travel in the Twenty-First Century." In *Redefining Pilgrimage: New Perspectives on Historical and Contemporary Pilgrimages*, edited by Antón M. Pazos, 7–32. New York: Routledge, 2016.

Badone, Ellen, and Sharon R. Roseman. "Approaches to the Anthropology of Pilgrimage and Tourism." In *Intersecting Journeys: The Anthropology of Pilgrimage and Tourism*, edited by Ellen Badone and Sharon R. Roseman, 1–23. Urbana: University of Illinois Press, 2004.

Baker, Kimball. *Go to the Worker: America's Labor Apostles*. Marquette WI: Marquette University Press, 2010.

Bakhtin, Mikhail. *Rabelais and His World*. Translated by Hélène Iswolsky. 1968. Reprint, Bloomington: Indiana University Press, 1984.

Balch, Robert W., and Margaret Gilliam. "Devil Worship in Western Montana: A Case Study in Rumor Construction." In *The Satanism Scare*, edited by James T. Richardson, Joel Best, and David Bromley, 249–62. New York: Aldine de Gruyter, 1991.

Basrudin, Azza. *Humanizing the Sacred: Sisters in Islam and the Struggle for Gender Justice in Malaysia*. Seattle: University of Washington Press, 2016.

Beavis, Mary Ann. "Christian Goddess Spirituality and Thealogy." *Feminist Theology* 24, no. 2 (2016): 125–38.

Bednarowski, Mary Farrell. *The Religious Imagination of American Women*. Bloomington: Indiana University Press, 1999.

Bell, Catherine. *Ritual: Perspectives and Dimensions*. New York: Oxford University Press, 1997.

———. *Ritual Theory, Ritual Practice*. Oxford: Oxford University Press, 1992.

Bell, Linda. *Rethinking Ethics in the Midst of Violence: A Feminist Approach to Freedom*. Lanham MD: Rowman & Littlefield, 1993.

Bender, Courtney. *Heaven's Kitchen: Living Religion at God's Love We Deliver*. Chicago: University of Chicago Press, 2003.

———. *The New Metaphysicals: Spirituality and the American Religious Imagination*. Chicago: University of Chicago Press, 2010.

Bendroth, Margaret Lamberts. *Fundamentalism and Gender, 1875–Present*. New Haven: Yale University Press, 1993.

Benhabib, Selya. "The Generalized and the Concrete Other: The Kohlberg-Gilligan Controversy and Moral Theory." In *Women and Moral Theory*, edited by Eva Feder Kittay and Diana T. Meyers, 154–77. New York: Rowman & Littlefield, 1987.

Bennett, James B. "'Until This Curse of Polygamy Is Wiped Out': Black Methodists, White Mormons, and Constructions of Racial Identity in the Late Nineteenth Century." *Religion and American Culture* 21, no. 2 (2011): 167–94.

Berger, Helen A. *A Community of Witches: Contemporary Neo-Paganism and Witchcraft in the United States*. Columbia: University of South Carolina Press, 1999.

Berger, Helen A., Evan A. Leach, and Leigh S. Shafer. *Voices from the Pagan Census: A National Survey of Witches and Neo-Pagans in the United States*. Columbia: University of South Carolina Press, 2003.

Berger, Peter L. "The Desecularization of the World: A Global Overview." In *The Desecularization of the World: Resurgent Religion and World Politics*, edited by Peter L. Berger, 1–18. Grand Rapids MI: Eerdmans, 1999.

———. "Secularization and Desecularization." In *Religions of the Modern World: Traditions and Transformations*, edited by Linda Woodhead, Paul Fletcher, Hiroko Kawanami, and David Smith, 291–98. New York: Routledge, 2002.

Bey, Hakim. *T.A.Z.: The Temporary Autonomous Zone, Ontological Anarchy, Poetic Terrorism*. New York: Autonomedia, 1991.

Bhardwaj, Surinder M., and Gisbert Rinschede. "Pilgrimage—A World Wide Phenomenon." In *Pilgrimage in World Religions*, edited by Surinder M. Bhardwaj and Gisbert Rinschede, 11–20. Berlin: Dietrich Reimer, 1988.

Bielo, James S. *Emerging Evangelicals: Faith, Modernity, and the Desire for Authenticity*. New York: New York University Press, 2011.

———. "Materializing the Bible: Ethnographic Methods for the Consumption Process." *Practical Matters: A Journal of Religious Practices and Practical Theology*, May 4, 2016. http://wp.me/p6QAmj-EB (accessed May 11, 2016).

Boddy, Janice. *Wombs and Alien Spirits: Women, Men, and the Zār Cult in Northern Sudan*. Madison: University of Wisconsin Press, 1989.

Bordon, Sandra L. "Communitarian Journalism and the Common Good: Lessons from *The Catholic Worker*." *Journalism* 15, no. 3 (2014): 273–88.

Bouma, Beverley. "Jesus Was a Feminist: An Institutional Ethnography of Feminist Christian Women." *Illumine* 5, no. 1 (2006): 1–10.

Braude, Ann. "Faith, Feminism and History." In *The Religious History of American Women: Reimagining the Past*, edited by Catherine A. Brekus, 232–52. Chapel Hill: University of North Carolina Press, 2007.

———. *Radical Spirits: Spiritualism and Women's Rights in Nineteenth-Century America*. Boston: Beacon Press, 1989.

———, ed. *Transforming the Faiths of Our Fathers: Women Who Changed American Religion*. New York: Palgrave Macmillan, 2004.

————. "Women's History *Is* American Religious History." In *Retelling U.S. Religious History*, edited by Thomas Tweed, 87–107. Berkeley: University of California Press, 1997.

Brauner, Sigrid. "Cannibals, Witches, and Shrews in the 'Civilizing Process.'" In *"Neue Welt" / "Dritte Welt": Interkulturelle Beziehungen Deutschlands zu Latinamerika und der Karibik*, edited by Sigrid Bauschinger and Susan L. Cocalis, 1–27. Tübingen: Francke, 1995.

Bremer, Thomas S. "Touristic Angle of Vision: Tourist Studies as a Methodological Approach for the Study of Religions." *Religion Compass* 8, no. 12 (2014): 371–79.

Bridgehead. "History." n.d. http://www.bridgehead.ca/pages/history (accessed January 6, 2017).

Brock, Rita Nakashima. *Journeys by Heart: A Christology of Erotic Power*. New York: Crossroad, 1988.

Brown, Karen McCarthy. *Mama Lola: A Vodou Priestess in Brooklyn*. Berkeley: University of California Press, 1991.

Brown, Keith R. *Buying into Fair Trade: Culture, Morality, and Consumption*. New York: New York University Press, 2013.

Bruce, Steve. *God Is Dead: Secularization in the West*. Oxford: Wiley-Blackwell, 2002.

Brunner, Claudia. "Occidentalism Meets the Female Suicide Bomber: A Critical Reflection on Recent Terrorism Debates. A Review Essay." *Signs* 32, no. 4 (2007): 957–71.

Bubeck, Diemut. *Care, Gender, and Justice*. New York: Oxford University Press, 1995.

Budapest, Zsuzsanna Emese. *The Holy Book of Women's Mysteries*. Oakland CA: Z. E. Budapest and Susan B. Anthony Coven No. 1, 1979.

Bunyan, John. *The Pilgrim's Progress*. Edited by W. R. Owens. Oxford: Oxford University Press, 2003.

Burack, Cynthia. *Tough Love: Sexuality, Compassion, and the Christian Right*. Albany NY: State University of New York Press, 2014.

Bustos, Alejandro. "Outside the Fence: Young Activists Inspired Despite Violence of Protest." Canadian Press, April 21, 2001. http://www.segabg.com/article.php?id=178011 (accessed January 5, 2017).

Butler, Anthea D. *Women in the Church of God in Christ: Making a Sanctified World*. Chapel Hill: University of North Carolina Press, 2007.

Butler, Judith. *Gender Trouble: Feminism and the Subversion of Identity*. New York: Routledge, 1990.

————. *Precarious Life: The Powers of Mourning and Violence*. London: Verso, 2004.

Bynum, Carolyn Walker. *Holy Feast, Holy Fast: The Religious Significance of Food to Medieval Women*. Berkeley: University of California Press, 1987.

Byrne, Carol. *The Catholic Worker Movement (1933–1980): A Critical Analysis.* Bloomington IN: AuthorHouse, 2010.

Byrne, Julie. *The Other Catholics: Remaking America's Largest Religion.* New York: Columbia University Press, 2016.

Cannon, Mae Elise. *Just Spirituality: How Faith Practices Fuel Social Action.* Downers Grove IL: InterVarsity Press, 2013.

Cantarow, Ellen. "Not Tears Alone." *Technology Review* 91 (October 1988): 16–17.

Carrette, Jeremy R., and Richard King. *Selling Spirituality: The Silent Takeover of Religion.* New York: Routledge, 2005.

Carter, Michael S. "A 'Traitorous Religion': Indulgences and the Anti-Catholic Imagination in Eighteenth Century New England." *Catholic Historical Review* 99, no. 1 (2013): 52–77.

Casanova, José. "Nativism and the Politics of Gender in Catholicism and Islam." In *Gendering Religion and Politics: Untangling Modernities,* edited by Hanna Herzog and Ann Braude, 21–50. New York: Palgrave, 2009.

Castelli, Elizabeth A., and Rosamond C. Rodman, eds. *Women, Gender, Religion: A Reader.* New York: Palgrave, 2001.

Catholic Worker. "Home." n.d. http://www.catholicworker.org (accessed January 18, 2017).

Cavanaugh, William T. "Colonialism and Religious Violence." In *Religion and the Secular: Historical and Colonial Formations,* edited by Timothy Fitzgerald, 241–62. London: Equinox, 2007.

Chakrabarty, Dipesh. *Provincializing Europe: Postcolonial Thought and Historical Difference.* Princeton NJ: Princeton University Press, 2000.

Charles, Larry, dir. *Religulous.* Produced by Thousand Words. Distributed by Blue Sky Media, 2008. Film.

Chernus, Ira. "Dorothy Day and the Catholic Worker Movement." In *American Nonviolence: The History of an Idea,* 145–60. Maryknoll NY: Orbis Books, 2004.

Chireau, Yvonne. *Black Magic: Religion and the African American Conjuring Tradition.* Berkeley: University of California Press, 2003.

Cho, Sumi, Kimberlé Williams Crenshaw, and Leslie McCall. "Toward a Field of Intersectionality Studies: Theory, Applications, and Praxis." *Signs* 38, no. 4 (2013): 785–810.

Chossudovsky, Michel. "The Quebec Wall." *Jackson Progressive,* April 18, 2001. http://www.jacksonprogressive.com/issues/trade/chossudovskyquebec.html (accessed January 4, 2017; site discontinued; available at https://www.nadir.org/nadir/initiativ/agp/free/chossudovsky/quebec.htm).

Chrisjohn, Roland, and Sherri Young, with Michael Maraun. *The Circle Game: Shadows and Substance in the Indian Residential School Experience in Canada*. Penticton BC: Theytus Books, 2005.

Christ, Carol. *The Laughter of Aphrodite: Reflections on a Journey to the Goddess*. San Francisco: Harper & Row, 1987.

———. "Musings on the Goddess and Her Cultured Despisers Provoked by Naomi Goldenberg." *Feminist Theology* 13, no. 2 (2005): 143–49.

———. *Rebirth of the Goddess: Finding Meaning in Feminist Spirituality*. Reading MA: Addison-Wesley, 1997.

Churchill, Ward. *Pacifism as Pathology: Reflections on the Role of Armed Struggle in North America*. Winnipeg: Arbeiter Ring Publishing, 1998.

Cimino, Richard, and Christopher Smith. *Atheist Awakening: Secular Activism and Community in America*. Oxford: Oxford University Press, 2014.

Citizens of Bolivia, Canada, United States, India, and Brazil. "The Cochabamba Declaration." Archives of Global Protests, December 8, 2000. http://www.nadir.org/nadir/initiativ/agp/free/imf/bolivia/cochabamba .htm (accessed January 4, 2017).

Clarke, Kamari Maxine. *Fictions of Justice: The International Criminal Court and the Challenge of Legal Pluralism in Sub-Saharan Africa*. Cambridge: Cambridge University Press, 2009.

Clarke, L. "Women in Islam." In *Women and Religious Traditions*, edited by Leona M. Anderson and Pamela Dickey Young, 193–224. New York: Oxford University Press, 2010.

Clarot, Franck, et al. "Lethal Head Injury Due to Tear-Gas Cartridge Gunshots." *Forensic Science International* 137, no. 1 (October 2003): 45–51.

"Cleanup Crews Erase Memory of Summit Protests." CBC News, April 24, 2001. http://www.cbc.ca/news/canada/cleanup-crews-erase-memory -of-summit-protests-1.294556 (accessed January 4, 2017).

Clifton, Chas. *Her Hidden Children: The Rise of Wicca and Paganism in America*. Lanham MD: Alta Mira Press, 2006.

Cobble, Dorothy Sue, Linda Gordon, and Astrid Henry. *Feminism Unfinished: A Short, Surprising History of American Women's Movements*. New York: Liveright, 2014.

Cogliano, Francis D. *No King, No Popery: Anti-Catholicism in Revolutionary New England*. Westport CT: Greenwood Press, 1995.

Cohen, Erik. "Pilgrimage and Tourism: Convergence and Divergence." In *Sacred Journeys: The Anthropology of Pilgrimage*, edited by Alan Morinis, 47–64. Westport CT: Greenwood Press, 1992.

Cohn, Norman. *Europe's Inner Demons: An Enquiry Inspired by the Great Witch-Hunt*. Sussex: Sussex University Press, 1975.

Coleman, Kristy S. *Re-riting Woman: Dianic Wicca and the Feminine Divine*. Lanham MD: AltaMira, 2009.

Coleman, Simon. "Do You Believe in Pilgrimage? *Communitas*, Contestation, and Beyond." *Anthropological Theory* 2, no. 3 (2002): 355–68.

———. "Pilgrim Voices: Authoring Christian Pilgrimage." In *Pilgrim Voices: Narrative and Authorship in Christian Pilgrimage*, edited by Simon Coleman and John Elsner, 1–16. New York: Berghahn Books, 2003.

Coleman, Simon, and John Eade. "Introduction: Reframing Pilgrimage." In *Reframing Pilgrimage: Cultures in Motion*, edited by Simon Coleman and John Eade, 1–25. New York: Routledge, 2004.

Coleman, Simon, and John Elsner. "Tradition as Play: Pilgrimage to 'England's Nazareth.'" *History and Anthropology* 15, no. 3 (September 2004): 273–88.

Collier-Thomas, Bettye. *Jesus, Jobs, and Justice: African American Women and Religion*. New York: Random House, 2010.

Collins, Patricia Hill. *Black Feminist Thought: Knowledge, Consciousness, and the Politics of Empowerment*. New York: Routledge, 1990.

———. "Black Women and Motherhood." In *Justice and Care: Essential Readings in Feminist Ethics*, edited by Virginia Held, 117–38. Boulder CO: Westview Press, 1995.

———. "Intersectionality's Definitional Dilemmas." *Annual Review of Sociology* 41 (2015): 1–20.

———. *On Intellectual Activism*. Philadelphia: Temple University Press, 2013.

Common Frontiers Canada. "Building a Hemispheric Social Alliance in the Americas." http://www.commonfrontiers.ca/Current_Activities /Hemispheric.html#1 (accessed January 4, 2017).

———. "The FTAA: It's Hazardous for Your Health." http://www .commonfrontiers.ca/oldsite/call-out_eng_colour%20_final.pdf (accessed January 4, 2017).

Connolly, William E. "Belief, Spirituality, and Time." In *Varieties of Secularism in a Secular Age*, edited by Michael Warner, Jonathan VanAntwerpen, and Craig Calhoun, 126–44. Cambridge: Harvard University Press, 2010.

Conway, Janet. "Civil Resistance and the 'Diversity of Tactics' in the Anti-Globalization Movement: Problems of Violence, Silence, and Solidarity in Activist Politics." *Osgoode Law Journal* 41, nos. 2–3 (2003): 505–30.

———. "Ethnographic Approaches to the World Social Forum." In *Insurgent Encounters: Transnational Activism, Ethnography, and the Political*, edited by Jeffrey S. Juris and Alex Khasnabish, 267–92. Durham NC: Duke University Press, 2013.

Corrigan, John, and Lynn S. Neal. *Religious Intolerance in America: A Documentary History*. Chapel Hill: University of North Carolina Press, 2010.

Council of Canadians / Conseil des Canadiens. "Remembering Water Justice Activist Kimy Domico." June 2, 2015. http://canadians.org/blog/remembering -water-justice-activist-kimy-pernia-domico (accessed January 6, 2017).

Cowan, Doug E. *Cyberhenge: Modern Pagans on the Internet*. New York: Routledge, 2005.

Coy, Patrick G. "An Experiment in Personalist Politics: The Catholic Worker Movement and Nonviolent Action." *Peace & Change* 26, no. 1 (January 2001): 78–94.

Craig, David M. "Debating Desire: Civil Rights, Ritual Protest, and the Shifting Boundaries of Public Reason." *Journal of the Society of Christian Ethics* 27, no. 1 (2007): 157–82.

Craig, Robert H. *Religion and Radical Politics: An Alternative Christian Tradition in the United States*. Philadelphia: Temple University Press, 1992.

Crenshaw, Kimberlé. "Demarginalizing the Intersection of Race and Sex: A Black Feminist Critique of Antidiscrimination Doctrine, Feminist Theory and Antiracist Politics." *University of Chicago Legal Forum* 140, no. 1 (1989): 139–67.

———. "From Private Violence to Mass Incarcerations: Thinking Intersectionally about Women, Violence and State Control." *UCLA Law Review* 59 (2012): 1418–73.

———. "Mapping the Margins: Intersectionality, Identity Politics and Violence against Women of Color." *Stanford Law Review* 43 (1991): 1241–99.

Crouch, Dave. "The Bolsheviks and Islam." *International Socialism: A Quarterly Journal of Socialist Theory* 110 (Spring 2006). http://isj.org.uk /the-bolsheviks-and-islam/.

Crowley, Aleister. *Magick: Liber Alba: Book 4*. San Francisco: Weiser Books, 1998.

"Cruelty to Cat Lands Art Student in Court." CBC News, July 27, 2001. http:// www.cbc.ca/news/canada/cruelty-to-cat-lands-art-student-in-court -1.295034 (accessed January 6, 2017).

Cuso International. "Our History." 2017. http://www.cusointernational.org /about-cuso/our-history (accessed January 6, 2017).

Daly, Mary. *Beyond God the Father: Toward a Philosophy of Women's Liberation*. Boston: Beacon Press, 1973.

———. *Gyn/Ecology: The MetaEthics of Radical Feminism*. Boston: Beacon Press, 1978.

―――. *Outercourse: The Be-Dazzling Voyage: Containing Recollections from My Logbook of a Radical Feminist Philosopher (Be-ing an Account of my Time/ Space Travels and Ideas—Then, Again, Now, and How)*. San Francisco: HarperSanFrancisco, 1992.

Danaher, Kevin, and Jason Mark. *Insurrection: Citizen Challenges to Corporate Power*. New York: Routledge, 2003.

Daro, Vinci. "The Edge Effects of Alter-Globalization Protests." In *Insurgent Encounters: Transnational Activism, Ethnography, and the Political*, edited by Jeffrey S. Juris and Alex Khasnabish, 171–95. Durham NC: Duke University Press, 2013.

"Dave." "Are Cats for True Christians? (Is it appropriate for a Christian to own a cat, in light of their past pagan religious affiliation and the medical information that is now coming to light?)" JW Files, n.d. http://www .jwfiles.com/wt_ex_jw_corner/cats.htm (accessed January 6, 2017).

Davie, Jody Shapiro. *Women in the Presence: Constructing Community and Seeking Spirituality in Mainline Protestantism*. Philadelphia: University of Pennsylvania Press, 1995.

Dawkins, Richard. *Brief Candle in the Dark: My Life in Science*. New York: Ecco, 2015.

―――. *The God Delusion*. Boston: Houghton Mifflin, 2006.

―――. *The Magic of Reality: How We Know What's Really True*. New York: Free Press, 2011.

―――. "Who Is 'Belittling' What?" Richard Dawkins Foundation for Reason and Science, August 6, 2014. https://richarddawkins.net/2014/08 /who-is-belittling-what/ (accessed January 5, 2017).

De B'Béri, Boulou Ebanda. "The Politics of Knowledge: The Promised Land Project and Black Canadian History as a Model of Historical 'Manufactur-ation.'" In *The Promised Land: History and Historiography of the Black Experience in Chatham-Kent's Settlements and Beyond*, edited by Boulou Ebanda de B'Béri, Nina Reid-Maroney, and Handel Kashope Wright, 17–39. Toronto: University of Toronto Press, 2014.

DeCarlo, Jacqueline. *Fair Trade: Beginner's Guide*. Oxford: One World Publications, 2007.

Dennett, Daniel C. *Breaking the Spell: Religion as a Natural Phenomenon*. New York: Viking, 2006.

DeRogatis, Amy. *Saving Sex: Sexuality and Salvation in American Evangeli-calism*. New York: Oxford University Press, 2015.

Derrida, Jacques. *Politics of Friendship*. Translated by George Collins. New York: Verso, 1997.

De Waal, Frans, *The Bonobo and the Atheist: In Search of Humanism among the Primates*. New York: Norton, 2013.

Diamant, Anita. *The Red Tent*. New York: Picador USA, 1997.

DiManno, Rosie. "Unspeakable Horror of the Cat Torturers." *Toronto Star*, April 15, 2002, A2.

Di Matteo, Enzo. "Foggy over Tear Gas Safety." *Now*, May 17, 2001. http://www.nowtoronto.com/news/story.cfm?content=127434 (accessed January 5, 2017).

Dodds, Susan. "Dependence, Care, and Vulnerability." In *Vulnerability: New Essays in Ethics and Feminist Philosophy*, edited by Catriona Mackenzie, Wendy Rogers, and Susan Dodds, 181–203. New York: Oxford University Press, 2014.

Donaldson, Laura E. "On Medicine Women and White Shame-ans: New Age Native Americanism and Commodity Fetishism as Pop Culture Feminism." In *Women, Gender, Religion: A Reader*, edited by Elizabeth A. Castelli and Rosamond C. Rodman, 237–53. New York: Palgrave, 2001.

Dubisch, Jill. "Encountering Gods and Goddesses: Two Pilgrimages in Greece." *Crosscurrents* 59, no. 3 (2009): 283–99.

———. "Epilogue: The Many Faces of Mary." In *Moved by Mary: The Power of Pilgrimage in the Modern World*, edited by Anna-Karina Hermkens, Willy Jansen, and Catrien Notermans, 227–38. Aldershot: Ashgate, 2009.

———. *In a Different Place: Pilgrimage, Gender, and Politics at a Greek Island Shrine*. Princeton NJ: Princeton University Press, 1995.

Dufferin Grove News. "About Us." January 31, 2005. http://www.dufferinpark.ca/aboutus/wiki/wiki.php (accessed January 4, 2017).

———. "Home." http://dufferinpark.ca/home/wiki/wiki.php (accessed January 4, 2017).

Duncan, Carol. *This Spot of Ground: Spiritual Baptists in Toronto*. Waterloo ON: Wilfrid Laurier Press, 2008.

Dunn, Maryjane. "Historical and Modern Signs of 'Real' Pilgrims on the Road to Santiago de Compostela." In *The Camino de Santiago in the 21st Century*, edited by Samuel Sánchez y Sánchez and Annie Hesp, 13–35. New York: Routledge, 2015.

DuPlessis, Rachel Blau, and Ann Snitow, eds. *The Feminist Memoir Project: Voices from Women's Liberation*. New York: Crown Publishing, 1998.

Durkheim, Émile. *The Elementary Forms of Religious Life*. Translated by Joseph Ward Swain. 1915. Reprint, New York: Free Press, 1965.

Eade, John, and Michael J. Sallnow. "Introduction." In *Contesting the Sacred: The Anthropology of Christian Pilgrimage*, edited by John Eade and Michael J. Sallnow, 1–29. London: Routledge, 1991.

Eagleton, Terry. "Lunging, Flailing, Mispunching." *London Review of Books*, October 19, 2006, 32–34.

Echols, Alice. *Daring to Be Bad: Radical Feminism in America, 1967–1975.* Minneapolis: University of Minnesota Press, 1989.

Eisler, Riane. *The Chalice and the Blade: Our History, Our Future.* Cambridge: Harper & Row, 1987.

Elisha, Omri. *Moral Ambition: Mobilization and Social Outreach in Evangelical Megachurches.* Berkeley: University of California Press, 2011.

Eller, Cynthia. *Gentlemen and Amazons: The Myth of Matriarchal Prehistory, 1861–1900.* Berkeley: University of California Press, 2011.

———. *Living in the Lap of the Goddess: The Feminist Spirituality Movement in America.* New York: Crossroad, 1993.

———. *The Myth of Matriarchal Prehistory: Why an Invented Past Won't Give Women a Future.* Boston: Beacon Press, 2000.

Ellis, Marc H. *A Year at the Catholic Worker.* New York: Paulist Press, 1978.

Engelke, Matthew. "Christianity and the Anthropology of Secular Humanism." *Current Anthropology* 55, no. 10 (2014): 297–300.

Erzen, Tanya. *Straight to Jesus: Sexual and Christian Conversions in the Ex-Gay Movement.* Berkeley: University of California Press, 2006.

Evans, Sara M., ed. *Journeys That Opened Up the World: Women, Student Christian Movements, and Social Justice, 1955–1975.* New Brunswick NJ: Rutgers University Press, 2003.

———. *Personal Politics: The Roots of Women's Liberation in the Civil Rights Movement.* New York: Vintage Books, 1979.

Falwell, Jerry. Interview with Pat Robertson. *The 700 Club.* Christian Broadcasting Network, September 13, 2001.

Fatovic, Clement. "The Anti-Catholic Roots of Liberal and Republican Conceptions of Freedom in English Political Thought." *Journal of the History of Ideas* 66, no. 1 (2005): 37–58.

Fedele, Anna. "Créativité et incertitude dans les nouveaux rituels contemporains." *Social Compass* 61, no. 4 (2014): 497–510.

———. *Looking for Mary Magdalene: Alternative Pilgrimage and Ritual Creativity at Catholic Shrines in France.* New York: Oxford University Press, 2013.

Fedele, Anna, and Kim Knibbe. "Introduction: Gender and Power in Contemporary Spirituality." In *Gender and Power in Contemporary Spirituality: Ethnographic Approaches,* edited by Anna Fedele and Kim E. Knibbe, 1–27. New York: Routledge, 2013.

Fenton, Elizabeth. "Birth of a Protestant Nation: Catholic Canadians, Religious Pluralism, and National Unity in the Early U.S. Republic." *Early American Literature* 41, no. 1 (2006): 29–57.

Fessenden, Tracy. *Culture and Redemption: Religion, the Secular, and American Literature.* Princeton NJ: Princeton University Press, 2007.

———. "Disappearances: Race, Religion, and the Progress Narrative of U.S. Feminism." In *Secularisms*, edited by Janet R. Jakobsen and Ann Pellegrini, 139–61. Durham NC: Duke University Press, 2008.

———. "Gendering Religion." *Journal of Women's History* 14, no. 1 (2002): 163–69.

Fife, Wayne. "Extending the Metaphor: British Missionaries as Pilgrims in New Guinea." In *Intersecting Journeys: The Anthropology of Pilgrimage and Tourism*, edited by Ellen Badone and Sharon R. Roseman, 140–59. Chicago: University of Illinois Press, 2004.

Fineman, Martha Albertson. "The Vulnerable Subject: Anchoring Equality in the Human Condition." *Yale Journal of Law and Feminism* 20, no. 1 (2008): 1–23.

Finley, Nancy J. "Political Activism and Feminist Spirituality." *Sociological Analysis* 54, no. 4 (Winter 1991): 349–62.

Fitzgerald, Timothy. "Encompassing Religion, Privatized Religions and the Invention of Modern Politics." In *Religion and the Secular: Historical and Colonial Formations*, edited by Timothy Fitzgerald, 211–40. London: Equinox, 2007.

Flusty, Steven. *De-Coca-Colonization: Making the Globe from the Inside Out.* New York: Routledge, 2004.

Food Not Bombs. "Home." http://www.foodnotbombs.net/new_site/ (accessed January 4, 2017).

Ford, Heidi A. "Hierarchical Inversions, Divine Subversions: The Miracles of Râbi'a al-Ádawîya." *Journal of Feminist Studies in Religion* 15, no. 1 (1999): 5–24.

Foster, Lawrence. *Women, Family, Utopia: Communal Experiments of the Shakers, the Oneida Community, and the Mormons.* Syracuse: Syracuse University Press, 1991.

Foucault, Michel. *Discipline and Punish: The Birth of the Prison.* Translated by Alan Sheridan. 1977. Reprint, New York: Vintage, 1995.

Fox, Richard Wightman. "The Culture of Liberal Progressivism, 1875–1925." *Journal for Interdisciplinary History* 23, no. 3 (1993): 639–60.

Frankenberg, Ruth. *White Women, Race Matters.* Minneapolis: University of Minnesota Press, 1993.

Frankfurter, David. "Beyond Magic and Superstition." In *People's History of Christianity*, vol. 2: *Late Ancient Christianity*, edited by Virginia Burrus, 255–84. Minneapolis: Fortress, 2005.

———. *Evil Incarnate: Rumors of Demonic Conspiracy and Ritual Abuse in History.* Princeton NJ: Princeton University Press, 2006.

Franklin, V. P., and Bettye Collier-Thomas. "For the Race in General and Black Women in Particular: The Civil Rights Activities of African American Women's Organizations, 1915–1950." In *Sisters in the Struggle: African American Women in the Civil Rights–Black Power Movement*, edited by

Bettye Collier-Thomas and V. P. Franklin, 21–41. New York: New York University Press, 2001.

Fraser, Nancy. "Rethinking the Public Sphere: A Contribution to the Critique of Actually Existing Democracy." In *Habermas and the Public Sphere*, edited by Craig Calhoun, 109–42. Cambridge MA: MIT Press, 1992.

———. *Scales of Justice: Reimagining Political Space in a Globalizing World.* New York: Columbia University Press, 2009.

Frederick, Marla F. *Between Sundays: Black Women and Everyday Struggles of Faith.* Berkeley: University of California Press, 2003.

Frey, Nancy. *Pilgrim Stories: On and Off the Road to Santiago.* Berkeley: University of California Press, 1998.

Friedel, Tracy L. "Understanding the Nature of Indigenous Youth Activism in Canada: Idle No More as a Resumptive Pedagogy." *South Atlantic Quarterly* 114, no. 4 (2015): 878–91.

Friedman, Marilyn. "Beyond Caring: The De-Moralization of Gender." In *Justice and Care: Essential Readings in Feminist Ethics*, edited by Virginia Held, 61–78. Boulder CO: Westview Press, 1995.

Frink, Sandra. "Women, the Family, and the Fate of the Nation in American Anti-Catholic Narrative, 1830–1860." *Journal of the History of Sexuality* 18, no. 2 (2009): 237–64.

Fuller, Robert. *Spiritual, but Not Religious: Understanding Unchurched America.* Oxford: Oxford University Press, 2001.

Gallant, Sarah Marie. "Imagination, Empowerment and Imaginary Figures." In *Feminist Spirituality: The Next Generation*, edited by Chris Klassen, 13–32. Lanham MD: Lexington Books, 2009.

Gandhi, Leela. *Affective Communities: Anticolonial Thought, Fin-de-Siècle Radicalism, and the Politics of Friendship.* Durham NC: Duke University Press, 2006.

Gasaway, Brantley W. *Progressive Evangelicals and the Pursuit of Social Justice.* Chapel Hill: University of North Carolina Press, 2014.

Geertz, Clifford. "Religion as a Cultural System." In *The Interpretation of Cultures: Selected Essays*, 87–125. New York: Basic Books, 1973.

Gerber, Lynne. *Seeking the Straight and Narrow: Weight Loss and Sexual Reorientation in Evangelical America.* Chicago: University of Chicago Press, 2011.

Gilkes, Cheryl Townsend. *"If It Wasn't for the Women . . .": Black Women's Experience and Womanist Culture in Church and Community.* Maryknoll NY: Orbis Books, 2001.

Gilligan, Carol. "Do the Social Sciences Have an Adequate Theory of Moral Development?" In *Social Science as Moral Inquiry*, edited by Norma Haan,

Robert N. Bellah, Paul Rabinow, and William M. Sullivan, 33–51. New York: Columbia University Press, 1983.

———. *In a Different Voice: Psychological Theory and Women's Development*. Cambridge: Harvard University Press, 1982.

———. "Moral Orientation and Moral Development." In *Justice and Care: Essential Readings in Feminist Ethics*, edited by Virginia Held, 31–46. Boulder CO: Westview Press, 1995.

Gillis, Stacy, Gillian Howie, and Rebecca Munford, eds. *Third Wave Feminism: A Critical Exploration*. Houndmills, Basingstoke, Hampshire: Palgrave Macmillan, 2007.

Gilmore, Lee. "Embers, Dust, and Ashes: Pilgrimage and Healing at the Burning Man Festival." In *Pilgrimage and Healing*, edited by Jill Dubisch and Michael Winkelman, 155–78. Tucson: University of Arizona Press, 2005.

———. "Fires of the Heart: Ritual, Pilgrimage and Transformation at Burning Man." In *AfterBurn: Reflections on Burning Man*, edited by Lee Gilmore and Mark Van Proyen, 43–64. Albuquerque: University of New Mexico Press, 2005.

Gimbutas, Marija. *Civilization of the Goddess*. San Francisco: HarperSanFrancisco, 1991.

———. *Goddesses and Gods of Old Europe, 7000–3500 B.C.* Berkeley: University of California Press, 1974.

Ginsburg, Faye D. *Contested Lives: The Abortion Debate in an American Community*. Berkeley: University of California Press, 1989.

Gluck, Sherna Berger, et al. "Whose Feminism, Whose History? Reflections on Excavating the History of (the) U.S. Women's Movement(s)." In *Community Activism and Feminist Politics: Organizing across Race, Class and Gender*, edited by Nancy A. Naples, 31–56. New York: Routledge. 1998.

Goldberg, Michelle. "Tear Gas Is an Abortifacient. Why Won't the Anti-Abortion Movement Oppose It?" *Nation*, August 19, 2014. http://www.thenation.com/blog/181318/tear-gas-abortifacient-why-wont-anti-abortion-movement-oppose-it# (accessed January 5, 2017).

Goldenberg, Naomi. *The Changing of the Gods: Feminism and the End of Traditional Religions*. Boston: Beacon Press, 1979.

Goodchild, Philip. *Capitalism and Religion: The Price of Piety*. New York: Routledge, 2002.

———. *The Theology of Money*. Durham NC: Duke University Press, 2009.

Gordon, Linda. "Black and White Visions of Welfare: Women's Welfare Activism, 1890–1945." *Journal of American History* 78, no. 2 (1991): 559–90.

———. *The Great Arizona Orphan Abduction*. Cambridge: Harvard University Press, 2009.

Gosse, Van. *Rethinking the New Left: An Interpretive History*. New York: Palgrave, 2005.

Graeber, David. *Debt: The First 5000 Years*. Brooklyn: Melville House, 2011.

———. *Direct Action: An Ethnography*. Edinburgh: AK Press, 2009.

Graveline, Fyre Jean. "IDLE NO MORE: Enough Is Enough!" *Canadian Social Work Review / Revue canadienne de service social* 29, no. 2 (2012): 293–300.

Grayson, Deborah R. "'Necessity Was the Midwife of Our Politics': Black Women's Health Activism in the 'Post'–Civil Rights Era." In *Still Lifting, Still Climbing: African American Women's Contemporary Activism*, edited by Kimberly Springer, 131–48. New York: New York University Press, 1999.

Gregorič Bon, Nataša. "Secular Journeys, Sacred Places: Pilgrimage and Homemaking in Himarë/Himara Area of Southern Albania." In *Pilgrimage, Politics and Place-Making in Eastern Europe: Crossing the Borders*, edited by John Eade and Mario Katić, 135–49. Farnham, UK: Routledge, 2016.

Grewal, Inderpal, and Caren Kaplan. *An Introduction to Women's Studies: Gender in a Transnational World*. Boston: McGraw-Hill, 2006.

Griffin, Wendy. "Goddess Spirituality and Wicca." In *Her Voice, Her Faith: Women Speak on World Religions*, edited by Arvind Sharma and Katherine K. Young, 243–82. Boulder CO: Westview Press, 2003.

———. "Webs of Women: Feminist Spiritualities." In *Witchcraft and Magic: Contemporary North America*, edited by Helen A. Berger, 55–80. Philadelphia: University of Pennsylvania Press, 2005.

Griffith, R. Marie. *Born Again Bodies: Flesh and Spirit in American Christianity*. Berkeley: University of California Press, 2004.

———. *God's Daughters: Evangelical Women and the Power of Submission*. Berkeley: University of California Press, 1997.

Grimes, Ronald L. *The Craft of Ritual Studies*. Oxford: Oxford University Press, 2013.

———. *Ritual Criticism: Case Studies in Its Practice, Essays on Its Theory*. Columbia: University of South Carolina Press, 1990.

———. *Symbol and Conquest: Public Ritual and Drama in Santa Fe, New Mexico*. Ithaca NY: Cornell University Press, 1976.

Grow, Matthew J. "The Whore of Babylon and the Abomination of Abominations: Nineteenth-Century Catholic and Mormon Perceptions and Religious Identity." *Church History* 73, no. 1 (2004): 139–67.

Gürsel, Esra Demir. "Regulating Women's Bodies in the Jurisprudence of the European Court of Human Rights." In *Religion, Gender, and the Public Sphere*, edited by Niamh Reilly and Stacey Scriver, 155–67. New York: Routledge, 2014.

Gutiérrez, Gustavo. *A Theology of Liberation: History, Politics, and Salvation.* Maryknoll NY: Orbis Books, 1973.

Habermas, Jürgen. *Between Facts and Norms.* Translated by William Rehg. Cambridge MA: MIT Press, 2001.

———. *The Structural Transformation of the Public Sphere.* Translated by Thomas Burger and Frederick Lawrence. Cambridge MA: MIT Press, 1989.

Hall, David D., ed. *Lived Religion in America: Toward a History of Practice.* Princeton NJ: Princeton University Press, 1997.

Hammer, Juliane. *American Muslim Women, Religious Authority, and Activism: More than a Prayer.* Austin: University of Texas Press, 2012.

———. "To Work for Change: Normativity, Feminism, and Islam." *Journal of the American Academy of Religion* 84, no. 1 (2016): 98–112.

Handleman, Kali, ed. *The Revealer: A Review of Religion and Media.* Website. Center for Religion and Media, New York University. https://wp.nyu.edu /therevealer/ (accessed January 18, 2017).

Hankin, Steven M., and Colin N. Ramsay. "Investigation of Accidental Secondary Exposure to cs Agent." *Clinical Toxicology* 45, no. 4 (May 2007): 409–11.

Hankins, Barry. *American Evangelicals: A Contemporary History of a Mainstream Religious Movement.* Lanham MD: Rowman & Littlefield, 2008.

Harris, Duchess. "From the Kennedy Commission to the Combahee River Collective: Black Feminist Organizing 1960–1980." In *Sisters in the Struggle: African American Women in the Civil Rights–Black Power Movement,* edited by Bettye Collier-Thomas and V. P. Franklin, 280–305. New York: New York University Press, 2001.

Harris, Sam. *The End of Faith: Religion, Terror, and the Future of Reason.* New York: Norton, 2004.

———. *Letter to a Christian Nation.* New York: Knopf, 2006.

———. *Waking Up: A Guide to Spirituality without Religion.* New York: Simon & Schuster, 2014.

Hart, Stephen. *Cultural Dilemmas of Progressive Politics: Styles of Engagement among Grassroots Activists.* Chicago: University of Chicago Press, 2001.

Hassan, Riffat. "Feminist Theology as a Means of Combating Injustice toward Women in Muslim Communities and Culture." In *Evil and the Response of World Religion,* edited by William Cenkner, 80–95. St. Paul MN: Paragon House, 1997.

———. "Riffat Hassan." In *Transforming the Faiths of Our Fathers: Women Who Changed American Religion,* edited by Ann Braude, 173–97. New York: Palgrave Macmillan, 2004.

"Head of Animal Group Defends TIFF over Cat Doc." *Toronto Globe and Mail*, September 8, 2004. http://www.theglobeandmail.com/arts/head-of -animal-group-defends-tiff-over-cat-doc/article1003693/ (accessed January 6, 2017).

Hedges, Chris. *I Don't Believe in Atheists*. New York: Free Press, 2008.

Heelas, Paul. "The Spiritual Revolution: From 'Religion' to 'Spirituality.'" In *Religions of the Modern World: Traditions and Transformations*, edited by Linda Woodhead, Paul Fletcher, Hiroko Kawanami, and David Smith, 357–77. New York: Routledge, 2002.

Heinrich, Uwe. "Possible Lethal Effects of CS Tear Gas on Branch Davidians during the FBI Raid on the Mount Carmel Compound near Waco, Texas." Office of U.S. Special Counsel John C. Danforth, Washington DC, April 19, 1993. http://www.veritagiustizia.it/docs/gas_cs/CS_Effects_Waco.pdf (accessed January 5, 2017).

Held, Virginia. "Care and Justice in the Global Context." *Ratio Juris* 17, no. 2 (June 2004): 141–55.

———. *The Ethics of Care: Personal, Political, Global*. New York: Oxford University Press, 2006.

———. "Feminist Moral Inquiry and the Feminist Future." In *Justice and Care: Essential Readings in Feminist Ethics*, edited by Virginia Held, 153–78. Boulder CO: Westview Press, 1995.

———. "Taking Care: Care as Practice and Value." In *Setting the Moral Compass: Essays by Women Philosophers*, edited by Cheshire Calhoun, 59–71. New York: Oxford University Press, 2004.

Heller, Dana. *Cross-Purposes: Lesbians, Feminists, and the Limits of Alliance*. Bloomington: Indiana University Press, 1997.

Herzog, Hanna, and Ann Braude, eds. *Gendering Religion and Politics: Untangling Modernities*. New York: Palgrave, 2009.

Hewitt, Nancy A., ed. *No Permanent Waves: Recasting Histories of U.S. Feminism*. New Brunswick NJ: Rutgers University Press, 2010.

Hidayatullah, Aysha A. *Feminist Edges of the Qur'an*. New York: Oxford University Press, 2014.

Higginbotham, Evelyn Brooks. *Righteous Discontent: The Women's Movement in the Black Baptist Church, 1880–1920*. Cambridge: Harvard University Press, 1993.

Hiltebeitl, Alf, and Kathleen M. Erndl, eds. *Is the Goddess a Feminist? The Politics of South Asian Goddesses*. New York: New York University Press, 2000.

Hitchens, Christopher. *God Is Not Great: How Religion Poisons Everything*. New York: Twelve, 2007.

———. *Morality*. New York: Hachette, 2012.

Hoodfar, Homa. "The Veil in Their Minds and on Our Heads: Veiling Practices and Muslim Women." In *Women, Gender, Religion: A Reader*, edited by Elizabeth A. Castelli and Rosamond C. Rodman, 420–46. New York: Palgrave, 2001.

hooks, bell. *Ain't I a Woman: Black Women and Feminism*. Boston: South End Press, 1981.

Hu, Howard, MD, MPH, et al. "Tear Gas: Harassing Agent or Toxic Chemical Weapon?" *Journal of the American Medical Association* 262, no. 5 (August 1989): 660–63.

Hutton, Ronald. "Paganism and Polemic: The Debate over the Origins of Modern Pagan Witchcraft." *Folklore* III, no. 1 (2000): 103–17.

———. *The Triumph of the Moon: A History of Modern Pagan Witchcraft*. Oxford: Oxford University Press, 1999.

Hyndman-Rizk, Nelia. "Return to Hadchit: The Virtual, Spiritual and Temporal Dimensions of Pilgrimage." In *Pilgrimage in the Age of Globalization: Constructions of the Sacred and Secular in Late Modernity*, edited by Nelia Hyndman-Rizk, 170–201. Newcastle upon Tyne: Cambridge Scholars, 2012.

Ignatiev, Noel. *How the Irish Became White*. New York: Routledge, 1995.

Imam, Aysha M. "The Muslim Religious Right ('Fundamentalists') and Sexuality." In *Good Sex: Feminist Perspectives from the World's Religions*, edited by Patricia Beattie Jung, Mary E. Hunt, and Radhika Balakrishnan, 15–30. New Brunswick NJ: Rutgers University Press, 2002.

International Centre for Human Rights and Democratic Development. "John Humphrey Freedom Award Past Winners: Mr. Kimy Pernía Domicó (Colombia) and Angélica Mendoza de Ascarza (Peru)." http://www.dd-rd.ca/site/humphrey_award/index.php?id=610&subsection=past_winners (accessed March 2, 2008; site discontinued).

Isasi-Díaz, Ada María. *En la Lucha / In the Struggle: Elaborating a Mujerista Theology*. Minneapolis: Fortress, 2004.

———. *Mujerista Theology: A Theology for the Twenty-First Century*. Maryknoll NY: Orbis Books, 1996.

Ivakhiv, Adrian. "Green Pilgrimage: Problems and Prospects for Ecological Peacebuilding." In *Pilgrims and Pilgrimages as Peacemakers in Christianity, Judaism and Islam*, edited by Antón M. Pazos, 85–103. Burlington VT: Ashgate, 2013.

Jackson, Jerma A. *Singing in My Soul: Black Gospel Music in a Secular Age*. Chapel Hill: University of North Carolina Press, 2004.

Jacobs, Janet. "Women-Centered Healing Rites: A Study of Alienation and Reintegration." In *In Gods We Trust: New Patterns of Religious Pluralism in*

America, edited by Thomas Robbins and Dick Anthony, 373–83. New Brunswick NJ: Transaction Publications, 1993.

Jaggar, Alison M. *Feminist Politics and Human Nature*. Lanham MD: Rowman & Littlefield, 1983.

Jakobsen, Janet R., and Pellegrini, Ann. "Introduction: Times like These." In *Secularisms*, edited by Janet R. Jakobsen and Ann Pellegrini, 1–35. Durham NC: Duke University Press, 2008.

———. "World Secularisms at the Millennium: Introduction." *Social Text* 18, no. 3 (2000): 1–27.

Jay, Nancy. *Throughout Your Generations Forever: Sacrifice, Religion, and Paternity*. Chicago: University of Chicago Press, 1992.

Jenkins, Philip. *The New Anti-Catholicism: The Last Acceptable Prejudice*. New York: Oxford University Press, 2003.

Jenson, Jane. "Was It for 'Want of Courage?' The Ebbing of Canada's Maternal Feminism after Entering the Electoral Institutions." In *Going Public: National Histories of Women's Enfranchisement and Women's Participation within State Institutions*, edited by Mary F. Katzenstein and Hege Skejie, 15–44. Oslo: Institute for Social Research, 1990.

Johnson, Elizabeth A. *She Who Is: The Mystery of God in Feminist Theological Discourse*. New York: Crossroad, 2002.

Johnson, Paul Christopher. "Toward an Atlantic Genealogy of 'Spirit Possession.'" In *Spirited Things: The Work of "Possession" in Afro-Atlantic Religions*, edited by Paul Christopher Johnson, 23–46. Chicago: University of Chicago Press, 2014.

Johnson, Paul Christopher, and Mary Keller. "The Work of Possession(s)." *Culture and Religion* 7, no. 2 (2006): 111–22.

Jones, Timothy W. "Social Motherhood and Spiritual Authority in a Secularizing Age: Moral Welfare Work in the Church of England, 1883–1961." *Feminist Theology* 23, no. 2 (2015): 143–55.

Joskowicz, Ari. *The Modernity of Others: Jewish Anti-Catholicism in Germany and France*. Redwood City CA: Stanford University Press, 2013.

"J.R., U.S.A." "Are Cats for True Christians? (Is it appropriate for a Christian to own a cat, in light of their past pagan religious affiliation and the medical information that is now coming to light?)" Paradise Cafe Discussions, July 10, 2007. http://www.paradisecafediscussions.net/showthread.php?tid=1861 (accessed January 6, 2017).

Jung, Patricia Beattie, Mary E. Hunt, and Radhika Balakrishnan, eds. *Good Sex: Feminist Perspectives from the World's Religions*. New Brunswick NJ: Rutgers University Press, 2002.

Juris, Jeffrey S. "Reflections on #Occupy Everywhere: Social Media, Public Space, and Emerging Logics of Aggregation." *American Ethnologist* 39 (2012): 259–79.

———. "Violence Performed and Imagined." *Critique of Anthropology* 25, no. 4 (2005): 413–32.

Kaell, Hillary. "Notes on Pilgrimage and Pilgrimage Studies." *Practical Matters Journal*, May 4, 2016.

———. *Walking Where Jesus Walked: American Christians and Holy Land Pilgrimage.* New York: New York University Press, 2014.

KAIROS. "Be Not Afraid—40 Years of Bold Witness to Ecumenical Social Justice." May 6, 2013. http://www.kairoscanada.org/who-we-are/be-not-afraid/ (accessed January 3, 2017).

———. "Home." 2016. http://www.kairoscanada.org/ (accessed January 4, 2017).

Kaminer, Wendy. *I'm Dysfunctional, You're Dysfunctional: The Recovery Movement and Other Self-Help Fashions.* Reading MA: Addison-Wesley, 1992.

Kane Paula. "Stigmatic Cults and Pilgrimage: The Convergence of Private and Public Faiths." In *Christian Homes: Religion, Family and Domesticity in the 19th and 20th Centuries*, edited by Tine Van Osselaer and Patrick Pasture, 104–25. Leuven, Belgium: Leuven University Press, 2014.

Keane, Webb. *Christian Moderns: Freedom and Fetish in the Mission Encounter.* Berkeley: University of California Press, 2007.

Kedar, Karyn D. "Metaphors of God." In *New Jewish Feminism: Probing the Past, Forging the Future*, edited by Elyse Goldstein, 35–41. Woodstock VT: Jewish Lights Publishing, 2009.

Keller, Mary. *The Hammer and the Flute: Women, Power and Spirit Possession.* Baltimore: Johns Hopkins University Press, 2002.

Kenny, Stephen. "A Prejudice That Rarely Utters Its Name: A Historiographical and Historical Reflection upon North American Anti-Catholicism." *American Review of Canadian Studies* 32, no. 4 (2002): 639–72.

Kent, Tara E. "The Confluence of Race and Gender in Women's Sexual Harassment Experiences." In *Gender Violence: Interdisciplinary Perspectives*, edited by Laura L. O'Toole, Jessica R. Schiffman, and Margie L. Kiter Edwards, 172–80. New York: New York University Press, 2007.

Kenyon, Susan M. *Spirits and Slaves in Central Sudan: The Red Wind of Sennar.* New York: Palgrave Macmillan, 2012.

King, Sarah. *Fishing in Contested Waters: Place and Community in Burnt Church / Esgenoopetitj.* Toronto: University of Toronto Press, 2014.

Klassen, Chris. "The Colonial Mythology of Feminist Witchcraft." In *Between the Worlds: Readings in Contemporary Neopaganism*, edited by Sian Reid, 361–80. Toronto: Canadian Scholars Press, 2006.

———. "Confronting the Gap: Why Religion Needs to Be Given More Attention by Women's Studies." *Third Space: A Journal for Emerging Feminist Scholars* 3, no. 1 (2003): 5–25.

Klassen, Pamela E. *Blessed Events: Religion and Homebirth in America*. Princeton NJ: Princeton University Press, 2001.

———. "Procreating Women and Religion: The Politics of Spirituality, Healing, and Childbirth in America." In *Religion and Healing in America*, edited by Linda L. Barnes and Susan S. Sered, 71–88. New York: Oxford University Press, 2004.

———. "Ritual Appropriation and Appropriate Ritual: Christian Healing and Adaptations of Asian Religions." *History and Anthropology* 16, no. 3 (September 2005): 377–91.

———. *Spirits of Protestantism: Medicine, Healing and Liberal Christianity*. Berkeley: University of California Press, 2011.

Klassen, Pamela, Shari Goldberg, and Danielle Lefabvre, eds. *Women and Religion*. Vols. 1–4. New York: Oxford University Press, 2009.

Klejment, Anne, and Alice Klejment. *Dorothy Day and the Catholic Worker: A Bibliography and Index*. New York: Garland, 1986.

Klejment, Anne, and Nancy L. Roberts, eds. *American Catholic Pacifism: The Influence of Dorothy Day and the Catholic Worker Movement*. Westport CT: Praeger, 1996.

Knibbe, Kim. "Obscuring the Role of Power and Gender in Contemporary Spiritualties." In *Gender and Power in Contemporary Spirituality: Ethnographic Approaches*, edited by Anna Fedele and Kim E. Knibbe, 179–94. New York: Routledge, 2013.

Koehlinger, Amy. "'Are You the White Sisters or the Black Sisters?' Women Confounding Categories of Race and Gender." In *The Religious History of American Women: Reimagining the Past*, edited by Catherine A. Brekus, 253–78. Chapel Hill: University of North Carolina Press, 2007.

Kosek, Joseph Kip. *Acts of Conscience: Christian Nonviolence and Modern American Democracy*. New York: Columbia University Press, 2009.

Kuikman, Jacoba. "Women in Judaism." In *Women and Religious Traditions*, edited by Leona M. Anderson and Pamela Dickey Young, 43–74. New York: Oxford University Press, 2010.

Laidlaw, Stuart. "The Battle of St. Jean." *Toronto Star*, April 23, 2001, A16.

Latour, Bruno. *We Have Never Been Modern*. Translated by Catherine Porter. Cambridge: Harvard University Press, 1993.

Laughlin, Kathleen A., and Jacqueline L. Castledine, eds. *Breaking the Wave: Women, Their Organizations, and Feminism, 1945–1985*. New York: Routledge, 2011.

LaVey, Anton Szandor. *The Satanic Bible*. New York: Avon Books, 1969.

Lears, Jackson. *Fables of Abundance: A Cultural History of Advertising in America*. New York: Basic Books, 1994.

——. *No Place of Grace: Antimodernism and the Transformation of American Culture, 1880–1920*. Chicago: University of Chicago Press, 1981.

Leclair, Louise. "Carnivals against Capital: Rooted in Resistance." In *Representing Resistance: Media, Civil Disobedience, and the Global Justice Movement*, edited by Andy Opel and Donnalyn Pompper, 3–15. Westport CT: Praeger Publishers, 2003.

Leite, José Corrêa. *The World Social Forum: Strategies of Resistance*. Translated by Traci Romine. Chicago: Haymarket Books, 2005.

Levitt, Laura. "Other Moderns, Other Jews: Revisiting Jewish Secularism in America." In *Secularisms*, edited by Janet R. Jakobsen and Ann Pellegrini, 107–38. Durham NC: Duke University Press, 2008.

Levy, Barrie. *Women and Violence*. Berkeley: Seal Press, 2008.

Lewis, James R, ed. *Magical Religion and Modern Witchcraft*. Albany: State University of New York Press, 1996.

Lilla, Mark. *The Stillborn God: Religion, Politics, and the Modern West*. New York: Knopf, 2007.

Lincoln, Eric C., and Lawrence H. Mamiya. *The Black Church in the African American Experience*. Durham NC: Duke University Press, 1990.

Lindkvist, Linde. "The Politics of Article 18: Religious Liberty in the Universal Declaration of Human Rights." *Humanity: An International Journal of Human Rights, Humanitarianism, and Development* 4, no. 3 (2013): 429–47.

Littman, Lynne, dir. *In Her Own Time*. Center for Visual Anthropology, University of Southern California, in association with Embassy Television, 1985. Film.

Llewellyn, Dawn. "Across Generations: Women's Spiritualties, Literary Texts, and Third Wave Feminism." In *Feminist Spirituality: The Next Generation*, edited by Chris Klassen, 179–200. Lanham MD: Lexington Books, 2009.

Llewellyn, Dawn, and Marta Trzebiatowska. "Secular and Religious Feminisms: A Future of Disconnection?" *Feminist Theology* 21, no. 3 (May 2013): 244–58.

Llewellyn, Kristina R. "Teaching June Cleaver, Being Hazel Chong: An Oral History of Gender, Race and National 'Character.'" In *Feminist History in Canada: New Essays on Women, Gender, Work, and Nation*, edited by Catherine Carstairs and Nancy Janovicek, 178–99. Vancouver: UBC Press, 2013.

Loades, Ann. *Feminist Theology: Voices from the Past*. Cambridge: Polity Press, 2001.

Lock, Charles. "Bowing Down to Wood and Stone: One Way to Be a Pilgrim." In *Pilgrim Voices: Narrative and Authorship in Christian Pilgrimage*, edited by Simon Coleman and John Elsner, 110–32. New York: Berghan Books, 2003.

Loenen, Titia. "Safeguarding Religious Freedom and Gender Equality: The Case against Uniform European Human Rights Standards." In *Religion, Gender, and the Public Sphere*, edited by Niamh Reilly and Stacey Scriver, 136–42. New York: Routledge, 2014.

Loney, James. *Captivity: 118 Days in Iraq and the Struggle for a World without War*. Toronto: Knopf Canada, 2011.

Long, Charles H. *Significations: Signs, Symbols, and Images in the Interpretation of Religion*. Philadelphia: Fortress Press, 1986.

Loomba, Ania. *Colonialism/Postcolonialism*. London: Routledge, 2005.

Lorde, Audre. "An Open Letter to Mary Daly." In *Sister Outsider: Essays and Speeches*, 66–71. Berkeley: Crossing Press, 1984.

Löwy, Michael. "Marxism and Religion: Opiate of the People?" *New Socialist: Ideas for Radical Change* 51 (May–June 2005): 19–23.

Luhrmann, Tanya M. *Persuasions of the Witch's Craft: Ritual Magic in Contemporary England*. Cambridge: Harvard University Press, 1989.

Lyon, Sarah, and Mark Moberg, eds. *Fair Trade and Social Justice: Global Ethnographies*. New York: New York University Press, 2010.

Mackenzie, Catriona. "The Importance of Relational Autonomy and Capabilities for an Ethics of Vulnerability." In *Vulnerability: New Essays in Ethics and Feminist Philosophy*, edited by Catriona Mackenzie, Wendy Rogers, and Susan Dodds, 33–59. New York: Oxford University Press, 2014.

Mackenzie, Catriona, Wendy Rogers, and Susan Dodds. "Introduction: What Is Vulnerability and Why Does It Matter for Moral Theory?" In *Vulnerability: New Essays in Ethics and Feminist Philosophy*, edited by Catriona Mackenzie, Wendy Rogers, and Susan Dodds, 1–29. New York: Oxford University Press, 2014.

MacKinnon, Catharine A. "Intersectionality as Method: A Note." *Signs* 38, no. 4 (Summer 2013): 1019–30.

Maddrell, Avril, Veronica della Dora, Alessandro Scafi, and Heather Walton. *Christian Pilgrimage, Landscape and Heritage*. New York: Routledge, 2014.

Magliocco, Sabina. "Ritual Is My Chosen Art Form: The Creation of Ritual as Folk Art among Contemporary Pagans." In *Magical Religion and Witchcraft*, edited by James R. Lewis, 93–120. Albany: State University of New York Press, 1996.

———. *Witching Culture: Folklore and Neo-Paganism in America*. Philadelphia: University of Pennsylvania Press, 2004.

Maher, Bill. Interview with Conan O'Brien. *Late Night with Conan O'Brien*. NBC, January 4, 2008.

Mahmood, Saba. "Can Secularism Be Other-Wise?" In *Varieties of Secularism in a Secular Age*, edited by Michael Warner, Jonathan VanAntwerpen, and Craig Calhoun, 282–99. Cambridge: Harvard University Press, 2010.

———. *Politics of Piety: The Islamic Revival and the Feminist Subject*. Princeton NJ: Princeton University Press, 2005.

———. *Religious Difference in a Secular Age: A Minority Report*. Princeton NJ: Princeton University Press, 2016.

Marks, Lynne. "Challenging Binaries: Working-Class Women and Lived Religion in English Canada and the United States." *Labor: Studies in Working-Class History of the Americas* 6, no. 1 (2009): 107–25.

Marotti, Arthur F. *Religious Ideology and Cultural Fantasy: Catholic and Anti-Catholic Discourses in Early Modern England*. South Bend IN: University of Notre Dame Press, 2005.

Marx, Karl. *Marx on Religion*. Edited by John Raines. Philadelphia: Temple University Press, 2002.

Marx, Karl, and Friedrich Engels. *The Communist Manifesto*. Translated by Samuel Moore, edited by Joseph Katz. 1848. Reprint, New York: Washington Square, 1964.

Massa, Mark S. *Anti-Catholicism in America: The Last Acceptable Prejudice*. New York: Crossroad, 2003.

Masuzawa, Tomoko. *The Invention of World Religions, or, How European Universalism Was Preserved in the Language of Pluralism*. Chicago: University of Chicago Press, 2005.

Mattingly, Carol. "Uncovering Forgotten Habits: Anti-Catholic Rhetoric in Nineteenth-Century American Women's Literacy." *College Composition and Communication* 58, no. 2 (2006): 160–81.

McClary, Susan. "Same as It Ever Was: Youth Culture and Music." In *Rock She Wrote: Women Write about Rock, Pop, and Rap*, edited by Evelyn McDonnell and Ann Powers, 440–54. New York: Delta, 1995.

McEwan, Melissa. "The Point, You Are Proving It." *Shakesville*, July 5, 2011. http://www.shakesville.com/2011/07/point-you-are-proving-it.html (accessed January 5, 2017).

McFague, Sallie. *Super, Natural Christians: How We Should Love Nature*. Minneapolis: Fortress Press, 1997.

McKanan, Dan. *The Catholic Worker after Dorothy: Practicing the Works of Mercy in a New Generation*. Collegeville MN: Liturgical Press, 2008.

————. *Touching the World: Christian Communities Transforming Society*. Collegeville MN: Liturgical Press, 2007.

Merry, Sally Engle. *Gender Violence: A Cultural Perspective*. Malden MA: Wiley-Blackwell, 2009.

Miller, Sarah Clark. "A Kantian Ethic of Care?" In *Feminist Interventions in Ethics and Politics*, edited by Barbara S. Andrew, Jean Keller, and Lisa Schwartzman, 111–27. Oxford: Rowman & Littlefield, 2005.

Milloy, John Sheridan. *A National Crime: The Canadian Government and the Residential School System, 1879 to 1986*. Winnipeg: University of Manitoba Press, 1999.

Mitchell, Kerry. *Spirituality and the State: Managing Nature and Experience in America's National Parks*. New York: New York University Press, 2016.

Mitchell, Timothy. *Colonising Egypt*. 1988. Reprint, Berkeley: University of California Press, 1991.

Mitchell, W. J. T., Bernard E. Harcourt, and Michael Taussig. *Occupy: Three Inquiries into Disobedience*. Chicago: University of Chicago Press, 2013.

Mizruchi, Susan L. "The Place of Ritual in Our Time." In *Religion and Cultural Studies*, edited by Susan L. Mizruchi, 56–79. Princeton NJ: Princeton University Press, 2001.

Moallem, Minoo. "Transnationalism, Feminism, and Fundamentalism." In *Women, Gender, Religion: A Reader*, edited by Elizabeth A. Castelli and Rosamond C. Rodman, 119–45. New York: Palgrave, 2001.

Moghissi, Haideh. *Feminism and Islamic Fundamentalism: The Limits of Postmodern Analysis*. London: Zed Books, 1999.

Mohanty, Chandra Talpade. "Under Western Eyes: Feminist Scholarship and Colonial Discourses." In *Third World Women and the Politics of Feminism*, edited by Chandra Talpade, Ann Russo, and Lourdes Torres, 51–80. Bloomington: Indiana University Press, 1991.

Mollenkott, Virginia Ramey. "Virginia Ramey Mollenkott." In *Transforming the Faiths of Our Fathers*, edited by Ann Braude, 55–72. New York: Palgrave Macmillan, 2004.

Moloney, Deirdre M. *American Catholic Lay Groups and Transatlantic Social Reform in the Progressive Era*. Chapel Hill: University of North Carolina Press, 2002.

Moody, Linda A. *Women Encounter God: Theology across the Boundaries of Difference*. Maryknoll NY: Orbis Books, 1996.

Moore, R. Laurence. *Religious Outsiders and the Making of Americans*. New York: Oxford University Press, 1986.

Morinis, Alan. "Introduction: The Territory of the Anthropology of Pilgrimage." In *Sacred Journeys: The Anthropology of Pilgrimage*, edited by Alan Morinis, 1–30. London: Greenwood Press, 1992.

Morris, Aldon. "The Black Church in the Civil Rights Movement: The SCLC as the Decentralized Radical Arm of the Black Church." In *Disruptive Religion: The Force of Faith in Social Movement Activism*, edited by Christian Smith, 29–59. New York: Routledge, 1996.

Morrow, Diane Batts. *Persons of Color and Religious at the Same Time: The Oblate Sisters of Providence, 1828–1860*. Chapel Hill: University of North Carolina Press, 2002.

Moslener, Sara. *Virgin Nation: Sexual Purity and American Adolescence*. Oxford: Oxford University Press, 2015.

Mouffe, Chantal. *The Return of the Political*. London: Verso, 1993.

Moynaugh, Maureen, and Nancy Forestell. General Introduction. In *Documenting First Wave Feminisms*, Vol. 1: *Transnational Collaborations and Crosscurrents*, edited by Maureen Moynaugh and Nancy Forestell, xix–xxv. Toronto: University of Toronto Press, 2012.

Muir, Elizabeth, and Marilyn Färdig Whiteley. "Introduction: Putting Together the Puzzle of Canadian Women's Christian Work." In *Changing Roles of Women in the Church in Canada*, edited by Elizabeth Muir and Marilyn Färdig Whiteley, 3–18. Toronto: University of Toronto Press, 1995.

Mullin, Amy. *Reconceiving Pregnancy and Childcare: Ethics, Experience and Reproductive Labor*. Cambridge: Cambridge University Press, 2005.

Mutume, Gumisai. "Quebec Braces for Anti-Globalisation Protests." Inter Press Service, April 19, 2001. http://www.ipsnews.net/2001/04 /finance-quebec-braces-for-anti-globalisation-protests/ (accessed January 4, 2017).

Najmabadi, Afsaneh. "(Un)Veiling Feminism." In *Secularisms*, edited by Janet R. Jakobsen and Ann Pellegrini, 39–57. Durham NC: Duke University Press, 2008.

Naples, Nancy A., ed. *Women's Activism and Globalization: Linking Local Struggles and Transnational Politics*. New York: Routledge, 2002.

Neitz, Mary Jo. "In Goddess We Trust." In *In Gods We Trust: New Patterns of Religious Pluralism in America*, edited by Thomas Robbins and Dick Anthony, 353–72. New Brunswick NJ: Transaction Publications, 1990.

Nepstad, Sharon Erickson. *Convictions of the Soul: Religion, Culture, and Agency in the Central America Solidarity Movement*. New York: Oxford University Press, 2004.

———. *Religion and War Resistance in the Plowshares Movement.* New York: Cambridge University Press, 2008.

Nightmare, M. Macha. *Pagan Pride: Honoring the Craft of Earth and Goddess.* New York: Citadel, 2004.

———. *Witchcraft and the Web: Weaving Pagan Traditions On-Line.* Toronto: ECW Press, 2001.

Noddings, Nel. *Caring: A Feminine Approach to Ethics and Moral Education.* 1984. Reprint, Berkeley: University of California Press, 2003.

Nolan, Mary Lee, and Sidney Nolan. *Christian Pilgrimage in Modern Western Europe.* Chapel Hill: University of North Carolina Press, 1989.

Northup, Lesley A. *Ritualizing Women: Patterns of Spirituality.* Cleveland: Pilgrim Press, 1997.

Olajos, E. J., and H. Salem. "Riot Control Agents: Pharmacology, Toxology, Biochemistry and Chemistry." *Journal of Applied Toxicology* 21, no. 5 (2001): 355–91.

O'Neill, William O. *The New Left: A History.* Arlington Heights IL: Harlan Davidson, 2001.

Ontario Coalition against Poverty. "About." 2016. https://ocaptoronto .wordpress.com/ (accessed January 6, 2017).

On the Ground Collective. *Health and Safety at Militant Actions.* Version 1.3. Syracuse NY: On the Ground, 2001.

Organizing Autonomous Telecoms. "Home." http://www.tao.ca/ (accessed January 4, 2017).

Orleck, Annelise. *Common Sense and a Little Fire: Women and Working Class Politics in the United States, 1900–1965.* Chapel Hill: University of North Carolina Press, 1995.

Orsi, Robert. *History and Presence.* Cambridge: Harvard University Press, 2016.

———. "Snakes Alive: Resituating the Moral in the Study of Religion." In *Women, Gender, Religion: A Reader,* edited by Elizabeth A. Castelli and Rosamond C. Rodman, 98–118. New York: Palgrave, 2001.

———. *Thank You, St. Jude: Women's Devotion to the Patron Saint of Hopeless Causes.* New Haven: Yale University Press, 1996.

———. "U.S. Catholics between Memory and Modernity: How Catholics Are American." In *Catholics in the American Century: Recasting Narratives of U.S. History,* edited by R. Scott Appleby and Kathleen Sprows Cummings, 10–42. Ithaca NY: Cornell University Press, 2012.

Ostling, Michael. "Babyfat and Belladonna: Witches' Ointment and the Contestation of Reality." *Magic, Ritual and Witchcraft* 11, no. 1 (2016): 30–72.

———. *Between the Devil and the Host: Imagining Witchcraft in Early Modern Poland.* Oxford: Oxford University Press, 2011.

O'Toole, Laura L., Jessica R. Schiffman, and Margie L. Kiter Edwards. "The Roots of Male Violence." In *Gender Violence: Interdisciplinary Perspectives,* edited by Laura L. O'Toole, Jessica R. Schiffman, and Margie L. Kiter Edwards, 3–10. New York: New York University Press, 2007.

Owen, Alex. *The Darkened Room: Women, Power, and Spiritualism in Late Victorian England.* Philadelphia: University of Pennsylvania Press, 1990.

Oxfam Canada. "Introduction to Oxfam." 2016. http://www.oxfam.ca/about /introduction (accessed January 6, 2017).

———. "Key Milestones in the History of OXFAM Canada." September 13, 2005. https://www.oxfam.ca/who-we-are/history/oxfam_canada _milestones.pdf (accessed February 19, 2007; page discontinued).

Panetta, Alexander. "Quebec Judge Rules That Security Fence at Summit of the Americas Can Stay." Canadian Press, April 18, 2001.

———. "Violence Blamed on Black Bloc: Group Came to Prominence at Seattle Riots." *Toronto Star,* April 21, 2001.

Parrish, Marilyn McKinley, and Edward W. Taylor. "Seeking Authenticity: Women and Learning in the Catholic Worker Movement." *Adult Education Quarterly* 57, no. 3 (May 2007): 221–47.

Pascoe, Peggy. *Relations of Rescue: The Search for Female Moral Authority in the West, 1874–1939.* New York: Oxford University Press, 1990.

———. *What Comes Naturally: Miscegenation Law and the Making of Race in America.* New York: Oxford University Press, 2009.

Pasulka, Diana Walsh. "The Eagle and the Dove: Constructing Catholic Identity through Word and Image in Nineteenth-Century United States." *Material Religion* 4, no. 3 (2008): 306–25.

Pateman, Carole. *The Disorder of Women: Democracy, Feminism, and Political Theory.* Stanford CA: Stanford University Press, 1989.

Pearson, Joanne. *Wicca and the Christian Heritage: Ritual, Sex and Magic.* London: Routledge, 2007.

Pellauer, Mary D. *Toward a Tradition of Feminist Theology: The Religious Social Thought of Elizabeth Cady Stanton, Susan B. Anthony, and Anna Howard Shaw.* Brooklyn: Carlson, 1991.

Peskowitz, Miriam. "Unweaving: A Response to Carol. P. Christ." In *Women, Gender, Religion: A Reader,* edited by Elizabeth A. Castelli and Rosamond C. Rodman, 40–45. New York: Palgrave, 2001.

Petrunic, Josipa. "Activist Groups Demand Quebec City Inquiry." *Toronto Globe and Mail,* May 22, 2001.

Phillips, Kevin. *American Theocracy: The Peril and Politics of Radical Religion, Oil, and Borrowed Money in the 21st Century.* New York: Penguin, 2007.

Pike, Sarah M. *Earthly Bodies, Magical Selves: Contemporary Pagans and the Search for Community*. Berkeley: University of California Press, 2001.

———. *New Age and Neopagan Religions in America*. New York: Columbia University Press, 2004.

Plaskow, Judith. *The Coming of Lilith: Essays on Feminism, Judaism, and Sexual Ethics 1972–2003*. Edited by Judith Plaskow and Donna Berman. Boston: Beacon Press, 2005.

———. *Standing Again at Sinai: Judaism from a Feminist Perspective*. San Francisco: Harper & Row, 1990.

Porter, Jennifer E. "Pilgrimage and the IDIC Ethic: Exploring *Star Trek* Convention Attendance as Pilgrimage." In *Intersecting Journeys: The Anthropology of Pilgrimage and Tourism*, edited by Ellen Badone and Sharon R. Roseman, 160–79. Chicago: University of Illinois Press, 2004.

Preston, James J. "Spiritual Magnetism: An Organizing Principle for the Study of Pilgrimage." In *Sacred Journeys: The Anthropology of Pilgrimage*, edited by Alan Morinis, 31–46. Westport CT: Greenwood Press, 1992.

Pritchard, Elizabeth. "Agency without Transcendence." *Culture and Religion* 7, no. 3 (2006): 263–89.

Promey, Sally M. "The Public Display of Religion." In *The Visual Culture of American Religions*, edited by David Morgan and Sally M. Promey, 27–48. Berkeley: University of California Press, 2001.

Puar, Jasbir K. *Terrorist Assemblages: Homonationalism in Queer Times*. Durham NC: Duke University Press, 2007.

"Quebec City: Anti-FTAA Activists Scout Out the Terrain." *Montreal Gazette*, March 26, 2001. http://www.infoshop.org/octo/ftaa_news.html (accessed October 1, 2003; page discontinued).

Raging Grannies International. "Herstory." n.d. http://raginggrannies.org /herstory/ (accessed January 4, 2017).

Rawls, John. *A Theory of Justice*. Cambridge MA: Belknap Press, 1971.

Razak, Arisika. "Her Blue Body: A Pagan Reading of Alice Walker Womanism." *Feminist Theology* 18, no. 1 (2009): 92–116.

Reader, Ian. "Conclusions." In *Pilgrimage in Popular Culture*, edited by Ian Reader and Tony Walter, 230–33. London: Macmillan Press, 1993.

———. "Introduction." In *Pilgrimage in Popular Culture*, edited by Ian Reader and Tony Walter, 1–27. London: Macmillan Press, 1993.

Reading, Anna. "Singing for My Life: Memory, Nonviolence, and the Songs of Greenham Common Women's Peace Camp." In *Cultural Memories of Nonviolent Struggles: Powerful Times*, edited by Anna Reading and Tamar Katriel, 147–65. New York: Palgrave Macmillan, 2015.

Reid-Maroney, Nina. "History, Historiography, and the Promised Land Project." In *The Promised Land: History and Historiography of the Black Experience in Chatham-Kent's Settlements and Beyond*, edited by Boulou Ebanda de B'Béri, Nina Reid-Maroney, and Handel Kashope Wright, 62–70. Toronto: University of Toronto Press, 2014.

Reilly, Niamh. "Introduction: Religion Gender and the Public Sphere: Mapping the Terrain." In *Religion, Gender, and the Public Sphere*, edited by Niamh Reilly and Stacey Scriver, 1–17. New York: Routledge, 2014.

Reiser, Andrew Chamberlin. *The Chautauqua Moment: Protestants, Progressives, and the Culture of Modern Liberalism*. New York: Columbia University Press, 2003.

Richardson, James T., Joel Best, and David Bromley, eds. *The Satanism Scare*. New York: Aldine de Gruyter, 1991.

Riegle, Rosalie G., ed. *Dorothy Day: Portraits by Those Who Knew Her*. Maryknoll NY: Orbis Books, 2003.

Riley, Denise. *"Am I That Name?" Feminism and the Category of "Women" in History*. Minneapolis: University of Minnesota Press, 1988.

Roberts, Jo. "Dancing into the Revolution: Reflections on Quebec City and the Continuing Struggle against Globalization." *The Mustard Seed: The Toronto Catholic Worker Community* 11, no. 1 (Winter 2002): 1.

Robinson, Martin. "Pilgrimage and Mission." In *Explorations of a Christian Theology of Pilgrimage*, edited by Craig Bartholomew and Fred Hughes, 170–83. New York: Routledge, 2004.

Robinson, Thomas A., and Lanette D. Ruff. *Out of the Mouths of Babes: Girl Evangelists in the Flapper Era*. New York: Oxford University Press, 2012.

Roediger, David R. *The Wages of Whiteness: Race and the Making of the America Working Class*. 1991. Reprint, New York: Verso, 2007.

Roof, Wade Clark. *A Generation of Seekers: The Spiritual Journeys of the Baby Boom Generation*. New York: HarperCollins, 1993.

Rountree, Kathryn. "Goddess Pilgrims as Tourists: Inscribing the Body through Sacred Travel." *Sociology of Religion* 63, no. 4 (2002): 475–96.

Rouse, Carolyn Moxley. *Engaged Surrender: African American Women and Islam*. Berkeley: University of California Press, 2004.

Roy, Carole. *The Raging Grannies: Wild Hats, Cheeky Songs, and Witty Actions for a Better World*. Montreal: Black Rose Books, 2004.

Roy, Jody M. *Rhetorical Campaigns of the 19th Century Anti-Catholics and Catholics in America*. Lewiston NY: Edwin Mellen Press, 2000.

Ruddick, Sara. "Making Connections between Parenting and Peace." *Journal for the Association for Research on Mothering* 3, no. 2 (Fall–Winter 2001): 7–20.

———. *Maternal Thinking: Toward a Politics of Peace*. New York: Ballantine, 1989.

Ruether, Rosemary Radford. *America, Amerikkka: Elect Nation and Imperial Violence*. London: Equinox, 2007.

———. *Goddesses and the Divine Feminine: A Western Religious History*. Berkeley: University of California Press, 2005.

———. "Response to Naomi Goldenberg." *Feminist Theology* 13, no. 2 (2005): 151–53.

———. "Rosemary Radford Ruether." In *Transforming the Faiths of Our Fathers*, edited by Ann Braude, 73–84. New York: Palgrave Macmillan, 2004.

Said, Edward. *Orientalism*. New York: Random House, 1978.

Salmonsen, Jone. *Enchanted Feminism: Ritual, Gender and Divinity among the Reclaiming Witches of San Francisco*. New York: Routledge, 2002.

Sands, Kathleen. "Feminisms and Secularisms." In *Secularisms*, edited by Janet R. Jakobsen and Ann Pellegrini, 308–29. Durham NC: Duke University Press, 2008.

Santos, Boaventura de Sousa. *The Rise of the Global Left: The World Social Forum and Beyond*. London: Zed Books, 2006.

Satter, Beryl. *Each Mind a Kingdom: American Women, Sexual Purity, and the New Thought Movement, 1875–1920*. Berkeley: University of California Press, 1999.

Savage, Barbara Dianne. *Your Spirits Walk beside Us: The Politics of Black Religion*. Cambridge: Harvard University Press, 2008.

Sax, William S. *Mountain Goddess: Gender and Politics in a Himalayan Pilgrimage*. Oxford: Oxford University Press, 1991.

Schissel, Bernard, and Terry Wotherspoon. "The Legacy of Residential Schools." In *Inequality in Canada: A Reader on the Intersections of Gender, Race, and Class*, edited by Valerie Zawilski and Cynthia Levine-Rasky, 188–207. Don Mills ON: Oxford University Press, 2005.

Schmidt, Leigh Eric. *Restless Souls: The Making of American Spirituality*. San Francisco: Harper, 2005.

Schüssler Fiorenza, Elisabeth. *In Memory of Her: A Feminist Reconstruction of Christian Origins*. New York: Crossroad, 1983.

Schweitzer, Don, ed. *The United Church of Canada: A History*. Kitchener ON: Wilfrid Laurier University Press, 2011.

Scott, Dayna Nadine. "The Forces That Conspire to Keep Us 'Idle.'" *Canadian Journal of Law and Society* 28, no. 3 (2013): 425–28.

Scott, Joan Wallach. *The Politics of the Veil*. Princeton NJ: Princeton University Press, 2007.

———. "Sexularism: On Secularism and Gender Equality." In *The Fantasy of Feminist History*, 91–116. Durham NC: Duke University Press, 2011.

Sered, Susan Starr. *Priestess, Mother, Sacred Sister: Religions Dominated by Women*. New York: Oxford University Press, 1994.

———. *Women as Ritual Experts: The Religious Lives of Elderly Jewish Women in Jerusalem*. New York: Oxford University Press, 1992.

Seymour-Smith, Charlotte, ed. "Cosmology." *Dictionary of Anthropology*. Boston: G. K. Hall, 1986.

Sharlet, Jeffrey. *The Family: The Secret Fundamentalism at the Heart of American Power*. New York: HarperCollins, 2008.

———. "Jesus plus Nothing: Undercover among America's Secret Theocrats." *Harper's*, March 2003.

———. "Sex as a Weapon: Decoding the Literature of the Christian Men's Movement." Nerve.com, April 25, 2005. www.nerve.com/dispatches /sharlet/sexasaweapon/ (accessed January 18, 2017).

———. "Soldiers for Christ: Inside America's Most Powerful Mega-Church." *Harper's*, May 2005.

Sharma, Arvind, and Katherine K. Young, eds. *Her Voice, Her Faith: Women Speak on World Religions*. Boulder CO: Westview Press, 2003.

Shukrallah, Hala. "The Impact of the Islamic Movement in Egypt." In *Feminism in the Study of Religion: A Reader*, edited by Darlene M. Juschka, 180–97. London: Continuum, 2001.

Slote, Michael. *Morals from Motives*. New York: Oxford University Press, 2001.

Smith, Barbara. "'Feisty Characters' and 'Other People's Causes': Memories of White Racism and U.S. Feminism." In *The Feminist Memoir Project: Voices from Women's Liberation*, edited by Rachel Blau DuPlessis and Ann Snitow, 477–81. New York: Three Rivers Press, 1998.

Smith, Christian. "Correcting a Curious Neglect, or Bringing Religion Back In." In *Disruptive Religion: The Force of Faith in Social Movement Activism*, edited by Christian Smith, 1–28. New York: Routledge, 1996.

———. *The Emergence of Liberation Theology: Radical Religion and Social Movement Theory*. Chicago: University of Chicago Press, 1991.

———. "Introduction: Rethinking the Secularization of American Public Life." In *The Secular Revolution: Power, Interests and Conflict in the Secularization of American Public Life*, edited by Christian Smith, 1–98. Berkeley: University of California Press, 2003.

Smith, Jonathan Z. *Imagining Religion: From Babylon to Jonestown*. Chicago: University of Chicago Press, 1982.

———. *Map Is Not Territory: Studies in the History of Religions*. Chicago: University of Chicago Press, 1993.

———. *To Take Place: Toward a Theory in Ritual*. Chicago: University of Chicago Press, 1987.

Sointu, Eeva, and Linda Woodhead. "Spirituality, Gender and Expressive Selfhood." *Journal for the Scientific Study of Religion* 47, no. 2 (2008): 259–76.

Spickard, James V. "Ritual, Symbol, and Experience: Understanding Catholic Worker House Masses." *Sociology of Religion* 66, no. 4 (2005): 337–57.

Spivak, Gayatri. "Can the Subaltern Speak?" In *Colonial Discourse and Post-Colonial Theory: A Reader*, edited by Williams, Patrick and Laura Chrisman, 90–111. New York: Columbia University Press, 1994.

Spretnak, Charlene, ed. *The Politics of Women's Spirituality: Essays on the Rise of Spiritual Power in the Feminist Movement*. Garden City NY: Anchor Books, 1982.

Srivastava, Sarita. "'You're Calling Me a Racist?' The Moral and Emotional Regulation of Antiracism and Feminism." *Signs* 31, no. 1 (2005): 29–61.

Stacey, Judith. *Brave New Families: Stories of Domestic Upheaval in the Late Twentieth Century*. New York: Basic Books, 1990.

Stacey, Judith, and Susan Elizabeth Gerrard. "We Are Not Doormats: The Influence of Feminism on Contemporary Evangelicals in the United States." In *Uncertain Terms: Negotiating Gender in American Culture*, edited by Faye Ginsberg and Anna Lowenhaupt Tsing, 98–117. Boston: Beacon Press, 1990.

Starhawk. *The Spiral Dance: A Rebirth of the Ancient Religion of the Great Goddess*. 1979. Reprint, San Francisco: HarperSanFrancisco, 1999.

———. *Truth or Dare: Encounters with Power, Authority, and Mystery*. San Francisco: Harper, 1987.

———. "Weaving a Web of Solidarity: A Feminist Action against Globalization." Nettime Archive, March 7, 2001. http://amsterdam.nettime.org /Lists-Archives/nettime-l-0103/msg00043.html (accessed January 4, 2017).

———. *Webs of Power: Notes from the Global Uprising*. Gabriola Island BC: New Society Publishers, 2002.

Starhawk, and M. Macha NightMare. *The Pagan Book of Living and Dying: Practical Rituals, Prayers, Blessings, and Meditations on Crossing Over*. San Francisco: HarperSanFrancisco, 1997.

Starr, Amory. *Global Revolt: A Guide to the Movements against Globalization*. London: Zed Books, 2005.

Stausberg, Michael. *Religion and Tourism: Crossroads, Destinations and Encounters*. New York: Routledge, 2011.

Stevenson, Garth. *Building Nations from Diversity: Canadian and American Experience Compared*. Montreal: McGill-Queens University Press, 2014.

Stevenson, Winona. "Colonialism and First Nations Women in Canada." In *Scratching the Surface: Canadian Anti-Racist Feminist Thought*, edited by Enkashi Dua and Angela Robertson, 49–82. Toronto: Women's Press, 1999.

Stoddard, Robert H. "Defining and Classifying Pilgrimages." In *Sacred Places, Sacred Spaces: The Geography of Pilgrimage*, edited by Robert H. Stoddard and Alan Morinis, 41–60. Baton Rouge: Louisiana State University Press, 1997.

Stoler, Ann. *Carnal Knowledge and Imperial Power: Race and the Intimate in Colonial Rule*. Berkeley: University of California Press, 2002.

Stout, Jeffrey. *Democracy and Tradition*. Princeton NJ: Princeton University Press, 2004.

Strange, Caroline. "From Modern Babylon to a City upon a Hill: Toronto's Social Survey Commission of 1915 and the Search for Sexual Order in the City." In *Queerly Canadian: An Introductory Reader in Sexuality Studies*, edited by Maureen Fitzgerald and Scott Rayter, 213–28. Toronto: Canadian Scholars Press, 2012.

———. *Toronto's Girl Problem: The Perils and Pleasures of the City, 1880–1930*. Toronto: University of Toronto Press, 1995.

Stuart, Alison. "The Right to Freedom of Religion: Equal Right or Male Right." In *Religion, Gender, and the Public Sphere*, edited by Niamh Reilly and Stacey Scriver, 180–91. New York: Routledge, 2014.

Styers, Randall. *Making Magic: Religion, Magic, and Science in the Modern World*. Oxford: Oxford University Press, 2004.

Swatos, William H., Jr., ed. *On the Road to Being There: Studies in Pilgrimage and Tourism in Late Modernity*. Boston: Brill, 2006.

Swerdlow, Amy. "Ladies' Day at the Capitol: Women Strike for Peace versus HUAC." In *Women's America: Refocusing the Past*, edited by Linda K. Kerber, Jane Sherron De Hart, and Cornelia Hughes Dayton, 471–86. New York: Oxford University Press, 2000.

———. *Women Strike for Peace: Traditional Motherhood and Radical Politics in the 1960s*. Chicago: University of Chicago Press, 1993.

Taves, Ann, and Courtney Bender. "Introduction: Things of Value." In *What Matters? Ethnographies of Value in a Not So Secular Age*, edited by Courtney Bender and Ann Taves, 1–33. New York: Columbia University Press, 2012.

Taylor, Charles. *The Ethics of Authenticity*. Cambridge: Harvard University Press, 1991.

———. *Modern Social Imaginaries*. Durham NC: Duke University Press, 2004.

———. *A Secular Age*. Cambridge MA: Belknap Press, 2007.

Taylor, Verta. *Rock-a-Bye-Baby: Feminism, Self-Help and Post-Partum Depression.* New York: Routledge, 1996.

Teish, Luisah. *Jambalaya: The Natural Woman's Book of Personal Charms and Practical Rituals.* New York: HarperOne, 1985.

Tessman, Lisa. *Burdened Virtues: Virtue Ethics for Liberatory Struggles.* Oxford: Oxford University Press, 2005.

Thirlwall, Gabe / Fish on Fridays. *Our Mother of Guadalupe.* Toronto: Fish on Fridays, n.d. Acquired by author April 21, 2001.

Thompson, Becky. *A Promise and a Way of Life: White Anti-Racist Activism.* Minneapolis: University of Minnesota Press, 2001.

Thorn, William J., Phillip M. Runkel, and Susan Mountin, eds. *Dorothy Day and the Catholic Worker Movement: Centenary Essays.* Marquette WI: Marquette University Press, 2001.

"Thousands Converge on Quebec as 'People's Summit' Gets Underway." CBC News, April 16, 2001. http://www.cbc.ca/news/canada/thousands-converge-on-quebec -as-people-s-summit-gets-underway-1.261253 (accessed January 5, 2017).

Tomlin, Graham. "Protestants and Pilgrimage." In *Explorations in a Christian Theology of Pilgrimage,* edited by Craig Bartholomew and Fred Hughes, 110–25. Burlington VT: Ashgate, 2003.

Tong, Rosemarie. *Feminist Thought: A More Comprehensive Introduction.* Boulder CO: Westview Press, 2013.

Tronto, Joan C. "Women and Caring: What Can Feminists Learn about Morality from Caring?" In *Justice and Care: Essential Readings in Feminist Ethics,* edited by Virginia Held, 101–77. Boulder CO: Westview Press, 1995.

Trullson, Asa. "Cultivating the Sacred: Gender, Power and Ritualization in Goddess-Oriented Groups." In *Gender and Power in Contemporary Spirituality: Ethnographic Approaches,* edited by Anna Fedele and Kim E. Knibbe, 28–45. New York: Routledge, 2013.

Truth and Reconciliation Commission of Canada. "Resources." n.d. http://www .trc.ca/websites/trcinstitution/index.php?p=9 (accessed January 9, 2017).

Tucker-Worgs, Tamelyn N. *The Black Mega-Church: Theology, Gender and the Politics of Public Engagement.* Waco TX: Baylor Press, 2011.

Tumbleson, Raymond D. *Catholicism in the English Protestant Imagination: Nationalism, Religion, and Literature, 1660–1745.* Cambridge: Cambridge University Press, 1998.

Turner, Victor. *Dramas, Fields, and Metaphors: Symbolic Action in Human Society.* Ithaca NY: Cornell University Press, 1974.

———. *The Ritual Process: Structure and Anti-Structure.* Chicago: Aldine, 1969.

Turner, Victor, and Edith Turner. *Image and Pilgrimage in Christian Culture: Anthropological Perspectives.* New York: Columbia University Press, 1978.

"A Turning Point for Activists: Summit of the Americas." Editorial. *Toronto Star*, April 25, 2001.

United Church of Canada. "Apology to Former Students of United Church Indian Residential Schools, and to Their Families and Communities (1998)." 2017. http://www.united-church.ca/social-action/justice -initiatives/apologies (accessed January 9, 2017).

———. "Justice and Reconciliation Fund." 2017. http://www.united-church .ca/social-action/justice-initiatives/justice-and-reconciliation-fund (accessed January 9, 2017).

———. "Social Action." 2017. http://www.united-church.ca/social-action (accessed January 18, 2017).

———. *Toward Justice and Right Relationship: A Beginning: A Study Guide for Congregations and Church Groups as They Explore the Legacy of Indian Residential Schools and Forge New Relationships with First Nations Peoples*. Toronto: United Church of Canada, Justice, Global, and Ecumenical Relations Unit, 2003.

———. "The Truth and Reconciliation Commission." 2017. http://www .united-church.ca/social-action/justice-initiatives/truth-and -reconciliation-commission (accessed January 9, 2017).

Valverde, Mariana. *The Age of Light, Soap and Water: Moral Reform in English Canada, 1885–1925*. 1991. Reprint, Toronto: McClelland and Stewart, 2008.

Van Osselaer, Tina. "Religion, Family and Domesticity in the Nineteenth and Twentieth Centuries: An Introduction." In *Christian Homes: Religion, Family and Domesticity in the 19th and 20th Centuries*, edited by Tina Van Osselaer and Patrick Pasture, 7–25. Leuven, Belgium: Leuven University Press, 2014.

Victor, Jeffery S. "The Dynamics of Rumor Panics about Satanic Cults." In *The Satanism Scare*, edited by James T. Richardson, Joel Best, and David Bromley, 221–36. New York: Aldine de Gruyter, 1991.

———. *Satanic Panic: The Creation of a Contemporary Legend*. Chicago: Open Court, 1993.

Vincett, Giselle. "The Fusers: New Forms of Spiritualized Christianity." In *Women and Religion in the West: Challenging Secularism*, edited by Kristen Aune, Sonya Sharma, and Giselle Vincett, 133–45. Aldershot: Ashgate, 2008.

———. "Generational Change in Goddess Feminism: Some Observations from the UK." In *Feminist Spirituality: The Next Generation*, edited by Chris Klassen, 139–58. Lanham MD: Lexington Books, 2009.

Wacker, Grant. "The Holy Spirit and the Spirit of the Age in American Protestantism, 1880–1910." *Journal of American History* 72, no. 1 (1985): 45–62.

Wadud, Amina. *Inside the Gender Jihad: Women's Reform in Islam*. Oxford: Oneworld Publications, 2006.

———. *Qur'an and Woman: Reading the Sacred Text from a Woman's Perspective*. New York: Oxford University Press, 1999.

Wald, Kenneth D. *Religion and Politics in the United States*. Lanham MD: Rowman & Littlefield. 2003.

Walker, Alice. *In Search of Our Mothers' Gardens: Womanist Prose*. San Diego: Harcourt Brace Jovanovich, 1984.

Walkom, Thomas. "Demonstrators' Dilemma to March to or Fro? Route of Final Rally Sparks Debate Fraught with Symbolism." *Toronto Star*, April 18, 2001, A6.

———. "How a Carnival Turned Ugly." *Toronto Star*, April 21, 2001.

———. "Quebec City's Carnival of Protest Ended in Tear Gas and Choking." *Toronto Star*, April 21, 2001.

Walton, Rivkah M. "Lilith's Daughters, Miriam's Chorus: Two Decades of Feminist Midrash." *Religion & Literature* 43, no. 2 (2011): 115–27.

Ward, Jule DeJager. *La Leche League: At the Crossroads of Medicine, Feminism, and Religion*. Chapel Hill: University of North Carolina Press, 2000.

Warne, Randi R. *Literature as Pulpit: The Christian Social Activism of Nellie McClung*. Waterloo ON: Wilfrid Laurier Press, 1993.

———. "Nellie McClung's Social Gospel." In *Changing Roles of Women in the Church in Canada*, edited by Elizabeth Muir and Marilyn Färdig Whiteley, 338–54. Toronto: University of Toronto Press, 1995.

Wasserstrom, Steven M. *Religion after Religion: Gershom Scholem, Mircea Eliade, and Henry Corbin at Eranos*. Princeton NJ: Princeton University Press, 1999.

Watson, Rebecca. "It Stands to Reason: Skeptics Can Be Sexist, Too." *Slate*, October 24, 2012. http://www.slate.com/articles/double_x/doublex /2012/10/sexism_in_the_skeptic_community_i_spoke_out_then_came _the_rape_threats.2.html (accessed January 5, 2017).

———. "The Privilege Delusion." *SkepChick*, July 5, 2011. http://skepchick .org/2011/07/the-privilege-delusion/ (accessed January 5, 2017).

Weintraub, Jeff. "The Theory and Politics of the Public/Private Distinction." In *Public and Private in Theory and Practice: Perspectives on a Grand Dichotomy*, edited by Jeff Weintraub and Krishan Kumar, 1–42. Chicago: University of Chicago Press, 1997.

Weisenfeld, Judith. *African American Women and Christian Activism: New York's Black YWCA, 1905–1945*. Cambridge: Harvard University Press, 1997.

———. "Invisible Women: On Women and Gender in the Study of African American Religious History." *Journal of Africana Religions* 1, no. 1 (2013): 133–49.

Wente, Margaret. "How Katie Got Her Man." *Toronto Globe and Mail*, March 13, 2003, A19.

"Where People Disappear." Editorial. *Ottawa Citizen*, February 15, 2008.

Wilcox, Melissa M. *Queer Women and Religious Individualism*. Bloomington: Indiana University Press, 2009.

———. "Spirituality, Activism, and the 'Postsecular' in the Sisters of Perpetual Indulgence." In *Religion, Gender and Sexuality in Everyday Life*, edited by Peter Nynäs and Andrew Kam-Tuck Yip, 37–50. Burlington VT: Ashgate, 2012.

———. "When Sheila's a Lesbian." *Sociology of Religion* 63, no. 4 (2002): 497–513.

Wilder, Charly. "I Don't Believe in Atheists: Interview with Chris Hedges." *Salon*, March 13, 2008. http://www.salon.com/books/int/2008/03/13 /chris_hedges/ (accessed January 18, 2017).

Williams, Daniel. *God's Own Party: The Making of the Christian Right*. Oxford: Oxford University Press, 2010.

Williams, Delores. "Delores Williams." In *Transforming the Faiths of Our Fathers: Women Who Changed American Religion*, edited by Ann Braude, 115–33. Boston: Beacon Press, 2004.

———. *Sisters in the Wilderness: The Challenge of Womanist God-Talk*. Maryknoll NY: Orbis Books, 1993.

Wilson, Bruce, and Frederick Clarkson, eds. *Talk to Action: Reclaiming History, Citizenship, and Faith*. Website. www.talk2action.org (accessed January 27, 2017).

Wilson, Robin Fretwell. "The Erupting Clash between Religion and the State over Contraception, Sterilization, and Abortion." In *Religious Freedom in America: Constitutional Roots and Contemporary Challenges*, edited by Allen D. Hertzke, 135–69. Norman: University of Oklahoma Press, 2015.

Winkelman, Michael, and Jill Dubisch. "Introduction: The Anthropology of Pilgrimage." In *Pilgrimage and Healing*, edited by Jill Dubisch and Michael Winkelman, ix–xxxvi. Tucson: University of Arizona Press, 2005.

Winter, Miriam Therese, Adair Lummis, and Allison Stokes. *Defecting in Place: Women Taking Responsibility for Their Own Spiritual Lives*. New York: Cross Road, 1995.

Wolffe, John. "Exploring the History of Protestant-Catholic Conflict." In *Protestant-Catholic Conflict from the Reformation to the Twenty-First Century: The Dynamics of Religious Difference*, edited by John Wolffe, 1–21. New York: Palgrave Macmillan, 2013.

Wollcott, Victoria. *Remaking Respectability: African American Women in Interwar Detroit*. Chapel Hill: University of North Carolina Press, 2001.

Women in Black. "Who Are Women in Black?" 2017. http://womeninblack .org/pagina-ejemplo/ (accessed January 5, 2017).

Woods, Allan. "Plea over Harper Colombia Visit." *Toronto Star*, July 11, 2007. https://www.thestar.com/news/canada/2007/07/11/plea_over_harper _colombia_visit.html (accessed May 3, 2017).

World Council of Churches. "History." 2017. http://www.oikoumene.org/en /about-us/wcc-history (accessed January 6, 2017).

Wotherspoon, Terry, and John Hansen. "The 'Idle No More' Movement: Paradoxes of First Nations Inclusion in the Canadian Context." *Social Inclusion* 1, no. 1 (2013): 21–36.

Wuthnow, Robert. *After Heaven: Spirituality in America since the 1950s*. Berkeley: University of California Press, 1998.

———. *Christianity and Civil Society: The Contemporary Debate*. Valley Forge PA: Trinity Press International, 1996.

———. *Sharing the Journey: Support Groups and America's New Quest for Community*. New York: Free Press, 1994.

Yellin, Jean Fagan. *Women and Sisters: Anti-Slavery Feminists in American Culture*. New Haven: Yale University Press, 1989.

Yip, Andrew Kam-Tuck, and Peter Nynäs. "Reframing the Intersection between Religion, Gender and Sexuality in Everyday Life." In *Religion, Gender and Sexuality in Everyday Life*, edited by Peter Nynäs and Andrew Kam-Tuck Yip, 1–16. Burlington VT: Ashgate, 2012.

York, Michael. "Contemporary Pagan Pilgrimages." In *From Medieval Pilgrimage to Religious Tourism: The Social and Cultural Economics of Piety*, edited by William H. Swatos Jr. and Luigi Tomasi, 137–58. Westport CT: Praeger, 2002.

———. *Pagan Theology: Paganism as a World Religion*. New York: New York University Press, 2003.

Young, Pamela Dickey. "Women in Christianity." In *Women and Religious Traditions*, edited by Leona M. Anderson and Pamela Dickey Young, 163–92. New York: Oxford University Press, 2010.

Yukich, Grace. "Boundary Work in Inclusive Religious Groups: Constructing Identity at the New York Catholic Worker." *Sociology of Religion* 71, no. 2 (2010): 172–96.

Yung, Judy. *Unbound Feet: A Social History of Chinese Women in San Francisco*. Berkeley: University of California Press, 1995.

Zack, Naomi. *Inclusive Feminism: A Third Wave Theory of Women's Commonality*. Lanham MD: Rowman & Littlefield, 2005.

Zatoun. "Zatoun Is Palestine in a Bottle." 2010. http://www.zatoun.com/ (accessed January 4, 2017).

Zwick, Mark, and Louise Zwick. *The Catholic Worker Movement: Intellectual and Spiritual Origins*. New York: Paulist Press, 2005.

Zwissler, Laurel. "In Memorium Maleficarum: Contemporary Pagan Mobilizations of the Burning Times." In *Emotions in the History of Witchcraft*, edited by Laura Kounine and Michael Ostling, 249–68. New York: Palgrave, 2016.

——. "Pagan Pilgrimage: New Religious Movements Research on Sacred Travel within Pagan and New Age Communities." *Religion Compass* 5, no. 7 (2011): 326–42.

——. "Second Nature: Contemporary Pagan Ritual Borrowing in Progressive Christian Communities." In "Feminism, Activism and Spirituality." Special issue, *Canadian Women's Studies / Cahier de la femme* 29, nos. 1–2 (2011): 16–23.

——. "Witches' Tears: Spiritual Feminism, Epistemology, and Witch Hunt Horror Stories." *The Pomegranate: International Journal of Pagan Studies* 18, no. 2 (2016): 176–204.

Index

activists *(continued)*
95–97; medics for, 228n119;
oppression and privilege
regarding, 10–13, 125, 136–38, 143,
146, 175–77, 200; personal agency
and resistance regarding, 174, 196–
97; progressivism and, 11, 59,
142–43, 199–200; recovery and
self-help movements concerning,
181; rituals and ritualizing
concerning, 70, 157–58, 201;
secularism and, 137, 196–97;
singing of songs by, 223n74;
spirituality vs. religion regarding,
41–42, 70, 125–28, 137–38, 141–43,
157–58, 201–2; stereotypes
concerning actions of, 70, 108–9,
118, 138, 230n149; violence vs.
nonviolence and, 228n108. *See
also* political activists
activities, 85–87, 100–102, 105, 234n77
affinity groups, 90, 115–16
African Americans, 9–10, 12–13, 175,
211nn36–37, 237n29. *See also*
women of color
African National Congress (ANC), 236n21
Afrocentric traditions, 12, 183
Age of Enlightenment. *See*
Enlightenment
Albanese, Catherine, 142–43
Alexander, M. Jacqui, 71, 183
al-Hibri, Azizah, 20
alienation. *See* oppression; repression
Amnesty International, 34, 73, 75–76,
180–81
anarchists, 88, 101, 105, 108–9, 126–
27, 148
ANC. *See* African National
Congress (ANC)
Anderson, Benedict, 103–4

androcentrism, 2, 7, 17–18, 24–25,
134–35, 140–41, 191. *See also*
misogyny
Angel (Catholic Church): as activist
and protester, 88; culture and,
127–28, 150, 152; regarding
journeys and pilgrimages, 96, 115,
116–17; languages and theologies
concerning, 149–50, 151–52, 155;
oppression and privilege
regarding, 107–9, 120, 177–78;
rituals and ritualizing concerning,
120–21, 150, 152; spirituality vs.
religion and, 127–28, 148–49,
151–52; tear gas and, 112; violence
vs. nonviolence and, 107, 108–9
Anglican Church. *See* Church of
England
animals, 179, 240n71
Annie (Clearwater United Church): at
Easter, 64; Goddess movement
and interpretations regarding,
152–54, 185, 235n111; health and
well-being concerning, 187; letter
writing by, 76, 180–81; membership and groups concerning, 34, 72
announcements, 54, 65, 71–73, 146, 167
anti-Catholicism, 129–30, 132,
231nn13–17, 232n33
anti-globalization. *See* Free Trade
Area of the Americas (FTAA);
global justice
Anzaldúa, Gloria, 12. *See also* feminist
theologies
apologies, 184–85, 242n104
apostolic succession, 235n118
art, 86, 87, 93, 240n71
artists, 117, 221n31
Asad, Talal, 104, 105, 131, 219n161
assaults. *See* abuses; violence

Catholicism: academic scholarship and religious studies regarding, 130, 132, 144–45, 232n33; conservatism and, 19–20, 144–46; modernity and, 129, 231n17; in Quebec City, 129, 231n16; rituals and religious traditions concerning, 71, 128, 130–31, 132, 137, 150, 152

Catholic Worker, 31, 217n146

Catholic Worker, Toronto: conservatism and, 144, 145–46; cosmologies of interconnection and, 40–41, 160–61, 187, 205; fair trade movement and, 179–80; health, well-being, and self-care concerning, 181, 187, 191–92, 205; homes and spaces for, 31–33, 67–68, 79, 160; International Socialists and, 191–92; members and demographics for, 31–34, 79, 160–61, 217n135; oppression and privilege regarding, 27, 121–22, 173–74; rites and rituals concerning, 47–48, 66–69, 71, 79, 81, 82, 140, 205; ritualizing and, 26–27, 45, 50, 51, 67–68, 77, 79, 80, 140; spiritual traditions and theologies for, 39, 183

cats, 179, 240nn71–72

centers, 57, 79, 85, 96, 98–102, 122–23, 146. *See also* spaces

ceremonies. *See* ecumenism; religious practices; religious traditions; ritual

changes: through energies and magic, 181, 192, 200, 201, 240n70, 243n122; healing, well-being, and self-care regarding, 162–63, 168, 187, 196, 200, 203; historical traditions and, 192–93, 201;

oppression and, 200, 243n120; through personal agency and resistance, 159–60, 196–97; through recovery and self-help movements, 181, 188, 200, 203, 205, 243n121; through rituals and ritualizing, 71, 77–82, 118–19, 121–22, 200–201, 205, 244n134; spirituality and, 133, 143, 162, 181, 187, 201–2; worldviews and, 160, 162–64, 167–68, 187–88, 192, 196–97, 200–201, 202–3. *See also* transformations

charity, 162–63, 167, 173

children: abuses and murders regarding, 184, 194–95; care and justice ethics concerning, 168, 170, 237n29; as members of communities, 31, 32, 33, 38, 184; rites and rituals concerning, 50, 52, 53, 57, 63–65, 179

Chireau, Yvonne, 183

Christ, Carol, 14

Christian Coalition. *See* Robertson, Pat

Christianity: academic scholarship and religious studies regarding, 18–19, 21, 22, 132, 199; animal deaths and, 179, 240n72; apostolic succession and, 235n118; cosmologies of interconnection and, 142–43, 162, 202, 205; ecumenism and, 236n21; Goddess movement and, 235n111; hierarchies and structures for, 102, 104–5, 147, 148, 202, 205; historical traditions and, 128–30, 142–43, 192–93; journeys and pilgrimages concerning, 115, 116; languages and theologies concerning, 14–15, 16, 150–51, 155, 202; oppression and privilege regarding, 120–23, 138, 175; personal agency and resistance concerning, 18–19, 29; public vs. private and, 5, 9–10, 27, 120–21, 136, 140, 155, 202; rituals and ritualizing regarding, 51, 67–69, 120–21, 123, 221nn32–33. *See also* religion; spirituality

Christian Peacemaker Team (CPT), 26, 60

Christine (Clearwater United Church), 34, 64, 72–73, 76, 153–54, 167, 180, 235n111

churches, 29–30, 38, 55–56, 141, 147, 201–2, 211n37. *See also specific churches and religions*

Churchill, Ward, 113

Church of England, 55, 68–69, 116, 129, 231nn13–14, 244n134

CIDA. *See* Canadian International Development Agency (CIDA)

circles, 52, 53–54, 56–59, 66, 93, 95. *See also* spaces

Civil Rights movements, 11, 22, 92, 134, 154, 215n111

classes, 5–6, 12, 71, 102–3, 105, 170–71, 193. *See also* hierarchies; social structures

Clay and Paper Theatre, 221n31

Clearwater United Church: committees and groups for, 34–35, 48, 71–76, 173; conservatism and, 146; cosmologies of interconnection and, 40–41, 77, 81–82, 152–54, 167, 185–86, 205; fair trade movement and, 89, 166–67, 179–80; health, well-being, and self-care concerning, 81–82, 181, 205; International Socialists and, 74, 77, 222n59; interpretations and,

185–86; leaders and pastors for, 34, 161, 164–67, 183–84; members and demographics for, 34–36, 217n135; oppression and privilege regarding, 27, 120–22, 154, 173–74, 176–78, 186; rites and rituals concerning, 45, 48, 49–51, 66–70, 71–73, 78, 79–80, 205; ritualizing and, 26–27, 35, 45, 51, 67–69, 77–80; spaces for, 35, 67–69, 77, 152–53; spirituality vs. religion and, 127, 128, 147, 149, 154, 155–56; spiritual traditions and theologies for, 150–51, 183–84, 185–86; worship services and announcements in, 35, 54, 71–73, 146, 167, 185–86

"The Cochabamba Declaration," 94

coexistence, 102–3, 109–10, 135–36, 160, 181–82. *See also* nonviolence

Cohen, Erik, 99

Coleman, Simon, 110

Collins, Patricia Hill, 171, 237n29

colonialism, 19, 183, 185

colonies, 129, 130, 131, 231n14

Columbia. *See* Republic of Columbia

combat, 86, 87, 107–9, 228n108

committees, 34–35, 47–48, 71–73

communitas, 84, 102–5

communities. *See* activist communities; political communities; religious communities

computer technology, 37, 88, 218n156. *See also* email; Listservs

conflicts. *See* combat; violence

conservatism: academic scholarship and religious studies regarding, 18–19, 22, 144–45, 199; languages and theologies concerning, 141–42, 156–57; personal agency and resistance regarding, 18–19, 29, 159. *See also* politics; the Right contemporary feminism. *See* feminism; third-wave feminism

Conway, Janet, 90

cosmologies of interconnection: activists and activist communities regarding, 42–43, 70, 80, 105, 160, 164–67, 190, 197; explication for, 42–43, 219n161; in global communities, 42, 70, 78–82, 105, 151–52, 160–64, 167–68, 200–202; healing, well-being, and self-care regarding, 42, 43, 70, 160, 168, 188–89, 196, 200, 203, 205; religion vs. spirituality and, 42–43, 70, 126, 128, 142–43, 151–54, 156, 162, 190, 194–97, 200–203; among religious communities, 42, 70, 151–54, 156, 158, 160–64, 167

courts, 184, 242n104

CPT. *See* Christian Peacemaker Team (CPT)

Craig, David M., 92, 141

Crenshaw, Kimberlé, 171

crossings, 67, 68–69, 125–26, 221n34. *See also* borders; boundaries; fences; peripheries

crowds, 86–87, 111, 112, 116, 176, 228n108

Crowley, Aleister, 179, 235n118, 240n70

cultural appropriation, 16, 49, 133, 173, 234n77

cultural conflicts, 5–6, 41–42, 121, 125–26, 129–30, 231n13

cultural feminism. *See* feminism

cultural feminists. *See* feminists

CUSO. *See* Canadian University Service Overseas (CUSO)

Daly, Mary, 14, 39

dancing: at demonstrations and protests, 86, 87, 91–92, 93; at holiday rituals, 57–59, 62–63, 66, 68, 81

danger, 110–14, 122–23, 193–94. *See also* risks

Daro, Vinci, 100, 228n108

Dawkins, Richard, 4, 134, 233n49

Day, Dorothy, 31

deaths, 179, 194, 220n21, 240n71. *See also* murders

deities, 14–15, 17, 37, 56, 57–58, 59. *See also* images

democracies, 4–5, 129–30, 135–36

demonstrations, 72–73, 74–75, 95–96, 138, 157–58, 201, 228n119

Derrida, Jacques, 171

destruction. *See* violence

Domicó, Kimy Pernía, 175–76

dominance. *See* empowerment; power

Dominionism. *See* conservatism; the Right

Donaldson, Laura E., 186

Douglas, Mary, 219n161

Dufferin Grove Park, 67, 220n30

Eade, John, 106, 110, 122

Easter: blessings and ritual during, 65–66, 79; cosmologies of interconnection and, 81–82; dancing and playing during, 62–63, 66, 68; hymns and songs for, 62–64, 65, 66, 68; lighting for, 59–62, 63–64, 68; prayers and wishes at, 61, 62, 64, 66–67; readings and reflections during, 61, 62, 64–65, 66; as rite and ritual, 51; symbolism for, 61, 62, 63, 64, 66–67, 68, 81

economies. *See* capitalism; fair trade movement

ecumenism, 68–69, 73–74, 89–90, 94, 164, 236n21

Egypt, 19, 29, 239n58

elements, 41, 45, 66–69, 117, 221nn32–33

Elisha, Omri, 170–71

email, 91, 191. *See also* computer technology; Listservs

empowerment: *communitas* and structures concerning, 103–4, 108, 147; oppression and privilege regarding, 10–11, 13, 14, 108, 143, 188–89; through rites and rituals, 46, 47, 78–79; self and self-help movements concerning, 143, 159, 162–63, 188–90. *See also* power

energies: changes and, 80–82, 181, 192, 200, 201, 243n122; empowerment and power through, 47, 58–59, 178–79, 181–82, 189–90; healing, well-being, and self-care concerning, 181, 187, 188, 192; historical traditions and, 185–86; magic and, 37, 179, 194–95, 240n70; rituals and, 93, 94–95, 119–20, 200

Enlightenment, 29–30, 129, 133, 136–37, 159–60, 192

ethics. *See* care ethics

ethnography. *See* methodology

European Court of Human Rights, 105

Evangelicalism, 104–5, 129, 136, 140, 142–43

Evans, Sara M., 215n111

experimentation, 68, 69, 117, 183–84, 221n39

fair trade movement, 73, 164–67, 170, 179–80, 195–96, 237n25. *See also* capitalism

Falwell, Jerry, 4–5, 210n10

Fatovic, Clement, 129

feminism: academic scholarship and, 21–22; cosmologies of interconnection and, 162–63, 200; healing, well-being, and self-care concerning, 14, 187, 193; liberalism and secularism regarding, 134–35, 154–55, 157, 210n12; recovery and self-help movements concerning, 243n121; spirituality vs. religion and, 126–28, 149, 154–56; waves of, 8, 9–13, 21–22, 154, 170, 188

feminist criticism, 7, 8, 13–14, 15, 17–21

feminists: academic scholarship and religious studies concerning, 17–19, 21–22, 84–85, 215n111, 222n66; care and justice ethics regarding, 160, 168–71, 196; conservatism and, 18–19, 29, 143, 159, 205; cosmologies of interconnection and, 43, 80, 156, 168, 200–203; demographics for, 28–30; healing, well-being, and self-care concerning, 168, 192, 196; Islam and, 132, 134–35, 149; oppression and privilege regarding, 6, 10–13, 28–30, 125, 134–35, 143, 202; personal agency and resistance concerning, 18–19, 29, 113, 159–60, 196–97, 222n66; progressivism and, 11, 143, 200,

feminists *(continued)*
204–5, 222n66; recovery and
self-help movements concerning,
181, 189, 200, 243n121; rites and
rituals regarding, 80, 84–85,
200–201; secularism and, 132,
134–35, 196–97, 202; spirituality
vs. religion regarding, 41–42,
139–41, 154–55, 200–203, 204–5
feminist theologies, 13–16, 26–27. *See
also* theologies
feminist theories, 7, 8, 13–14, 17–19,
29, 171
fences, 85–87, 89, 91–92, 93–94, 101–2,
113, 119. *See also* borders; boundaries; crossings; peripheries
Fenton, Elizabeth, 130
Fessenden, Tracy, 191
Fife, Wayne, 100–101
fights. *See* combat; violence
films, 240n71
First Nations, 40, 138, 183–86. *See also*
Aboriginal peoples; Native
Americans
first-wave feminism, 8, 9–10, 12, 21, 170
Flusty, Steven, 84, 104
Food Not Bombs, 88, 101
Foucault, Michel, 174
Franka (Clearwater United Church):
cosmologies of interconnection
and, 161–62, 164–68, 195–96; fair
trade movement and, 73, 164–67,
195–96; as leader and pastor, 34,
65, 161, 164–68, 183–84; World
Council of Churches and, 164–65,
236n21
Fraser, Nancy, 139
Frederick, Marla F., 30, 71, 175, 180, 196
freedom: through capitalism, 159–60;
Enlightenment and liberalism

regarding, 18, 159–60; personal
agency and, 18–19, 159, 174;
through resistance, 18–19, 29, 159,
174; secularism and, 18
free market. *See* capitalism
Free Trade Area of the Americas
(FTAA): camaraderie and solidarity concerning, 100–105, 107,
122–23; centers and sites
regarding, 85, 98–103, 106, 110;
dangers and risks concerning,
110–14, 121, 122–23, 174–76,
193–94; fences and peripheries
regarding, 85–87, 89–90, 91–92,
93–94, 99, 101–2, 119; journeys
and pilgrimages concerning, 97,
99–100, 106, 110, 114–17, 122–23,
226n79; People's Summit and,
85–87, 89–90, 174–76; rituals and
ritualizing regarding, 41, 83–85,
91–95, 112–13, 117–23, 226n79;
tactics and tear gas concerning,
86–88, 92, 95, 99, 106–8, 109,
111–12, 116, 178, 228n120
Frey, Nancy, 110
Friedman, Marilyn, 237n37
friendships. *See* relationships
Fry, Stephen, 134
FTAA. *See* Free Trade Area of the
Americas (FTAA)
fundamentalism, 143, 210n12

G8. *See* Group of Eight countries (G8)
G20. *See* Group of Twenty countries
(G20)
Gandhi, Leela, 171
Gandhi, Mahatma, 115
Gardiner, Gerald, 27, 240n70
gay marriages. *See* same-sex
marriages

hierarchies *(continued)*
  175, 178, 183–84, 201–2, 205;
  rituals and, 123, 205, 223n77;
  "summit-hoping" and, 225n52. *See
  also* classes; social structures
Higginbotham, Evelyn Brooks, 10
history, 128–33, 142–43, 154–55, 172,
  183–86, 201, 243n121
Hitchens, Christopher, 4, 134
Holy Spirit, 15, 142, 161
homeless people, 35, 59, 72, 74,
  239n66. *See also* poverty
homes: care and justice ethics
  regarding, 170–71, 237n37; gender
  and morality concerning, 9–10,
  170–71, 202; journeys and
  pilgrimages regarding, 115–16;
  politics and, 170–71; privilege and
  violence regarding, 177; reform
  and, 9–10, 202; relationships and,
  170–71, 202; religion in, 126–27,
  202; in Toronto Catholic Worker
  community, 31–33
homosexuality. *See* LGBTQ people
human rights, 20, 134, 142, 144, 165,
  180–81
hymns, 62–63, 64, 65, 66, 68, 93–94,
  183–84. *See also* singing; songs

iconography. *See* prayer cards
ideals. *See* worldview(s)
Idle No More movement, 40, 185, 203,
  242nn108–9
images, 14–15, 148, 156. *See also* deities
immigrants, 31, 35, 72, 74, 172–73,
  231n16
Indigenous peoples. *See* Aboriginal
  peoples; First Nations
individuals. *See* autonomy; personal
  agency; self

influences, 182
institutions, 27, 121, 123, 128, 136, 141,
  146, 173–74, 201–2. *See also*
  churches; governments
International Criminal Court, 104
International Socialists (IS), 74, 77,
  191–92, 193, 222n59. *See also*
  Marxism
interpretations: oppression through,
  20, 154; reform and, 26–27;
  religion vs. spirituality and, 34–35,
  144, 150, 151, 152–53, 157. *See also*
  readings
interventions, 176–80
invocations, 57–58
Irish people, 231n16
Islam: authority and, 132; feminists
  and, 132, 134–35, 149; human
  rights and, 20, 105; interpretations
  in, 20; misogyny and, 20; moral
  agency and self concerning, 180;
  oppression and privilege
  regarding, 120, 134–35, 233n49;
  personal agency and resistance
  concerning, 19, 29; religious
  traditions in, 14–15, 16, 20;
  secularism and, 134–35, 136, 138,
  149; socialism and, 244n134
Islamophobia, 132, 134–35, 149
Isle of Apples, 58–59

Jakobsen, Janet R., 5, 136, 137
Jenson, Jane, 9
Jones, Holly, 194–95, 220n21
Jones, Timothy W., 212n41
journeys, 96, 97–103, 110, 114–17,
  122–23. *See also* pilgrimages
Judaism, 14–15, 16
Judy (Clearwater United Church), 89,
  114–15, 121, 138, 147, 149, 155–56

Maurin, Peter, 31
McClary, Susan, 193
media, 55, 86, 87, 106, 113, 118, 176,
    228n108, 239n66, 240n71
medics, 228n119
meditations, 53, 94, 184. *See also*
    groundings; prayers
men, 10–12, 15, 57–58, 134–35, 168–69,
    228n108, 237n37
mesmerism, 182
methodology: common influences for,
    26–27, 38–41; cosmologies of
    interconnection and, 42–43,
    200–203, 219n161; demographics
    concerning, 28–30, 217nn135–36;
    inclusion criteria for, 24–27; methods
    and descriptions of, 1–2, 23–24;
    participant-observations for, 23–24,
    146, 216n127, 234n77; personal
    reflections regarding, 203–5
minds, 181–82. *See also* psychology
misogyny, 6, 7–8, 17, 20–21. *See also*
    androcentrism
Moberg, Mark, 237n25
modernity, 129, 132–33, 137, 139,
    231n17
Mollenkott, Virginia Ramey, 20
money, 55, 65, 159–60, 164, 166, 167,
    173–74, 179–80, 236n21
Moore, R. Laurence, 146
morality, 10, 43, 141, 168–71
Moral Majority, Inc. *See* Falwell, Jerry
Morinis, Alan, 97–98, 225n55
Mormonism, 4, 10, 19–20, 130–31, 135,
    215n102
Moslener, Sara, 143
mosque movement. *See* Islam
Mother Goddess religion. *See* Goddess
    movement

murders, 175, 194–95, 220n21,
    244n139. *See also* deaths
mysticism, 17, 156. *See also* magic
myths, 129–30, 159, 179

Native Americans, 113, 183, 185–86.
    See also Aboriginal peoples; First
    Nations
nature, 67–68, 150
negotiations, 50, 71, 108–9, 177–78,
    185, 231n16
neopaganism. *See* Goddess move-
    ment; Paganism, contemporary
Nestlé, 165
New Age movement, 139–40, 142–43,
    186, 234n77, 240n70
the New Left, 39–40, 191. *See also*
    the Left
new religious movements, 10, 11–12,
    26–27, 36–37
Nicaragua, 166, 167
NightMare, M. Macha, 23, 217n128
Night of Dread, 67, 221n31
Noddings, Nel, 168, 169
nonviolence, 87–88, 97, 106–8, 113,
    118–19. *See also* coexistence
norms, 18–19, 159, 169–70, 174,
    222n66, 236n2
North America: academic scholarship
    and religious studies in, 19, 21–22,
    130–32, 190; Catholicism in, 4, 27,
    129–32, 231n13; Christianity and
    Protestantism in, 3–5, 16, 27,
    120–21, 129–32, 142–43; colonies
    in, 129, 130, 131, 231n14; conserva-
    tism in, 5–6, 19, 142–43, 239n58;
    contemporary Paganism and
    Wicca in, 16, 27, 36–37, 121,
    218n152; cultural conflicts in, 5–6,
    121, 125, 129, 129–30, 231n13; fair

Paganism *(continued)*
121–22, 123; rites and rituals for, 48–49, 71, 205, 221n32; ritualizing and, 26–27, 51, 78, 140; Samhain and, 51, 54–59, 66, 68, 81; spaces for, 47, 67–69, 152–53; spirituality vs. religion and, 126–27, 140, 147–48, 156, 218n152; Summer Solstice and, 51, 66–67, 68, 81. *See also* Goddess movement; Pagan collective; Wicca; Witchcraft

parades, 67, 102, 120–21, 226n79

participant-observation, 23–24, 146, 216n127, 234n77

Pascoe, Peggy, 9, 10

Pellegrini, Ann, 5, 136, 137

People's Summit, 85–87, 89–90, 175–76

peripheries, 71, 99, 101. *See also* borders; boundaries; crossings; fences

personal agency, 18–19, 78, 113, 159–60, 174, 196–97, 222n66, 236n2, 239n57. *See also* autonomy; self

Pike, Sarah M., 98

pilgrimages: centers and sites for, 95–96, 98, 100, 106; dangers of, 110, 113–14, 122–23; protests as, 84, 95–102, 106, 110, 113–17, 122–23, 201, 226n79; rituals and, 41, 84, 95, 98, 114, 117, 122–23, 201; shrines and, 96, 100, 116; spectators and, 226n79. *See also* journeys

pilgrims, 96, 98–99, 102–3, 110, 116, 122–23

playing, 53, 54, 68, 86, 87, 221n34

police: combat and, 86, 87, 107–9, 228n108; homeless people and, 239n66; oppression and privilege concerning, 107–9, 176–78; rituals

and, 85, 92, 93–94, 112–13, 118, 119; tactics and tear gas concerning, 86–87, 92, 99, 106–9, 111, 112, 178; violence vs. nonviolence and, 87, 106–9, 113, 118, 119, 176–77, 227n100

political activism, 141, 142–43, 168, 170–71, 196–97, 237n29. *See also* activism

political activists, 142, 146–47, 160, 175–77, 186–87, 196–97, 200–201. *See also* activists

political communities, 39–40, 125, 133, 134, 141–42, 156, 201

politics: academic scholarship and, 21–22, 84–85; churches and institutions regarding, 141, 145–47, 155–57, 201; classes and hierarchies concerning, 5–6, 103, 170–71, 201; cosmologies of interconnection and, 160–63, 168, 187, 196–97, 200–201, 204–5; healing, well-being, and self-care concerning, 143, 168, 186–89, 200; oppression and privilege concerning, 134–35, 137, 142–43, 186, 200, 222n66; of respectability, 9–10, 211nn36–37; rituals and ritualizing regarding, 47, 78, 80, 82–85, 140–41, 155, 200–201. *See also* conservatism; liberalism; Marxism

poor people. *See* homeless people; poverty

Porter, Jennifer E., 98

poverty, 165–66, 172, 176. *See also* homeless people

power: capitalism and fair trade regarding, 159–60, 164; care and justice ethics concerning, 160, 172, 196; centers of, 99–101, 146;

wcc. *See* World Council of
Churches (wcc)
weapons, 86, 111. *See also* tear gas
webs, 53–54, 66–67, 89, 91–92, 162
Weintraub, Jeff, 139
Weisenfeld, Judith, 9
well-being, 14, 42, 43, 82, 143, 160,
186–87, 196, 203. *See also* self-care;
self-help movements
white women: demographics for, 28,
29, 217n135; gender and sexism
regarding, 9, 12, 21–22, 191;
oppression and privilege
concerning, 12, 175–76, 178; rituals
by, 48–49, 183
Wicca, 12, 22, 27, 36–37, 218n152,
218n156. *See also* Paganism,
contemporary; Witchcraft
Winter, Miriam Therese, 144
Winter Solstice, 54–55
wishes, 53–54, 64, 67. *See also* prayers
Witchcraft, 27, 36–37, 114, 240n70. *See
also* Paganism, contemporary;
Wicca
Wolffe, John, 128
Womanism, 11–13, 16
women: care and justice ethics
concerning, 237n37; empowerment of, 10–11, 13, 14, 78, 143,
188–89; fair trade movement and,
237n25; images and symbolism
concerning, 2, 27, 91, 156;
oppression and privilege
regarding, 10, 20–21, 168–69,
175–76, 178, 233n49, 237n37;
power and, 7–8, 9–11, 91, 133, 135,
159, 174, 175, 243n121; in religious
communities, 18–19, 132–33,
140–41; rituals and ritualizing by,
71, 78, 140–41, 157–58; secularism

and, 132–36, 140–41, 154–55, 157.
See also gender; white women;
women of color
Women in Black, 119
women of color, 12–13, 21–22, 28, 30,
175–76, 211n37, 217nn135–36. *See
also* African Americans; First
Nations; Womanism
Women's Aglow Fellowship, 19, 29,
239n58
Women's March, 84, 178
WomynSpirit Festival, 55, 58, 91–92
Woodhead, Linda, 133
World Council of Churches (wcc),
164, 236n21
World Trade Organization (wto), 37,
83–84, 99–100, 226n79
worldview(s), 3–6, 29–30, 142–43,
145; coexistence as, 109–10, 160;
cosmologies of interconnection
concerning, 156, 158, 160, 162–63,
167, 190, 196, 202–3; healing,
well-being, and self-care
concerning, 160, 182, 187, 190, 192,
193, 196; historical traditions and,
129–32; journeys and pilgrimages
regarding, 84–85, 100–102, 115;
personal agency and resistance
concerning, 18–19, 160, 179–81,
196–97; recovery and self-help
movements regarding, 181–82;
rituals and, 45–46, 69–71, 84–85,
121–22, 140–41, 200–201; secularism and, 137–41, 157, 196–97,
202; spirituality vs. religion and,
125, 139–40, 142–43, 148–49, 162
wto. *See* World Trade Organization
(wto)
Wuthnow, Robert, 70, 243n122

Yarrow Collective: computer technology and Listservs for, 56–57, 167; cosmologies of interconnection and, 167, 194–95, 205; energies and, 47, 58–59, 81–82, 179, 194–95; fair trade movement and, 167, 179–80; healing, well-being, and self-care regarding, 181, 187, 196, 205; International Socialists and, 191–92; magic and mysticism regarding, 179, 194–95; members and leaders in, 36, 37–38, 48–49; oppression and privilege concerning, 173–74, 178–79, 243n120; rites and rituals for, 26–27, 45, 48–49, 68–69, 79, 80, 81, 205; Samhain and, 51, 54–59, 68, 81; spaces for, 38, 67, 68–69, 79, 194–95; spiritual traditions in, 183; Summer Solstice and, 51–54, 68, 194–95

York, Michael, 110, 117

Young Women's Christian Association (YWCA), 9–10

YWCA. See Young Women's Christian Association (YWCA)

Zacchaeus House, 31–32, 48, 59–60, 63, 145

In the Anthropology of Contemporary North America series:

America's Digital Army: Games at Work and War
Robertson Allen

Governing Affect: Neoliberalism and Disaster Reconstruction
Roberto E. Barrios

White Gold: An Ethnography of Breast Milk Sharing
Susan Falls

Mexicans in Alaska: An Ethnography of Mobility, Place, and Transnational Life
Sara V. Komarnisky

Holding On: African American Women Surviving HIV/AIDS
Alyson O'Daniel

Rebuilding Shattered Worlds: Creating Community by Voicing the Past
Andrea L. Smith and Anna Eisenstein

Religious, Feminist, Activist: Cosmologies of Interconnection
Laurel Zwissler

To order or obtain more information on these or other
University of Nebraska Press titles, visit nebraskapress.unl.edu.

CPSIA information can be obtained
at www.ICGtesting.com
Printed in the USA
FSHW011007120520
70167FS